The Battles that Shaped Indian History

The Battles that Shaped Indian History

Ajay and Monisha Singh

PENTAGON PRESS

The Battles that Shaped Indian History / **Ajay and Monisha Singh**

ISBN 978-81-8274-573-5

First Published in 2012

Published by

PENTAGON PRESS
206, Peacock Lane, Shahpur Jat
New Delhi-110049
Phones: 011-64706243, 26491568
Telefax: 011-26490600
email: rajan@pentagonpress.in
website: www.pentagonpress.in

Printed at Aegean Offset Printers, Greater Noida, U.P.

Dedicated
To
All Officers and Men
of
The Indian Armed Forces
May they emerge victorious
In all their battles

"Those who do not remember the lessons of history are condemned to relive them"

– George Santayana

Contents

Preface

The idea of this book has germinated for many years now. The battles of Indian history are a rich vein of information that we can draw upon even now and learn from the lessons that they contain. There is a need to understand our military history and have a clearer understanding of the battles that have taken place to shape our nation. This, in a way, will provide the insight to prepare ourselves for our future battles.

Warfare has evolved tremendously over the years. From the First Generation of warfare- a simple, muscular manner of war fighting, we have now evolved into the Fourth Generation of Warfare – a form of war fighting that is vastly different from the preceding ones. The manner of war fighting has changed with time, but have the basic principles really changed? Surprise holds as much weightage now as it did when Alexandra surprised Porus by crossing the swollen Jhelum River 2000 years ago. The importance of understanding and utilizing ground has the same relevance as it did earlier. Technology remains the prime determinant of warfare now as it was in the past. The technologies of composite bows, stirrups and gunpowder revolutionized the concept of war fighting in the past, just as cyber warfare and network centric warfare will shape it in this century. Yet while the concepts of war fighting will change, leadership and motivation are two attributes that will never lose their importance. After all even in today's era, can a Battlefield Management System replace the cool, composed leadership of General Sam Maneckshaw or the inspiring courage of a Babur or Rana Pratap? The principles and basic concepts of warfare remain constant and in understanding these concepts, we equip ourselves better for the warfare of the future.

I wish you all happy reading and hope that the book helps provide not only an interesting read but gives an insight into the major battles of Indian history and in doing so gives a perspective of the present and the future shape of warfare.

Ajay Singh

Acknowledgment

The book is the culmination of two years of research and writing. In the process we have been enriched, and enlightened. Through these pages we hope to give our readers a insight in India's rich military history and bring out the nuances of our momentous battles.

The book is for Ragini, our daughter, who has been the inspiration for these words – as she is for all our actions. She is not only our words, she is our very world.

We are grateful to our parents (both sets) for giving us the foundation, the values and the encouragement to pen these words. Had it not been for them, perhaps the thoughts through which the book took shape would never have been implanted.

There was so many who have contributed in making this book a reality. We are grateful to Akhil Chandra and his charming wife Sangeeta, for helping with the initial layout of the book. The maps have been prepared by them and they have helped make the battles come alive. The team of Arvind, Samir amd Arun were also largely instrumental in the research and preparation of the book. But we owe a special debt of gratitude to Mrs Sindhu Jayakumar, who cheerfully and incomplainingly converted reams upon reams of untidy, penciled scrawl into a neat, tight manuscript. We are also grateful to Harsh Negi, who helped design the manuscript copy and Prashant Kulkarni, who put it together in its final form.

But most of all, we are grateful to the Indian Army for giving us thirty glorious years in which these words germinated and eventually took shape. In a very small way, this book is an acknowledgment and a token to the huge debt of gratitude which we owe the army for the memories, the values and the wonderful times it has given us.

Ajay & Monisha Singh

1

The Battle of Jhelum River

Alexandra – *"And how do you wish to be treated?"*
Porus – *"As a king would another king!"*

❖ ❖ ❖

The battle of Jhelum River, or the Battle of Hydasphes, as the Greeks call it, was possibly the first recorded battle of Indian history. Most versions of the battle which are available to us have been recorded by Greek historians and present a rather biased perspective. This battle between the all-conquering army of Alexandra the Great and Porus, was the first battle between an Indian king and a foreign invader. Even though this battle was fought almost two and a half millennia ago, it still retains its lessons and its impact on Indian history is significant. In those days, India was not the India as we know it now. Its geographical boundaries extended along the Hindu Kush Mountains bordering present day Afghanistan to the West and along the mighty Himalayas to its North and Eastwards to the Brahmaputra. The Indian peninsula extended south towards the Indian Ocean, but for all practical purposes, India as an entity halted at the Vindhyas. South of the Vindhyas was virtually another civilization. By no stretch could this geographical landmass be called a nation. It was a motley collection of states ruled by satraps, each of whom boasted of their independent kingdoms and most of whom remained bitterly at war with each other. The mighty Gupta Empire flourished in the Indo-Gangetic plains, but the rest of Northern India was but a series of fragmented states. The Western borderlands comprising of Punjab, Sindh and Afghanistan were divided into two dozen or more independent principalities which in spite of a common culture were more often than not at war with each other. The major figure in the political landscape was Porus, the King of Pauravas who ruled in the area between the Jhelum and the Chenab rivers of undivided Punjab. It was on him that the onerous task of defending India from its first foreign invader fell.

When Alexandra reached the Hindu Kush Mountains in late 327 BC, he was at the zenith of his powers. In a brief, meteoric life of 30 years, he had unified the fragmented kingdoms of Ancient Greece and then swept through Asia, destroying the powerful Persian Empire. He had subjugated the warlords of Central Asia and occupied most of present day Uzbekistan and Kazakhstan. He now stood poised to extend his empire across the entire known world; across the Indus River, all the way down to the Indo-Gangetic plains and onto the shoreline of the great ocean which the Greeks believed to be the edge of the world.

By the winter of 327 BC, Alexandra's army stood poised on the banks of the Indus River (or the Sindhu River as it was known then). With his usual ingenuity he crossed it by merely harnessing his boats together and forming a pontoon bridge of sorts. Across the river, his army ravaged the Indus valley, the present day area of Pakistan's Swat and Buner, and captured the major cities of the Valley, Massaga; Bazira and Varana in quick succession. Most of the local rulers were soon subjugated and surrendered giving vast quantities of gold, silver and livestock as tribute. Alexandra's campaign in the Indus Valley was marked by great bloodshed and cruelty. Cities that resisted were wiped out and their inhabitants, men, women and children, massacred. Much of the loot was sent back to Greece and Alexandra's victorious army plunged inexorably deeper into India.

By March Alexandra reached Taxila, the then largest town in the Indus Valley. Here, Ambhi, the King of Taxila surrendered without a fight. Not only did he accept Alexandra's sovereignty willingly, he also gifted Alexandra three hundred talents of silver and a contingent of 3000 troops with which to wage his subsequent

Alexandra's Companion Cavalry – The finest Cavalry in the world of the time

battles. Abhisara, the ruler of Kashmir and Hazara also submitted willingly, while other kings of the area acquiesced and also provided five thousand troops to Alexandra. If only the kings had united together the combined armies would have been more than a match for Alexandra. But the rivalries and petty quarrels of these rulers eventually overrode national interests. Indian history, as it happened so often again after this, was to be shaped and decided, not by the valor of its armies but the fact that its rulers could never unite against a foreign invader.

The king of Taxila gave Alexandra another valuable gift; thirty war-elephants, hitherto never seen by the Greeks. These huge pachyderms were the mainstay of Indian armies and formed a formidable fighting machine. Heavily armored, they were encased in a sheath of leather and chain mail to protect their vulnerable sides. A protected *howdah* on the elephant's back allowed the riders to hurl spears and fire arrows. The one weak link was the mahout, the exposed driver who could be picked off with enemy arrows or spears. Alexandra was quick to realize their potential and more importantly was able to device his tactics to counter them. Targeting the mahout and then attacking the elephant's unprotected legs and underbelly would drive the animal mad with pain and make him totally out of control. An elephant running amok was likely to cause more damage to his own troops than to the enemy. The experience with elephants served Alexandra well and the tactics he devised were to be instrumental in his victory during the coming battle.

The strength of the opposing armies vary in different accounts. Greek historians have assessed Alexandra's army to have around 15000 cavalry and around 1,20,000 infantry. Many of these were mercenaries, but the core was based around 30,000 Macedonian and Greek troops who had repeatedly proven their mettle and shed blood in their march across two continents. At the helm was Alexandra himself, perhaps the greatest general the world has known; a master tactician of undisputed courage and skill who led from the front and whose brilliant victories against superior forces has given him an aura of invincibility. His eyes were fixed firmly on expanding his empire into the heartland of India and to the very limits of the known world. On the other hand, his opponent Porus led a comparatively smaller force, but his army was well-trained and equipped and knew they were fighting for their homes and hearths. He had managed to form an alliance of sorts with the neighboring kingdoms of Abhisara, Malvas and Kshudrahas and mustered together a force of around 20-30,000 infantry, 2500 cavalry, around 600 chariots and almost a hundred and fifty war-elephants. His elephant arm was the arm of decision, one which could form an

The elephant corps was the mainstay of the Indian Army

impregnable defensive line or an unstoppable assault wave. Even a single elephant could frighten enemy horses and thus they could be vital in neutralizing Alexandra's famed cavalry. Porus himself was a skilled and capable general. He was an imposing man – Greek historians describe him as being over six and a half feet tall with a regal, majestic bearing. Over the years he had built up his kingdom and acquired a reputation of immense personal valor and sound military generalship in its wake. Alexandra had sent emissaries to him and summoned him to accept his sovereignty; an offer which Porus scornfully refused, saying that he would meet him but at the battleground with his army and in arms. Now as his spies reported the news of Alexandra's advance, he moved out to defend his kingdom at its borders. Like all good military leaders he carefully chose his battleground. The site he chose was along the Jhelum River; a wide fast-flowing torrent, now swollen and even more formidable after the first rains of the season.

Alexandra began his march into the Punjab around May, preceded by scouts and local guides helpfully loaned by the king of Taxila.. Exhorting his troops in a soul-stirring address, he set out on the next phase of his campaign. His approach was marked by much bloodshed and a ruthless subjugation of all who dared stand up to him. He came into present day Indian Punjab by crossing the Nandana Pass on the foothills of the Himalaya Mountains near Chhamb and reached the only crossing place on the Jhelum River only to find it heavily guarded with Porus encamped on the other side.

Crossing the river which was in spate after unseasonal, torrential rains and with his every move being watched from the other side would have been military madness. Alexandra wisely chose to halt and set up camp on the Western bank of the River. The camp was large and deliberately elaborate, extending over nine kilometres wide and quite clearly visible from the other side. Alexandra wanted to create the impression that he intended to stay long. He also spread rumors that he was waiting for the river to subside before attempting a crossing, news which he knew would eventually reach Poros. While his deception plan was at work he conducted extensive reconnaissance to find alternative crossing sites. He also tasked his engineers to bring forward the boats that had been left behind on the Indus River. Each of these boats were cut and painstakingly brought forward carts. They were then reassembled in secrecy on the far banks of the Jhelum. In the long period of wait, the two armies sized each other and many individual and small-unit duels took place along the river. But neither side made a decisive move-at least not yet. As the armies waited Alexandra formulated his plan.

THE MAN

Alexandra – The greatest conqueror the world has known. By the time he was 30 he had expanded his empire across virtually the entire known world.

A master tactician, he developed the concepts of using cavalry in conjunction with the impregnable infantry phalanx. Was possibly the first exponent of the concepts of maneuver warfare.

Utilized the concepts of surprise and deception to the hilt. Led from the front.

His personnel courage and determination were exemplary. Was also known for his ruthlessness and cruelty, especially amongst his subjugated enemies.

His plan was simple. He intended to convince Poros that he was still waiting for the river to subside, while he would attempt to cross from an alternative site upstream. For days, his parties had moved up and down the river, attempting feint crossings on the river. Each feint crossing invariably attracted reaction from the Indian troops on the other side that would send detachments to counter them. Poros banked heavily on his elephants and had deployed them in pairs at each possible crossing site. Even the mere sight of those huge pachyderms unnerved the horses who had never seen these huge monsters in the previous campaigns. Meanwhile reconnaissance parties moved further ahead to find an alternate crossing place and one returned with news of a likely site around twelve kilometers upstream. Here the river was broader and thus much shallower. Better still, in the centre of the river was an island, the Adnana Island, which would not only screen the crossing, but also provide a temporary resting place for man and horse as they crossed the swollen river. Alexandra decided to cross using this site and then attack Porus army from the flank.

Alexandra divided his army in three parts for the coming battle He himself intended to lead the crossing of the Jhelum River at the head of around 13000 troops comprising of his favored Companion cavalry, the Macedonian cavalry and Scythian mounted archers. The bulk of the army was to remain in the camp under Kerateros, one of his seasoned generals, with around 3500 cavalry and 12000 infantry which was simulate normal activity and screen the move of Alexandra. The third element, placed under Meleager-another veteran. was to move with Alexandra till a half-way point and then lie hidden till Alexandra had crossed the river. As per the plan, Alexandra was to draw the bulk of Poros's forces against him and when they were engaged the balance of the Greek forces would cross the river in improvised rafts made of haystacks wrapped in animal skins. They were to attack Poros from the rear while he was engaged against Alexandra. It was a bold, audacious plan which hinged on surprise and skillful use of manuever. To counter this Poros' conventional wisdom had little to offer, except for the valor of his own troops who were fighting in their land and homes and for the safety of their own families.

Alexandra commenced his move to the crossing site under cover of a violent thunderstorm. He chose a long circuitous route which provided cover by low hills and concealed the move. In the camp, the campfires continued burning and normal hustle and bustle of soldiers and animals engaged in routine camp activity continued. The deception convinced Poros that the Greeks were not planning to attack and perhaps lulled him into complacency. Alexandra reached the Adnana crossing site just after midnight, with his move undetected. Here boats and improvised rafts had already been placed by his engineers which ferried the initial forces across. The bulk of the army however forded the swollen river on their horses. As the crossing began, the rain intensified which helped maintain surprise and prevented the Paurava sentries on the far bank from

THE MAN

Porus – Paurava king of western Punjab. Personally very courageous, he had acquired a reputation for personal valor and chivalry.

An able general who had led his army to many victories but was no match for Alexandra's tactical brilliance. His personal conduct after the battle ensured that he retained his kingdom.

noticing the move. The crossing itself was more difficult than they anticipated. Waters rose shoulder high and the force of the current swept away man and horse. Almost two hundred of his soldiers perished in the crossing, but by dawn, Alexandra was across and had established a bridgehead across the river with his infantry deployed in an impregnable phalanx, his archers supporting them from the rear and his cavalry along the flanks. The Greek phalanx was the most formidable deployment of the times, comprising of a tight formation of soldiers standing shoulder to shoulder with large shields called *haplons* covering themselves and their neighbors This overlapping layers of shields provided a tortoise like protection against enemy arrows and spears. Their principal weapon was a *sarissa*, a huge twenty four feet spear with a long blade which was wedged solidly in the ground to impale a charging horse at stand-off range. Each Phalangite wore armour consisting of a helmet, a breast-plate and greaves for their thighs and were lined up in sixteen rows with three feet intervals between the rows. Archers, slingers and javelin throwers were deployed in the rear and along the sides to fire at an advancing enemy. The actions of the phalanx were fine-tuned with the cavalry who were usually deployed on the rear or along the flanks. The Greek phalanx formed a solid line which could be used as an impregnable defensive position or moved forward inexorably in attack. Usually it formed the pivot to pin down an enemy while the cavalry maneuvered from the flanks or the rear on to the enemy.

By now Poros' scouts had detected the crossing and relayed the news to him. With the Greek army still deployed on the far bank opposite him, he was undecided as to where the main threat lay. He decided to remain behind with most of his army and sent his eldest son at the head of a covering force of a thousand troops to assess and counter the threat. Porus' son led his force with great speed and dash but as he approached the Greek positions he made a crucial tactical error. Firstly, he underestimated the strength opposite him. Then rather than adopt a blocking position on which additional troops could build up, he decided to charge the Greek positions. Even worse, rather than use his infantry and cavalry he led the charge with chariots. The results were disastrous. The soil was broken and churned up by rain, and the ground almost impassable. After the initial momentum of the charge, the chariots soon floundered and began sinking axle deep in the boggy earth. At this range they were easy pickings for enemy archers and a hail of arrows took a heavy toll of the riders. Porus son, valiantly leading the attack was killed in one of the first volleys and the leaderless force floundered. Alexandra now launched his cavalry from the flanks as his infantry closed in from the front. Surrounded from all sides and unable to maneuver, the contingent was soon decimated. The first clash of arms had begun with a decisive victory for the Greeks.

THE MOMENT

Alexandra's crossing of the Jhelum in bad weather and torrential rains changed the complexion of the battle. He emerged on Porus's flank and forced him to leave his prepared defenses on the Jhelum river and fight on the open Karri plain where his cavalry had an advantage.

With the vanguard destroyed, Alexandra moved southwards towards Poros' camp. As always he moved at a rapid pace, pushing men and horses beyond their limits. Within an hour he had reached the site of the Karri plain where he intended to fight his main battle on a ground which was suitable for his cavalry. His infantry formed the traditional phalanx at the edge of the plain. He himself was positioned on the left flank with the bulk of his cavalry, while a smaller cavalry contingent screened his right flank. On the far bank, the Greeks under General Kerateros, had established their siege guns and catapults and rained a constant volley of spears, arrows and boulders on the Indian positions across the river. Greek engineers were stealthily preparing rafts for the crossing with the simple expedient of using bundles of hay wrapped in canvas which was made water proof by smearing it with grease and animal fat. These improvised rafts would remain afloat long enough for the first waves to get across. The third element of Alexandra's army under

General Meleager, was also concealed and waiting to cross the Jhelum at the opportune time. Alexandra's elements were in place and so far everything seemed to be going as per plan.

On the other side, the few survivors of the covering force made their way back to Poros' camp and reported the news of the crossing. Poros realized that the main threat now came from his northern flank and not across the river and wheeled his huge army to meet the threat. His ponderous army redeployed sluggishly and moved northwards towards the Karri plain, leaving just a small contingent along with some elephants to guard the crossing site. As Poros approached the Greek deployment he decided to attack first. Once again they made the same mistake of attacking with chariots. The result was the same. Slowed down by the sodden earth, the initial attack was easily repulsed. Poros now halted his army around two kilometers from the Greek positions to counter Alexandra's impending attack. In the classical defensive deployment of the time, he extended his forces on a four kilometer wide frontage, with his left wing resting on the river. His deployment was based on around one hundred elephants each at an interval of around thirty to forty meters and the gaps between them covered by archers. The infantry was deployed behind the line of elephants while his chariots were in two rows on the two flanks. His cavalry was equally divided with around a thousand horsemen on each flank behind the line of chariots. With his left flank protected by the river, it may have been better to leave just a small force there and concentrate the bulk of his cavalry and chariots on the exposed right flank. As it was, his deployment was in anticipation of a frontal assault by Alexandra, as per the norms of war-fighting prevalent in India. He was still not attuned to the concept of the mobile battle in which Alexandra was a past master.

Poros was still in the process of forming-up when Alexandra made contact. His trained eye immediately noticed the strengths and weaknesses of his adversary's deployment and decided to attack it from its weakest point, its rear. He sent around two brigades of cavalry, under General Koinos in a wide out-flanking move, forcing Porus to shift some of his cavalry reserves to counter the emerging threat. Yet Koinos' cavalry did not attack the flank. It continued moving till it was way behind the line of Poros' deployment and then maneuvered towards the rear of his positions.

Koinos maneuver managed to catch the reserve cavalry as they were moving and a fierce encounter battle followed. Unfortunately, in those days, Indian tactics hinged around the use of war-elephants. Cavalry was still in its nascent form and had not developed adequately either in training or in tactics. On the other hand the famed Macedonian cavalry which was personally led by Alexandra was perhaps the best fighting force in the world. They had been hardened by three years of continuous warfare in which they had destroyed Persian, Turks, Uzbek, Bactrian and Egyptian forces and their tactics were fine-tuned and time-tested. Unlike the Indian cavalry they operated in all-arms teams and had a component of infantry, archers, catapult throwers and slingers. The Indian cavalry was soon halted and the chariots which supported them were unable to move in the wet earth of the Karri Plain. Within an hour, Poros' cavalry was virtually annihilated and the Greek cavalry held sway over the battlefield.

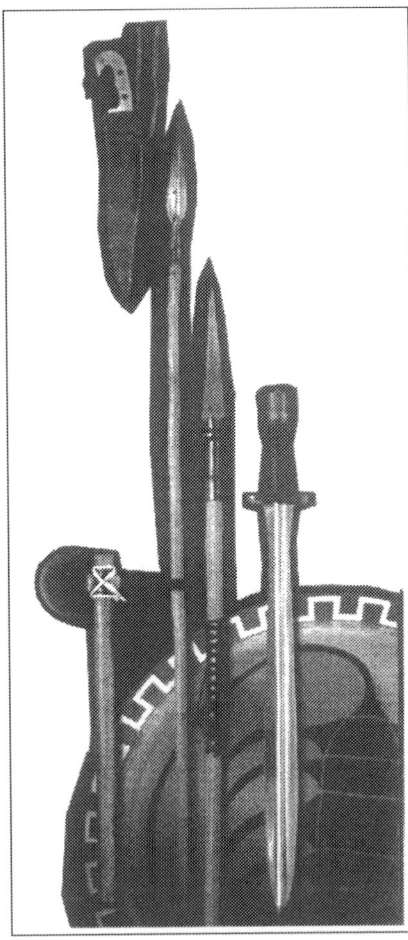

Greek Weapons of the Era

While the cavalry actions were underway, Alexandra's infantry moved forward in their formidable

Initial Deployment
ADNANA ISLAND
JHELUM RIVER
GREEK ARMY
RESERVE CAVALRY
INFANTRY PHALANX
COMPANION CAVALRY ALEXANDER
INITIAL DEPLOYMENT ON THE KARRI PLAIN
100 CHARIOTS
PORUS
200 ELEPHANTS
100 CHARIOTS
CAVALRY
INFANTRY
CAVALRY
PORUS' ARMY

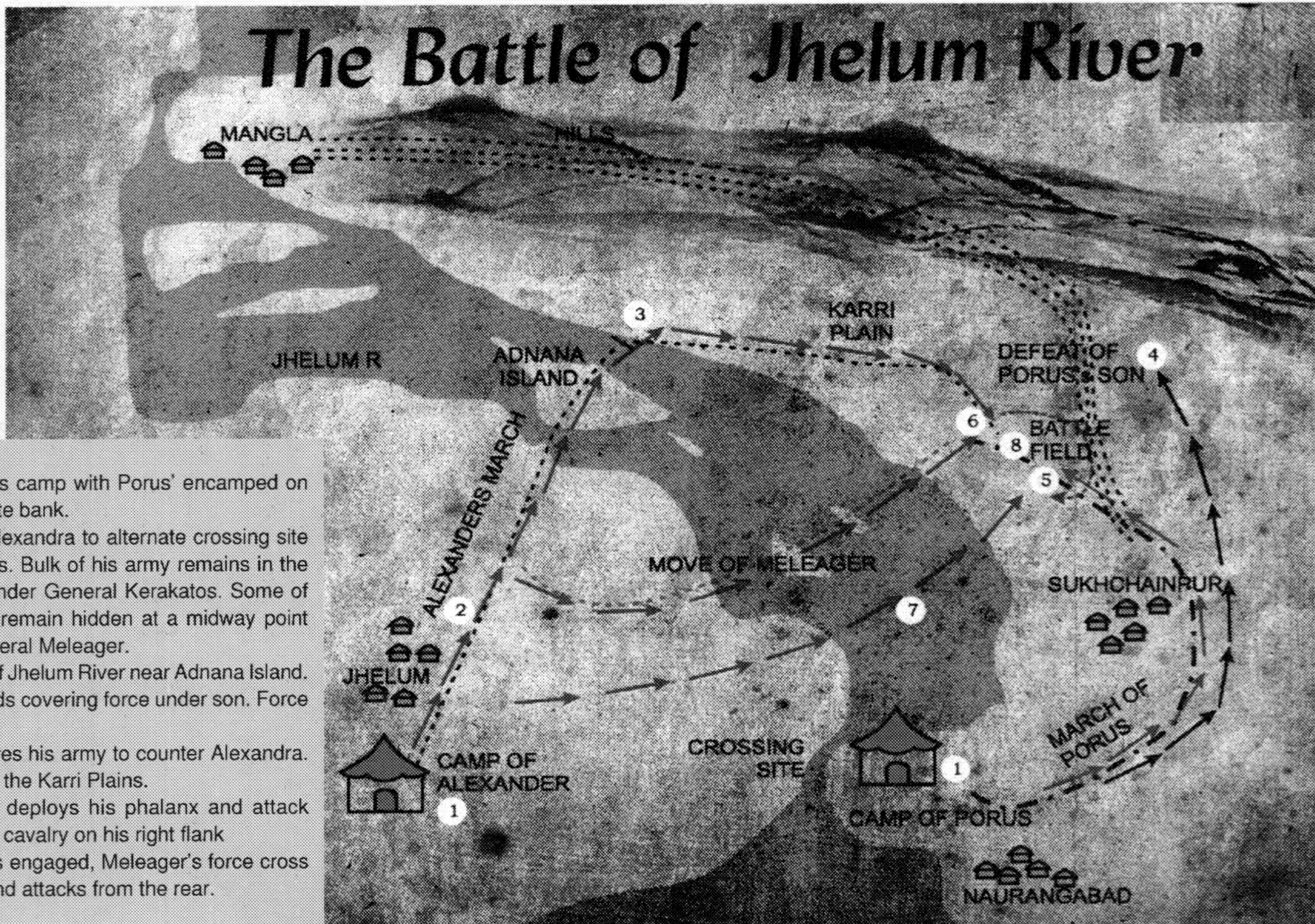

1. Alexandra's camp with Porus' encamped on the opposite bank.
2. Move of Alexandra to alternate crossing site in darkness. Bulk of his army remains in the camp to under General Kerakatos. Some of his forces remain hidden at a midway point under General Meleager.
3. Crossing of Jhelum River near Adnana Island.
4. Porus sends covering force under son. Force defeated.
5. Porus moves his army to counter Alexandra. Deploys in the Karri Plains.
6. Alexandra deploys his phalanx and attack Porus with cavalry on his right flank
7. With Porus engaged, Meleager's force cross the river and attacks from the rear.

phalanx formation. The phalanx slowly advanced towards the centre of the Indian deployment while the cavalry continued their attacks from the flanks and rear. Meanwhile the Greek infantry under Meleager which was hidden across the river, seized the moment and began crossing the Jhelum in small teams. By then Poros was heavily engaged against Alexandra's phalanx in his front and the sweeping cavalry in his rear and right flank to react to the new threat that was emerging. By around ten in the morning, Meleager's force was also across the Jhelum and deployed onto the left and rear of Poros' positions. Poros was gradually squeezed in from all sides. In the constricted space, with his cavalry reserves already gone, Poros had no choice but to charge with his elephants and infantry and try to break out from the ring which was closing around his army.

He led the break-out himself, mustering together his infantry and around fifty war-elephants. The force of his attack almost broke the Greek phalanx (which had never been broken in any battle before) due to the momentum of the charge and the panic caused by the sight of charging, trumpeting elephants. As the phalanx began giving ground, Alexandra changed tactics once again. He ordered the infantry to disperse from the tight formation of the phalanx and instead leave wide gaps in their lines through which the elephants could advance. The archers now targeted the exposed flanks and undersides of the elephants and began picking out their mahouts. The result was panic. Mad with pain and out of control, the elephants turned towards their own ranks causing the same mayhem amongst the Indian troops that they had wreaked on the Greek phalanx. Even worse, Poros second echelon which comprised of his chariot borne

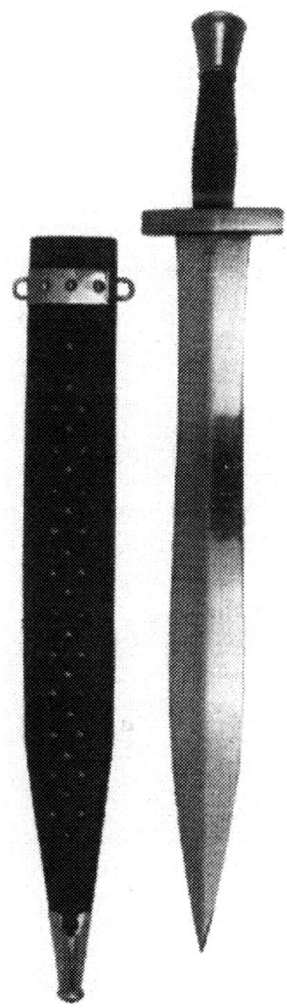

forces was cut off as they floundered in the rain-soaked mud. He was now in the midst of battle virtually without a reserve.

With the Indian elephants out of action, the cavalry decimated, the chariots floundering in the mud and the infantry unable to advance, Alexandra launched his *coup-de-main*. His own cavalry now wheeled towards the rear of the Indian positions. General Meleager's forces which by now had completely crossed the river, launched a general attack from the left onto Poros other flank. The broken phalanx was reformed and the Greek Infantry attacked from the front while the cavalry swept from the flanks and rear to cut off all lines of retreat. The battle now degenerated into a series of hand-to-hand duels and a general melee followed which lasted for almost six hours.

In spite of being hopelessly out-maneuvered, it seemed that Poros could still save the day as he valiantly rallied his troops. He himself set the example and led the break out through the Greek lines. He mahout was killed but he controlled his elephant himself and hurled "an endless stream of javelins with the force and distance of arrows." His presence might have tilted the scales when a well judged arrow struck him in the shoulder blade between his breast plate and the chain-mail of his body-armor. Though wounded and exhausted, he continued to battle, till his war-wounded elephant sank to his knees. Even though dismounted and severely wounded Poros was a formidable foe. He fought with sword and spear and prevented any of the enemy from closing in. His war-elephant tried to shield him and from Greek accounts even tried to pull out the exposed arrow which was lodged in the shoulder of his master.

The Indians held their own in the pitched battle that continued all day. Poros and his soldiers refused to cave in and casualties mounted on both sides, Alexandra sent the king of Taxila to persuade Poros to surrender. This enraged Poros even more as he considered the Taxila king to be a traitor and instead he hurled another spear forcing him to withdraw. Alexandra then approached personally and through an interpreter saluted his opponent, praised his valor and offered his condolences for the loss of both his sons who had fallen in the battle, The elder as head of the covering force, the younger who had tried to lead a break-out of the encircled infantry. After receiving an assurance that the remnants of his army would be spared and treated well, Poros finally agreed to a truce and allowed himself to be carried off and treated by Greek physicians.

THE WEAPONS

Alexandra relied primarily on his fast, heavily armed cavalry as his arm of decision. His infantry was well-equipped with long spears to form a defensive phalanx. Large shields, greaves and body armor provided ample protection to individual soldiers. His army was well equipped with catapults and siege guns to bombard Indian positions on other side of the river.

Porus relied largely on his armored elephants which when injured tended to become uncontrollable. His cavalry was not well developed and a greater emphasis was placed on chariots. In boggy ground chariots were usually unreliable.

Soldiers relied on swords, spears and long bows (which provided greater range but were unwieldy). The common soldiers had no body armor.

Yet, unfortunately, it was not the last act of the drama. As the Indian soldiers sheathed their weapons and began moving back towards their camp, the Greeks had managed to cross from the site of their own camp and moved towards the Karri Plain where unknown to them, the truce had just been negotiated. Their advance brought them in contact with the withdrawing Indians. It was approaching nightfall and as per Indian tradition, no fighting was done after dark. The Indian soldiers were unprepared for the Greek assault and the Paurava army suffered heavy casualties in this inopportune encounter before the Greek forces were finally called off and the truce re-established.

Alexandra, like the entire Greek army was impressed by the courage and valor of the Indians "the most formidable foe that we faced", wrote the Greek historian Plutarch. Poros personal conduct was equally impressive. In the previous battles with the Persians, their king Darius had fled the battlefield on two occasions, leaving his army to its fate once defeat was imminent. Poros fought on till the very end and refused to capitulate even when all seemed lost. At the end of the battle when asked, "And, how do you wish to be treated?" he replied "Like a king". Alexandra restored him to his throne and not only returned all his captured areas, but also gave him additional territories in return for acceptance of his regency.

By the end of the day, India's first battle against a foreign invader was over. As would be the case in future battles against foreign enemies a trend had begun. Fragmented rulers, in-fighting and betrayal, the use of large but cumbersome armies, conventional, predictable tactics and a disregard for technology would repeatedly ensure that the day belonged to the other side. Subsequent invasions by the Afghans, the Turks, the Mughals and the British would see

Indian armies succumb again and again to smaller armies utilizing superior tactics and employing better technology. This failing would bring India under foreign rule for over two millennia.

Alexandra's dominions in India now extended from the borders of present day Afghanistan up to the banks of the Jhelum. He wanted to continue his march through India upto the banks of the Ganges River and then to the ocean beyond which was the end of the known world. But his dreams of world conquest were thwarted not by any enemy, but by the fatigue of his own soldiers. Alexandra was halted at the banks of the Beas River, or the Hydrostes River as the Greeks called it., where his tired soldiers mutinied and refused to go further. Perhaps it was the memory of the bitter battle on the Jhelum and the knowledge that equally brave and even stronger armies lay in wait deeper that sapped the Greek spirit and will to fight. A frustrated Alexandra finally acquiesced to their demands and three months later began a long and painful march out of India and back to Greece.

The Impact of the Battle

What really was the impact of this battle on Indian history? Was it merely a skirmish, an exploratory foray into Indian territory or did it signal something more. It was definitely not just a mere skirmish nor was Alexandra's invasion just a foray. By the end of his campaign, he had advanced over 400 kilometers inside India, captured seven large towns and over seven thousand villages. As was his norm he established cities to commemorate his achievements and the city of Alexandria Nicaea (Meaning Alexandra's victory) was

established near the site of the battle. He raised another city, Alexandra Bucephela in memory of his faithful horse who had died as a result of a broken leg caused by a charging elephant. He left behind a Greek regent to oversee the captured territories and positioned large garrisons in the cities he founded. With their presence, foreign influence gradually seeped into India. There would be other such influences which would follow, leading to the immense diversity which exists in India.

The invasion also proved to be a precursor to other invasions. The Huns, the Afghans, the Turks the Mughals would ravage India in the coming centuries, changing its culture and geography. Many of the invaders emulated Alexandra and their tactics usually had a marked similarity with those used by Alexandra. His use of cavalry and his applications of the concepts of maneuver warfare would be emulated many times in the future by invaders such as Mohammed of Ghazni, Mohammed Ghori, Babur and others. The Indian armies unfortunately would not learn from this battle. The concepts of static positional warfare, based on elephants and sheer muscle power would remain unchanged for centuries. Nor would unconventional tactics or the use of new technologies be adopted. These failings would cost India dearly in the future.

But there was one unexpected positive fall-out. Alexandra's invasion in a way, gave birth to the Idea of India as a nation and not just a conglomeration of perpetually warring states. At that time two remarkable men were appearing on the political landscape. They were Chandragupta Maurya and his advisor Chanakya. He met Alexandra when he was camped in Taxila and was fired by his stories, especially of the unification of the Greek states. He too

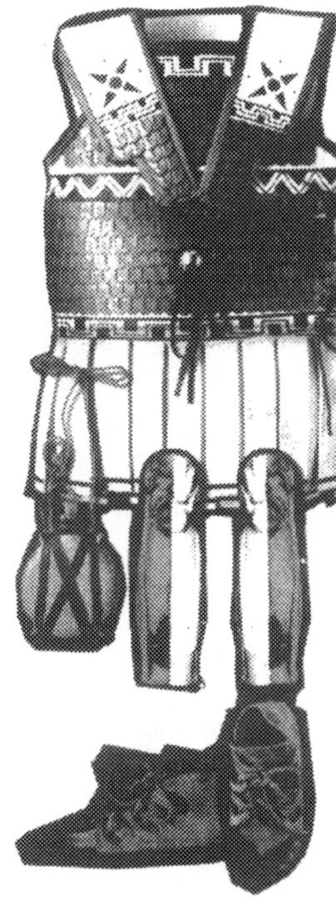
Greek Body Armour

dreamt of conquering all of India and making it a centralized entity under Mauryan rule. By the time Alexandra died three years later in 323 BC; Chandragupta had risen on the political firmament and was strong enough to challenge the authority of the Greek regent Seleucus. He evoked the cry of nationalism, perhaps for the first time in the history of India, to rouse its people against foreign rule. He defeated Seleucus soundly, drove away the Greek garrisons from their cities and recaptured Taxila and all of Punjab. Chandragupta followed up his initial victories and extended his empire further west up to the boundaries of Afghanistan. At its zenith, the Mauryan Empire extended from Kabul till the Bay of Bengal, and southwards till the Vindhya Mountains. For the first time in Indian history, a vast centralized state had arisen, giving shape to the contours of India as we know it now. The contours would change repeatedly, but the Idea of India had been established and would persevere. This was the lasting impact of Alexandra's invasion and indirect fallout of the bloody battle on the banks of the Jhelum River.

An artist's rendition of Prithiviraj Chauihan in full regalia

2

Victory and Debacle – The Battles of Tarain

"A night attack is the strategem of cowards" –
Rajput saying of the times.

❖ ❖ ❖

In the 12th century, the political landscape of India was distressingly familiar. Much of North India was under powerful Rajput rulers perpetually warring with each other. The Chahamanas or Chauhans were the dominant dynasty with its kingdom centred around Ajmer-Delhi and encompassing an area from Bihar in the West, Mewar in the South and the borders of Gujarat in the East. In Gujarat, the Chalukyas held sway,and were engaged in a continual tussle for supremacy with their neighbors. The equally powerful Gahadavalas of Kannauj dominated most of Bundelkhand while the Chandelas, Palas and Senas occupied smaller kingdoms in Orissa, Bihar and Bengal. It was a fragmented landscape with the powerful principalities in continual conflict with each other. In their fratricidal wars they remained oblivious to the menace that was brewing along the North Western borders.

India had not learnt from the experiences of the past. Over a century and half ago Mohammad Ghazni had launched eighteen devastating raids into India between 1000-1028 AD looting, killing, pillaging and converting. Each raid unleashed a trail of death and destruction but tragically it did not evoke a collective response. He systematically addressed one kingdom at a time in a series of annual raids that took him as far as Multan, Thaneshwar, Kannauj culminating in his final raid – the sack of the Somnath temple at Gujarat. Each of these raids took him further from his bases and deeper into hostile territory. A combined stand by the many states of medieval India would have not only halted Mohammed Ghazni, but could have virtually devastated his army. But in each case, the rulers stood idle watching their neighbor's house being burnt (at times with a sense of gleeful malice at their rival's discomfiture). The raids identified India as a soft target and though it did not establish the Ghazni dynasty on the throne of India, it set the tone for subsequent invasions. A century later another Mohammed; Shihabuddin Muizzuddin Mohammed Bin Sam of Ghor; or Mohammed Ghori as he is more commonly known, sought to emulate the feats of his namesake with even more disastrous consequence for the nation.

Mohammed Ghori came from the region between Herat and Ghazni, – modern day Turkey and Afghanistan. The turmoiled, intrigue ridden political atmosphere of Central Asia had made him a hard-boiled veteran at an early age. His childhood was replete with stories of the riches and easy plunder that lay waiting in India. Almost as soon as he reached adulthood, he had led a series of forays into Northern India advancing as far as the Indus, but they were mere probing attacks and not full-fledged raids. In 1175 he launched his first serious assault, crossing the Indus River for the first time and capturing Multan and Unch. He advanced deeper and soon annexed all of Sindh and its adjoining regions. With the initial victories easily attained, he now contemplated moving even further inward.

It was but natural that he would be drawn towards Gujarat and the vast riches that it held and in 1178, he planned his campaign. Gujarat was ruled by the Chalukyas, who were in a state of perpetual hostility with the Chauhans of Ajmer. Mohammed Ghori first tried to form an alliance with Prithviraj Chauhan, in which he proposed a division of the spoils if he was allowed to move through Chauhan territory on a direct route to Gujarat. His offer was rudely rebuffed. By some accounts Prithviraj was initially keen on attacking the

THE MAN

Prithiviraj Chauhan – Brave general, but over confident and impetuous. Through tactically strong, he lacked strategic foresight and could not consolidate an alliance against the foreign invader. He was too confident after his victory in the First Battle of Tarain. Allowed himself to be lulled into complacency with disastrous results.

Mohammed Ghori – His key trait was his determination. He did not let his initial defeats deter him. Changed his tactics after the first battle of Tarain with remarkable results. His single minded focus ensured victory in the Second Battle of Tarain.

invaders, but was dissuaded by his ministers on the misplaced premise that Ghori's attack on the Chalukyas would weaken them and enable him to consolidate his own power subsequently. This state of Chanakyan intrigue marked the political thinking of those times and these divisions amongst India's rulers emboldened foreign invaders to repeatedly raid India with impunity.

Although the direct route through Chauhan territory was denied to him, Ghori was not deterred. He took a long circuitous route through the Thar Desert and reached the outer fringes of the Chalukya Empire. Here at the borders he encountered their strong army, led by the dowager Queen Naikidevi who ruled on behalf of the boy-king Mularaja II. Naikidevi rode into battle with the young Maharaja on her lap and met the Ghori army at Gadarahatta, a valley in the area of present day Mount Abu. The Chalukyas knew their country well and were fighting for their land and survival. Their army was well-led, capable and the soldiers were known for their courage and skill with arms. Ghori's army was tired after forced marches of almost three months through the harsh desert and quite frankly were not prepared for such determined resistance. They had seriously under-estimated their opponent. The Chalukyas had chosen the battle-ground well. The open valley of Gadaraghata allowed the Chalukyas to fight a traditional, set-piece battle in which they were past masters and also prevented Ghori from using the mobility of his cavalry. After a fierce day-long battle, Mohammed Ghori's army was virtually decimated and he himself fled the field along with the shattered remnants of his army. At this juncture the fate of India would have been different had the Chalukyas followed the retreating army. Yet their cavalry was dispersed and could not concentrate in time to organize a vigorous pursuit. The misplaced concepts of fair-play too did not permit them to attack a defeated army. The retreating enemy was not pursued as they limped back and in spite of heavy casualties, Mohammed Ghori managed to withdraw his remnants in relatively good order across the border.

The events of Gujarat were observed with much interest by Prithviraj Chauhan even though he did not take any part in the battle. He was then at the height of his powers. Under his rule, the Chauhans had expanded their kingdom across much of present day Haryana, Punjab and Rajasthan. In the course of his conquest, he had made enemies with most of the powerful Rajput clans including the Chalukyas. When he heard of the rout of the Turkish army and followed its withdrawal across the Thar Desert, he made no attempt to intervene. Ghori was allowed to withdraw unhindered and made his way back to Ghazni, where he regrouped and consolidated his position. A threat which could have been crushed at inception was allowed to get away as the Indian rulers continued their squabbling and weakened each other in a series of inconclusive, fratricidal wars. The major threat which still loomed over the country was forgotten by their involvement with their own petty battles.

Mohammad Ghori

Prithviraj Chauhan

The First Battle of Tarain

In the years following his defeat and ignominious withdrawal from India, Mohammed Ghori was not idle. He rebuilt his army, enlisting the support of many tribal chiefs with promises of loot in Hindustan. This time he prepared with greater care and deliberation as he gradually developed the infrastructure for his next invasion of India. Prithviraj Chauhan too was equally busy in expanding his own empire. He had taken on the self-appointed title of "*Digvijay*" or world conqueror, but unfortunately his vision of the world encompassed only Northern India and the kingdoms adjoining his own empire. The dangers that lurked beyond these boundaries were conveniently ignored. Prithviraj's campaigns to expand the Chauhan empire brought him in direct conflict with most of the chiefs of the region including the Chalukyas of Gujarat and the Gahadavas of Kannuaj, the two most powerful dynasties of the time. The rivalries between the three kingdoms would have disastrous consequences for him and for India as such.

Bathinda Fort – Whose capture by Ghori was the first step of the conflict

Within a year Ghori was strong enough to launch another campaign into India. Just a year after his defeat at Gadaraghatta, he launched an expedition advancing in to Punjab. In 1179 he captured Peshawar and in 1181 he reached the gates of Lahore. He managed to capture Sialkot and defeated the Yamini dynasty, which then ruled the area of undivided Punjab, in a series of battles. Soon all of Punjab came under his yoke and his conquest now brought his borders in direct contact with the Chauhan Kingdom. Soon his gaze turned southwards once again. Yet, In spite of the threat brewing on his North Western borders, Prithviraj chose to ignore Ghori and continued to focus his energy and resources on his campaigns against the Chalukyas and Gahadavas. It was but a matter of time that border skirmishes erupted between the Chauhan and Ghori forces. Some historians claim that Prithviraj Chauhan defeated Mohammed Ghori seven times before the First Battle of Tarain but in all probability they were not full-fledged battles. Ghori's generals would have launched raids into the Chauhan Empire to test the defenses and perhaps nibble away at its territory. These raids were soundly repulsed by the Chauhan forces but did not deter Ghori in his plans for future conquest. These frontier clashes have been amplified to a great extent by some historians while others have chosen to discount them as being nothing more than skirmishes between border guards. Yet these clashes set the stage for the bigger battles to follow.

Things came to a head in the winter of 1190 when Mohammed Ghori captured the fortress of Tabarhindah, an important outpost on the borders of the Chauhan Empire. The exact location of the fortress has been lost in time, but it has been identified as being Bathinda The capture forced the local ruler to approach Prithviraj for help and the loss of this vital strongpoint finally galvanized him into action. In early 1191 he set out with a large army of over 200000 cavalry, 3000 elephants and a large contingent of infantry. He had mustered the support of most of the Rajput princes in the battle against the outsider and for once they were united in their cause. But significantly neither the Chalukyas nor the Gahadavas joined

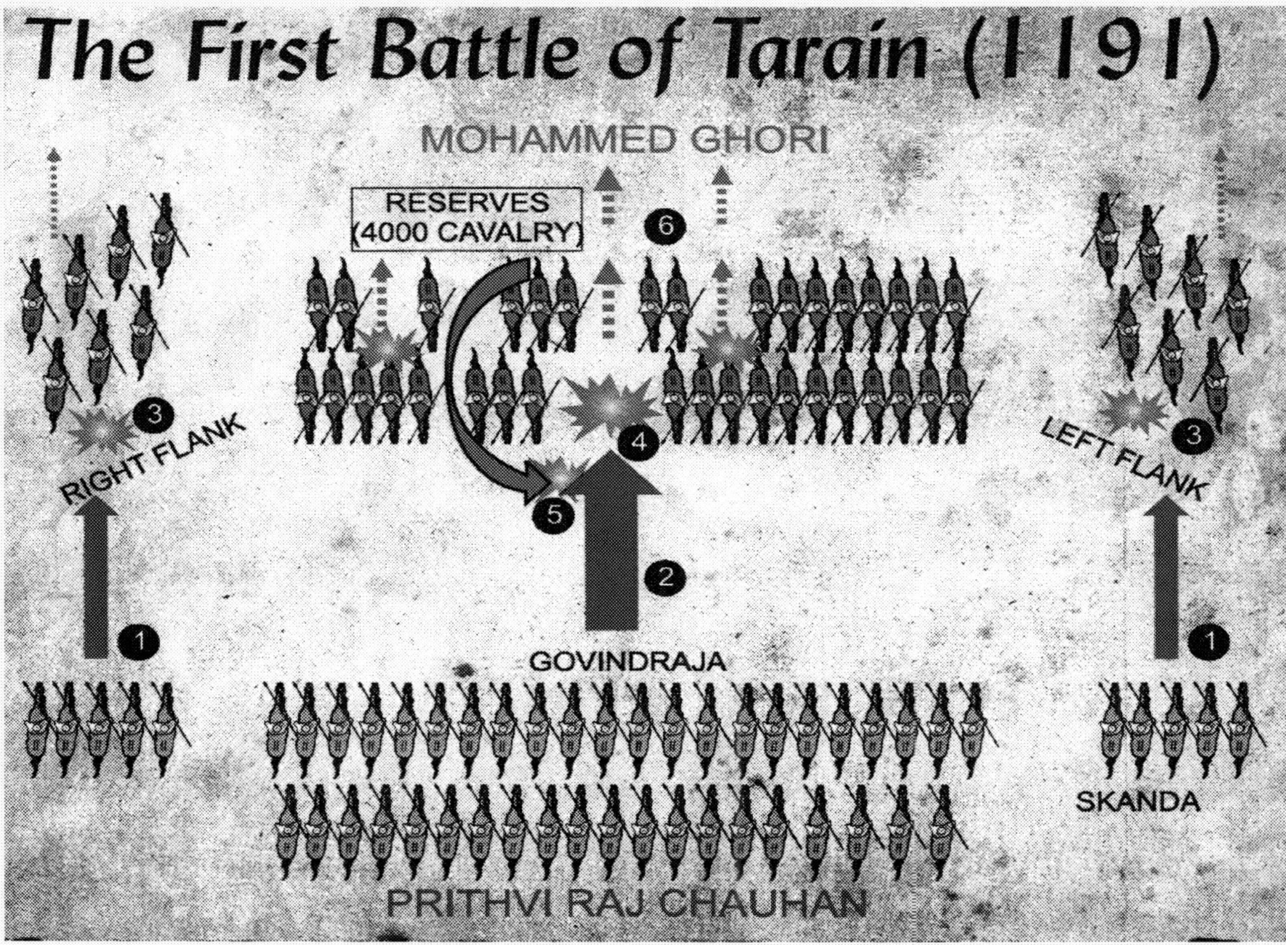

1. Initial attacks on both flanks by Rajput Army.
2. Attack on centre, led by Govindraja.
3. Break up of Ghori's flanks and their withdrawal.
4. Penetration of centre by Rajputs.
5. Counter attack by reserve Cavalry, led by Mohammed Ghori Counter attack fails and Ghori is injured.
6. Break up of centre and rout of Turkish army.

The Second Battle of Tarain (1192)

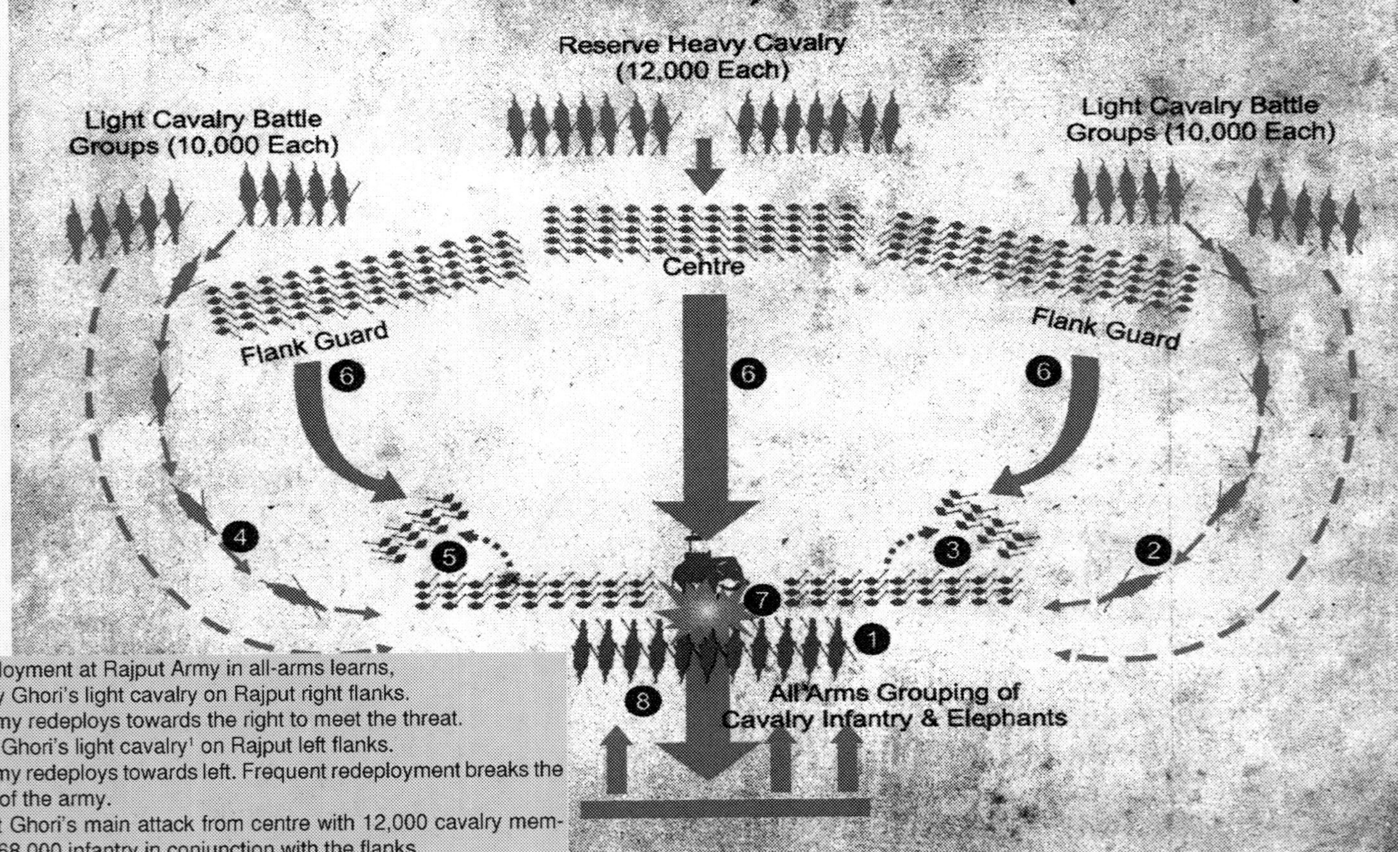

1. Initial deployment at Rajput Army in all-arms learns,
2. Attacks by Ghori's light cavalry on Rajput right flanks.
3. Rajput army redeploys towards the right to meet the threat.
4. Attack by Ghori's light cavalry[1] on Rajput left flanks.
5. Rajput army redeploys towards left. Frequent redeployment breaks the cohesion of the army.
6. Launch at Ghori's main attack from centre with 12,000 cavalry members and 68,000 infantry in conjunction with the flanks.
7. Ghori's attack breaks through Rajput formations, forms on the other side and attacks from the rear.

the cause. Mohammed Ghori had meanwhile reinforced his newly acquired fortress of Tabarhindah with a strong garrison of over 1200 cavalry and had stocked it sufficiently to withstand a prolonged siege. He himself camped with his army at Sirhind awaiting the arrival of Prithviraj and then marched to meet him in the first decisive encounter of the two armies.

The armies met at Tarain, now called Tirawari, an open plain in Haryana's Karnal district around a hundred and fifty kilometers West of Delhi. No exact estimates are available of the size of Ghori's forces, but in all probability the two armies would have been evenly matched. After all, Ghori would not have taken on the might of the powerful Chauhan Kingdom unless he himself was strong enough to contest it. The armies camped opposite each other for a fortnight and then organized themselves on the open plain of Tarain for the first of the fateful battles.

Ghori deployed his forces in the classical Turkish battle formation of the time. His main forces were arrayed in the centre, where he himself was positioned. The two wings of his army were entrusted to his Khurasami and Khalji generals, who were tasked to hold the flanks. His cavalry was deployed along the entire frontage to provide a readily available mobile force Yet in doing so he dispersed his cavalry unduly and did not retain a strong reserve for a crunch situation. This deployment was a little surprising, since

the Turkish concepts of war invariably hinged around maintaining a strong centralized cavalry reserve. Prithviraj too followed the traditional Indian deployment of that time – an Advance Guard, a strong Centre, two flanks, two flank guards and a rear guard; each composed of all arms teams with infantry, elephants, cavalry and chariots. On the open plain of Tarain the set-piece deployment allowed the Rajputs to exploit their strengths in conventional battle in which they were past masters.

Prithviraj took the initiative and launched the initial attacks with great force and skill. The main thrust of the attack was led by Skanda, one of his ablest generals, directed against the Turkish right flank. On the opposite flank an equally strong force was launched simultaneously. Prithviraj's plan was simple. He wanted to first break up the Turkish flanks and then simply roll from the sides towards the centre. The ferocity and determination of the Rajput attacks pushed back both wings of the Turkish army and gradually the flanks began to give way. The Rajput attacks pressed in squeezing the Turkish army from either flank. As the pressure intensified, the Turkish flanks broke and the troops fled from the battlefield exposing the centre to attack. It battle soon degenerated in to a fierce one-to-one personal combat in which no quarter was asked nor given. In this traditional form of combat, the Rajputs soon wrested their opponents. As the flanks collapsed and the exposed center came in the line of the Rajput assault, Ghori was advised to withdraw. But incensed at the sight of his flanks withdrawing without orders, he hurled himself along with his guards towards the centre of the Rajput attacks in a futile, last-ditch counter attack. His head-long charge got him face-to-face with Govindraja, the Governor of Delhi. In a desperate act he hurled his spear with full force towards his adversary seated in his howdah atop his war elephant. Govindraja managed to deflect the spear with his shield but the force of the impact broke two of his teeth. Govindraja responded in kind, hurling his spear with all his might. The height advantage of the elephant added to the momentum of the javelin which smashed into Mohammed Ghori's shoulders almost knocking him unconscious As Ghori swayed in his saddle, a Khalji foot soldier recognized him, jumped on his horse, held the falling king in his arms and guided him off the field of battle.

With Ghori gone the rest of the army disintegrated and a general rout followed. The victorious Rajputs pursued them for around forty kilometers or so but did not follow the chase with determination, allowing the bulk of the enemy to escape back into their own frontiers. Once again, their misplaced sense of chivalry did not permit an attack on a defeated enemy and Ghori was allowed to limp back with his broken army into the safety of his own dominions. One of the reasons for the failure of the pursuit was that the Rajputs had dispersed their cavalry along the entire frontage and did not have a strong mobile reserve for an effective pursuit which could have completed the destruction of the enemy.

The First Battle of Tarain was one of the greatest triumphs by an Indian army over a foreign invader, but like many of the earlier victories was not adequately followed up. In this battle, Mohammed Ghori played to the strength of his opponent, in spite of having been defeated in a similar battle against the Chalukyas just a few years ago. In conventional, static battle the Rajputs were superb. None could match them in skill, valor and the handling of personal arms Surprisingly, Ghori did not utilize the mobility of his cavalry, his traditional strength, at all. He deployed them in penny packets along the wings, keeping only a small force of around 4000 or so with him as an immediate reserve. This was too small a force to decide the outcome of the battle and once his wings collapsed there was little to restore the situation. A counter–attack on the flanks of the Rajput attacks by a strong cavalry force may have retrieved the situation but he simply did not have the resources. He generals too let him down. The Khalji and Khurasami troops who were entrusted with holding the flanks simple disintegrated and fled the battlefield, leaving the bulk of the army exposed and open to encirclement. Ghori's personal counter-attack to salvage the situation was too late. His force was not strong enough and by then his front had simply collapsed. His own fortuitous escape from the battlefield helped him to live and fight another day, but this day was lost. The disastrous defeat of the Turkish army could have been worse had the Rajputs chosen to follow up their attacks and decimate the remnants of the army in their scattered, demoralized withdrawal.

Flush with victory, Prithviraj now advanced and made contact with the fortress of Tabarhinda. It was a well-sited fortress and was well-defended by a strong garrison of around 1200 Turkish soldiers adequately stocked for a long siege. Storming the fort would have caused unacceptable causalities and moreover the Rajputs did not possess the siege catapults required to batter down the walls. They chose instead to invest it and wait for the defenders to run out of hope and provisions. It was long wait. Taharhinda held out for over a year – thirteen months to be precise – before the garrison finally surrendered and the frontiers of Prithviraj Chauhan's empire once again reached its original boundaries.

The Second Battle of Tarain

The rout of the Turkish army at Tarain affected both its principle actors differently. Mohammed Ghori withdrew to Ghazni and began plotting his return and revenge almost as soon as his injuries recovered. But the defeat rankled and thereafter, "he never slumbered in ease nor walked but in sorrow and anxiety." Back in Ghazni, the Khalji and Khurusami officers who were responsible for the unauthorized withdrawal of the flanks were publicly humiliated and dismissed. He then set about the task of forming a new army and built up a large force of Turks, Tajiks and Afghans. He armed and equipped them well and organized them into compact, well-trained formations and units. It took him a year and a half to be strong enough to return to India. Finally in the campaigning season of 1192, he was ready and marched back towards India with large force of over 1,20,000 well trained and equipped troops.

Prithviraj, on the other hand, spent an year of indolence. His easy victory had instilled a misplaced sense of self-confidence and now he discounted the threat from his North Western borders completely. He did not maintain any frontier guards or position any out-posts along the mountain passes of North Western India. He did not institute any form of early warning system. Instead he focused his energies on expanding the Chauhan empire and in quest of his title of "*Digvijay*", battled with most of the chiefs of Rajputana. He also picked up a bride on the way – none other than Sanyogita, the beautiful daughter of his old enemy, Raja Jayachand of Kannuaj. Relations between Kannauj and Ajmer had never been too cordial to begin with and degenerated further by the personal animosity of Jayachand and Prithviraj. Tradition attributes a more romantic cause to the hatred between the two powerful rulers. The bards of Rajasthan even today, sing of the love-story of Prithviraj and Sanyogita. Jayachand had organized a *swayamvar* ceremony in which Sanyogita was to choose her own husband amongst her many suitors. A host of nobility had assembled hoping to win the hand of the beautiful princess. Prithviraj, of course, was not invited and to spite him his statue was placed in the form of a sentry at the gate. As the ceremony began, Sanyogita ignored the assembled suitors and instead garlanded Prithviraj's statue selecting him as her husband. As she did so Prithviraj rushed forward on horseback and carried her back to Ajmer where they married with much pomp and ceremony. The story of the heroic abduction may have been exaggerated over time, but most scribes report that after his marriage he spent all his time with his new queen and had little interest in matters of administration and state. In his lethargy, he neglected his army and remained oblivious to the growing threat of Mohammed Ghori.

Ghori re-entered Punjab around March 1192 and soon captured both Peshawar and Lahore. With his position in Punjab secure he set out to expand his dominions deeper into India. He sent Prithviraj an emissary and offered to let him keep his kingdom if he accepted his sovereignty. The letter was treated with the contempt it deserved and ignored altogether. Prithviraj had awoken to the threat and yet was confident that he would be able to defeat Ghori once again. He assembled an army, of what has been estimated between 1,00,000 to 1,20,000 men and built up a confederation of chiefs and local rulers. Again the most powerful rulers of Northern India, Kannauj and the Chalukyas did not send any help. His army was much smaller than the force which had won so decisively at Tarain but in spite of that, Prithviraj remained supremely over-confident. He did not even consider it necessary to take his entire army with him in this campaign. His two most experienced generals, Skanda and Udayaraja, the prime architects of the first victory, were campaigning elsewhere but he did not feel it necessary to recall them. His minister, Someshwara advised him to wait and marshal more troops before confronting Ghazni, but the suggestion was rudely rebuffed. The trusted and capable minister was accused of treason and exiled in disgrace with his ears cut off. The humiliated minister joined Mohammed Ghori and provided detailed information about Prithviraj's order of battle, his tactics, state of preparations and the internal dissensions in the Rajput ranks. This vital information helped Ghori evolve his own plans.

Ghori began the campaign by first capturing the strategically vital Tabarhinda fort once again. The fortress fell without much resistance and flush with this early success, he advanced deeper into Chauhan territory. The two armies assembled at the field of Tarain and encamped in the familiar battle ground once again for a long period of wait. Prithviraj sent Ghori a letter asking him to be content with the area already captured and withdraw to prevent undue bloodshed. As a sop he even agreed to allow him to retain Tabarhinda. Ghori replied in a well-crafted letter stating that he had no authority to act on the proposal but would write to his elder brother at Ghazni for instruction. In the meantime, he proposed a truce. The language of the letter was obsequies and indicated a feeling of fear and insecurity which lulled the Rajputs into a misplaced sense of complacency. A temporary truce was established and the Rajputs let down their guard.

Truce or no truce, Ghori continued his preparations. While the Rajputs chose to spend their evenings in merry-making and feasting, his own scouts continually reconnoitered the camp and assessed their state of preparedness. The period of wait continued for a fortnight or so and then on the selected night, Ghori's army moved out silently from their camp, leaving their camp fires burning and depicting just enough activity to indicate that all was normal. The army marched all night and by dawn reached the rear of the

Rajput encampment. Just before day-break, they launched their attack on the unsuspecting camp.

Caught by surprise the Rajputs were initially caught off balance. But a sense of order was soon retained and they regrouped to fight back and keep their adversaries at bay. Fortunately for them, their cavalry was kept together at the centre of the camp and thus protected from the onslaught, The Rajputs assembled their entire cavalry and launched a furious counter-attack which pushed back the Turkish assault and forced them to withdraw with heavy casualties.

This was the decisive moment of the battle. If the Rajput cavalry had continued their attacks, the rest of the army could have formed up for a decisive attack while their enemy was off-balance. Instead, as at the First Battle of Tarain, they did not follow up the pursuit and withdrew back into their own lines after the attackers had been repelled. It was a crucial mistake. It allowed the enemy to regroup and reform for the main battle ahead.

Ghori had already prepared for this contingency. His troops withdrew in good order and reformed on the edge of the plain of Tarain in a compact and well-rehearsed battle array. This time his deployment hinged around his strongest force; his cavalry. He grouped his light cavalry into four battle groups of around 10,000 horsemen each which he deployed around the flanks. He retained his heavy cavalry of around 12,000 well-armed, heavily mailed horsemen as a central reserve, under his personal command. The bulk of the infantry was deployed in extended lines of sufficient depth to absorb the weight of any attack and provide the firm base from which his cavalry could sally out. He had learnt the lesson of his defeat well. Now rather than fight a conventional battle, he would

THE MOMENT

The turning moment was the launch of Ghori's heavy cavalry reserves, at the precise moment when the Rajput formations were disjointed by repeated attacks on the flanks. This powerful charge launched in conjunction with the light cavalry broke the Rajput ranks.

fight a battle of maneuver using the speed and mobility of his cavalry to break the Rajput deployment.

Prithviraj again formed up his army with the traditional deployment of an advance guard, a strong centre, two heavily protected flanks and a reserve (albeit not a very strong one). Each of his elements were composed of all-arms teams with infantry, cavalry, archers and elephants. However, he distributed his cavalry in squadron sized penny-packets across the entire frontage and did not maintain a strong enough mobile reserve for a concentrated decisive action. The dispersal of his cavalry implied that he was unable to react to the out-flanking maneuvers of the enemy and his own cavalry was largely relegated to a defensive role. The manner in which both sides utilised their cavalry; one in a concentrated manner in a largely offensive role, the other dispersed in purely defensive deployment would decide the outcome of the ensuing battle.

Ghori took the initiative. Just as the Rajput army completed lining up in its battle array, he launched one of his light cavalry groups onto the flanks of the formation. The size of the 10,000 strong cavalry force was magnified by the dust and noise and perhaps Prithviraj thought that the main attack was being launched on his flank. His large, ponderous formation turned to face the flank under attack. For a 1,00,000 strong force, complete with elephants, chariots, cavalry and foot soldiers shifting direction was a cumbersome feat in itself, even without enemy interference. As they turned, the formation became loose and ragged and lost its cohesion.

The huge maneuver of shifting direction was an exercise in futility. Even as they turned and braced to launch a counter-attack, the Turkish cavalry broke contact and withdrew back towards their lines without engaging in combat. The Rajputs now shifted formation once again to face their original front, where the large army of Mohammed Ghori awaited, fresh and intact. The same laborious process of changing direction began once again and when it was complete, the formation was loose and more ragged than before. Ghori now launched his second cavalry battle group on the opposite flank. Again the Rajput formation changed direction, again the Turkish cavalry withdrew without making contact, again the Rajputs chased an elusive, fleeing enemy and again the formation lost cohesion. This process went on four times during the day, frustrating the Rajput army, causing casualties and wearing down man and horse by its sequence of inconclusive actions. By late afternoon, the Rajputs were already tired and confused by the new tactics which they encountered. On the far side the Ghori army waited, the bulk of its troops still fresh and uncommitted, its formation intact and playing out a plan which they had undoubtedly rehearsed and practiced many times earlier.

In the afternoon, Mohammed Ghori launched his fifth and final flanking attack, only with a difference. His light cavalry battle-group now plunged deeper into the ranks of the Rajput formation and at the critical moment, Ghori launched his main attack. Placing himself at the head of his 12,000 strong, heavy cavalry and followed by almost 70,000 foot soldiers his attack tore into the centre of the now ragged Rajput formation. The heavy cavalry simply cut their way through the ranks into the rear. They reformed on the other side and then returned to launch yet another furious charge from the rear. The light cavalry continued its attacks on both flanks and the battleground turned into a melee of disorganized Rajput ranks fighting an enemy that surrounded them from all sides. The Rajput cavalry tried to launch their own counter-attacks, but it was too late. The cavalry was too dispersed and the attacks were simply not coordinated. By nightfall, 50-70000 Rajput soldiers fell on the battlefield with most of their leaders. Govindraja, the valiant governor of Delhi, who had played such a major role in the First Battle, was one of the many who fell, trying to lead an unsuccessful break-out. Prithviraj Chauhan was forced to leave the battlefield, but was pursued by the relentless Turks and captured near Sarsuti, (the site of modern day Sirsa) and taken to the Turkish camp.

The Aftermath of the Battle

The crushing defeat suffered at Tarain signaled the end of an era. Prithviraj Chauhan was captured and taken as a prisoner to

Ghazni Folk-lore provides an interesting story of his death. According to *Prithviraj Raso*, the chronicles of Prithviraj, Prithviraj was captured, tortured and blinded in Ghazni. There his court poet, Chand Bardai organized an archery display where the blind king would fire at a target using just sound. Mohammed Ghori himself was seated at the pride of place, on a balcony overlooking the archery court. As the blind king notched his arrow, Chand Bardai sounded a gong directly behind Ghori's seat. Prithviraj fired in that direction; the arrow sped and pierced his enemy beneath the heart, killing him instantly. Chand Bardai himself stabbed Prithviraj to death allowing him to die in a manner befitting a king.

The tale has gained credence over the year but in actuality Prithviraj was merely condemned to death by his captor. Ghori's own death took place years later, during one of his subsequent campaigns in India.

Ghori, followed up his initial conquests by placing his favorite general Qutb-ud-din Aibak on the throne of Delhi. It was to be just a regency but it paved the way for the establishment of the Delhi Sultanate and the beginning of Muslim rule in India.

Ghori's subsequent campaigns took him as far as Gujarat in 1195 He also defeated the powerful Gahadavala ruler Jayachandra (Prithviraj reluctant father in- law) and extended his area up to the banks of the Yamuna. It was only in 1206 that he met his end after a particularly brutal battle to quell the rebellion of the Khokars of Punjab. On his return from this campaign, he had encamped on the banks of the Indus River and was stabbed to death in his tent on the night of 15 March 1206 by a revengeful Khokar. But by then he had established Muslim rule in India in the form of Qutb-ud-din Aibak. The Delhi Sultanate would hold sway over North India virtually for another two hundred years.

The Rajput rulers meanwhile gradually declined. The three most powerful dynasties of the time; the Chauhans, the Gahadavalas and the Chalukyas had been defeated one by one in separate battles which destroyed their empires. Many of the smaller Rajput rulers chose to accept Muslim sovereignty and were allowed to retain their kingdoms, but the major kingdoms lost their powers irrevocably. The political ascendancy passed to the invaders who were now here to stay.

Analysis of the Battle

What really caused such conflicting results in the two battles? The first and most important reason was the manner in which they were fought and the strength of the two armies. In the First Battle, Prithviraj was undoubtedly better prepared and had assembled a larger army under his banner. In the Second, he was inferior in numbers as his most capable generals were out campaigning elsewhere. Altough exact details of the opposing armies are not available, the Ghori army was undoubedly larger than its opponent. The actions of the two adversaries reveal Mohammed Ghori confidence of his strength. His initial offer to Prithviraj was to accept his dominion – one he could have only made from a position of superiority. Prithviraj's counter offer proposed that Mohammed keep the areas he had already captured, including the prized fortress of Tabarhinda. He would have only made such a concession if he had been negotiating from a position of weakness. In all probability Prithviraj had been able to muster around 1,00,000 to 1,20,000 men in arms against around 1,50,000 to 2,00,000 held by his opponent. The caution which his ministers advised was due to the fact that he did not have sufficient troops to counter the large Turkish army. Yet in a spirit of bravado and over-confidence he ignored the advice and set out on the campaign when he was not fully prepared.

In the First Battle of Tarain both armies deployed conventionally and fought a traditional battle. Ghauri was unable to use the mobility of his cavalry and forced to fight a set-piece battle in which the Rajputs excelled. But the Rajputs squandered their hard-earned victory as they did not pursue the fleeing Turkish army and allowed it to live and fight another day. Ghori did not make the same mistake

THE TACTICS

The Rajputs adhered to the conventional tactics of the time, based on positional, static battle arrays. They did not hold any reserves which could retrieve an adverse situation. Ghori used the mobility of his cavalry by launching repeated attacks on the flanks, before launching a decisive blow from the centre. Skillful manuever decided the day.

in the second round. His deployment was designed to fight a fast, mobile battle which to negate the conventional skills of his opponent. The employment of cavalry made all the difference. The concentrated use of Turkish Cavalry and their skilful manuevering against the widely dispersed Rajput cavalry decided the day.

The equipping of the cavalry too played a major role. Ghori's cavalry were armed with light, composite, double curved bows made of wood-bark and animal bone meshed together to give a elastic hardness. The bow string was made from the large tendon of a buffalo or camel, sun-dried for many days to give it a tautness. This allowed it to propel an arrow at tremendous speeds over almost 650 yards against the range of 450 yards attained by a conventional bow. The added distance gave them the luxury of a stand-off range from where they could fire their arrows with relative impunity.

The deception measures taken by Ghori also played a major hand in the battle. His letter proposing a truce lulled the Rajputs into a false sense of complacency. Perhaps they did not take the threat seriously enough, or perhaps Prithviraj had simply become too over-confident after his first victory. Yet, truce or no truce, there was no excuse for not keeping adequate vigil on the Turkish camp or letting down their own guard. When the Turks attacked the unprepared Rajput camp at night they managed to attain total surprise which means that there was no early warning system in place. It is not that the stratagem of a night attack was new to Prithviraj. He had led one himself in his campaign against the Parmars of Abu just a year or so earlier. It should have been anticipated and the camp better prepared. Instead, Prithviraj was fast asleep even when the Ghori forces reached the vicinity of his tent. He has been severely criticized for this, "The king's behavior just before the Second Battle of Tarain was neither that of a hero, nor of a

great general, but that of a novice in the art of war and of a common reveler."

There were also strategic reasons for the defeat. The inability of the Rajput leaders to form alliances for one. The two most powerful rulers, the Chalukyas of Gujarat and the Gahadavalas of Kannauj did not join, nor did Prithviraj help them when they had been threatened. The fact that both the Chalukyas and the Chauhans defeated Ghori independently in two different battles – The Battle of Gadaraghata and in the First Battle of Tarain, indicates that the combined force of these two rulers would have been more than a match for Ghori's invaders. If only the three principle rulers of Northern India had combined they could here easily countered Ghori. However they ignored the external threat and focused on petty rivalries and old enmities. Perhaps one of the reasons for the indolence towards Ghori's actions was the fact, that before him, Muslim invaders had come repeatedly to raid, pillage and loot and in most cases the rulers had simply become inured to these raids. Perhaps mentally they compared it to an annual flooding of the rivers which came, devastated but withdrew leaving them to recover. The raids did not impact India as an entity but it did devastate individual kingdoms. But in the shifting political equations of that time, a raid on a neighboring kingdom ruler was not a cause of concern but an occasion to rejoice since it would increase their own influence. By the time the squabbling Chiefs realized the true nature of the external threat, it was simply too late. This time when the threat came it did not leave. Ghori's invaders left their representatives behind and established Muslim rule in India. The political landscape of India changed irrevocably. India would never be the same thereafter.

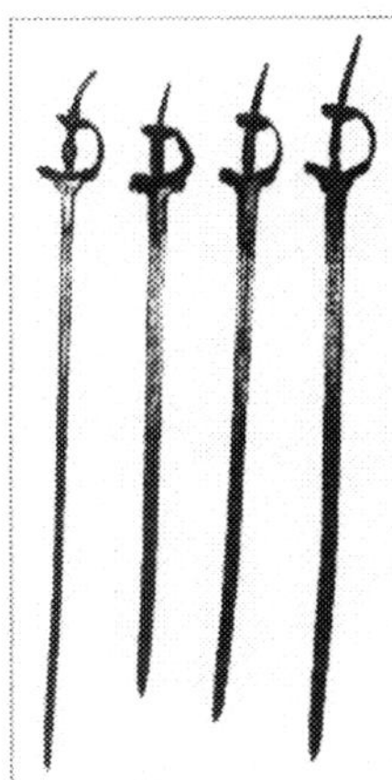

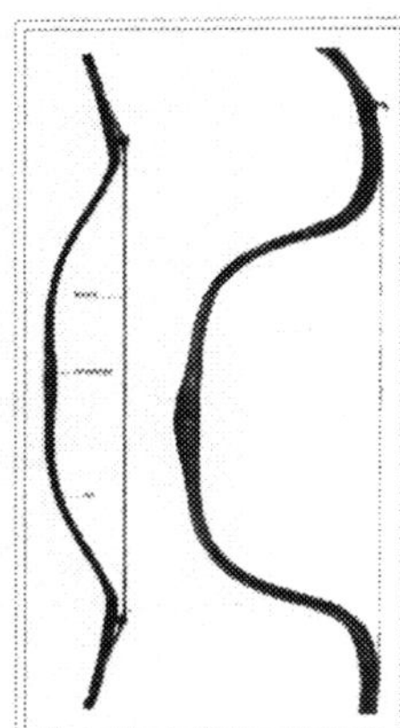

Babur directing an action in a critical moment in the battle. His cannon which played such a major role are in the foreground

3

The Carving of an Empire – The First Battle of Panipat

"The battle commenced when the sun was spear high and till midday when the enemy was completely broken and routed. This mighty army in the space of half a day lay in the dust",

– Babur, after the battle.

❖ ❖ ❖

If the Battle of Tarain signaled the establishment of Muslim rule in India, it did not really bring about much political stability. Dynasties came and went, the throne of Delhi changed hands repeatedly and the political landscape remained as disjointed and unclear as always. But in the 15th century another fortune seeker was drawn towards the riches of India. Like most before him, he came from the turmoil of Central Asia, whose perpetual turbulence repeatedly produced famed fighters. Like many of his predecessors, he would fight heavy odds, but unlike the others he would stay on to establish a dynasty that would rule India for over four hundred years. This man was Zahir-ud-Din Mohammed – Defender of the Faith – but was better known to future generations as Babur – or Tiger, the founder of the Mughal dynasty in India.

Babur came from a distinguished lineage. He was a descendent of Timur Lane and Chengis Khan, whose exploits he sought to emulate. Bought up in the turbulent quagmire of Central Asia he awoke to the harsh realities of power politics very early in life. At

Babur – Besides a brilliant general, he was also a scholar and a poet

THE MAN

Zahir ud din Mohammed Babur

Born on 14 February 1483 in Andijan Uzbekistan. A descendant of Timur Lane and Chengiz Khan. Ascended the throne of Ferghana in 1494 at the age fourteen.

A gifted general and skilled organizer. He organized his army in distinct arms. His ability to inspire his men was amply revealed during his dramatic address to the troops on the eve of battle at both Panipat and Khanua. Revolutionized warfare by the use of gunpowder and the incorporation of mobile warfare.

Was a man of great culture and learning. His memoirs, the *Baburnama* recounted his life in clear yet lyrical rose.

Died of illness on 26 December 1530. Buried in a simple grave in Kabul as per his will.

the age of eleven, his father Umar Shiekh Mirza the ruler of Fergana, a small province in Uzbekistan, died and he found himself in a struggle for succession for the throne. He was buffeted by uncles and relatives all claiming title to the throne. For two years he waged a constant battle of intrigue and deception to stave them off before finally consolidating his position and establishing himself firmly as the ruler of Fergana. He soon became strong enough to try to expand his kingdom and attacked Samarkhand, an adjoining kingdom which he had eyed covetously for long. After a siege of seven months he captured this prize and rode through its streets in triumph. But he was unable to enjoy his prize for long. Back home his brother

Gul rose in revolt and established himself on the throne of Ferghana. He rushed back to recover it and in doing so lost not only his own throne but his newly – won kingdom of Samarkhand as well – a kingdom which he held for all of 100days. By this time he was all of 15 yrs old and already a veteran of over a dozen battles.

For the next ten years Babur was "a king on a chessboard moved from place to place". He re-established himself on the throne of Fergana and more importantly managed to capture Kabul in 1504 when the ruler Ulugh Beg Mirza, his uncle, died leaving behind no successor. Babur seized the moment and raced towards the city, capturing it and claiming it for himself. More importantly he could stave off his competitors with a mixture of military skill and political intrigue and kept them at bay long enough to consolidate his hold on power. Now at the ripe age of 22 he had at last established a power base he could call his own and developed an appetite for more.

Ibrahim Lodhi

The Afghan ruler of Delhi. An ineffectual leader and a poor administrator. His rule was characterized by neglect and internal dissent.

Untested in battle. Had rarely led his men before the Battle of Panipat, choosing instead to rely on his generals.

Although he was not tactically gifted, he fought courageously at the Battle of Panipat and was the first Muslim ruler of Delhi to be killed on the battlefield.

Like most powerful chieftains of Central Asia, his eyes turned towards India and the vast riches that it held. After all he had an ancestry to emulate and had been brought up on stories of glorious raids and vast booties to be won. In 1505 he entered India for the first time and launched a border raid across the Khyber Pass. The raid was just a probing action for the subsequent expeditions which would follow. He followed this foray with five expeditions into India between 1519 and 1524 in which he looted enough to fill his treasury and more significantly gained the experience of battles in Indian conditions. He also used the period to modernize his army into a

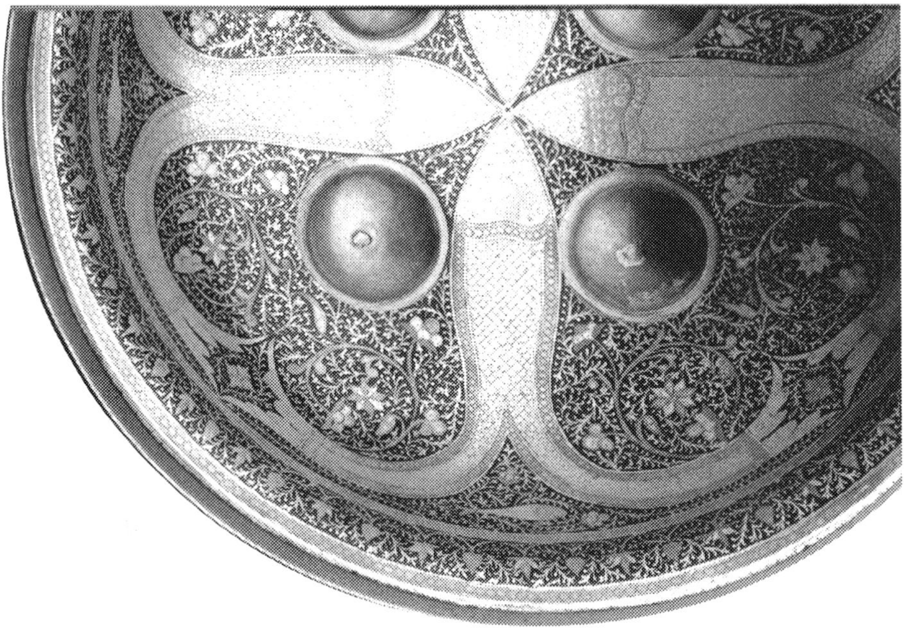

An ornately decorated Mughal shield

compact, well-trained force. He introduced muskets and cannons into his army and developed new tactics on the use of cavalry supported by infantry and artillery. India, always a soft target, was especially vulnerable at this juncture. It was rife with the internal dissensions and lacked a strong, effective power base. Ibrahim Lodi, the Afghan ruler of Delhi was a weak, unpopular king who concerned himself more with his personal pleasures than the affairs of state. The army was large, but poorly organized and equipped. The generals were not tested in battle and most had reached their ranks through favoritism, rather than merit. There was resentment amongst the local rulers against Ibrahim Lodi's unpopular rule and in 1523, Daulat Khan, the Afghan Governor of Punjab, approached Babur with an invitation to invade India. In 1524 Babur launched his first full-fledged invasion and advanced as far as Lahore. Yet he soon fell out with his ally, Daulat Khan over the division of the spoils. Prudently he withdrew to Kabul leaving behind a garrison at Lahore. Yet, his appetite had been whetted and in the next year he planned his subsequent and most crucial invasion of India.

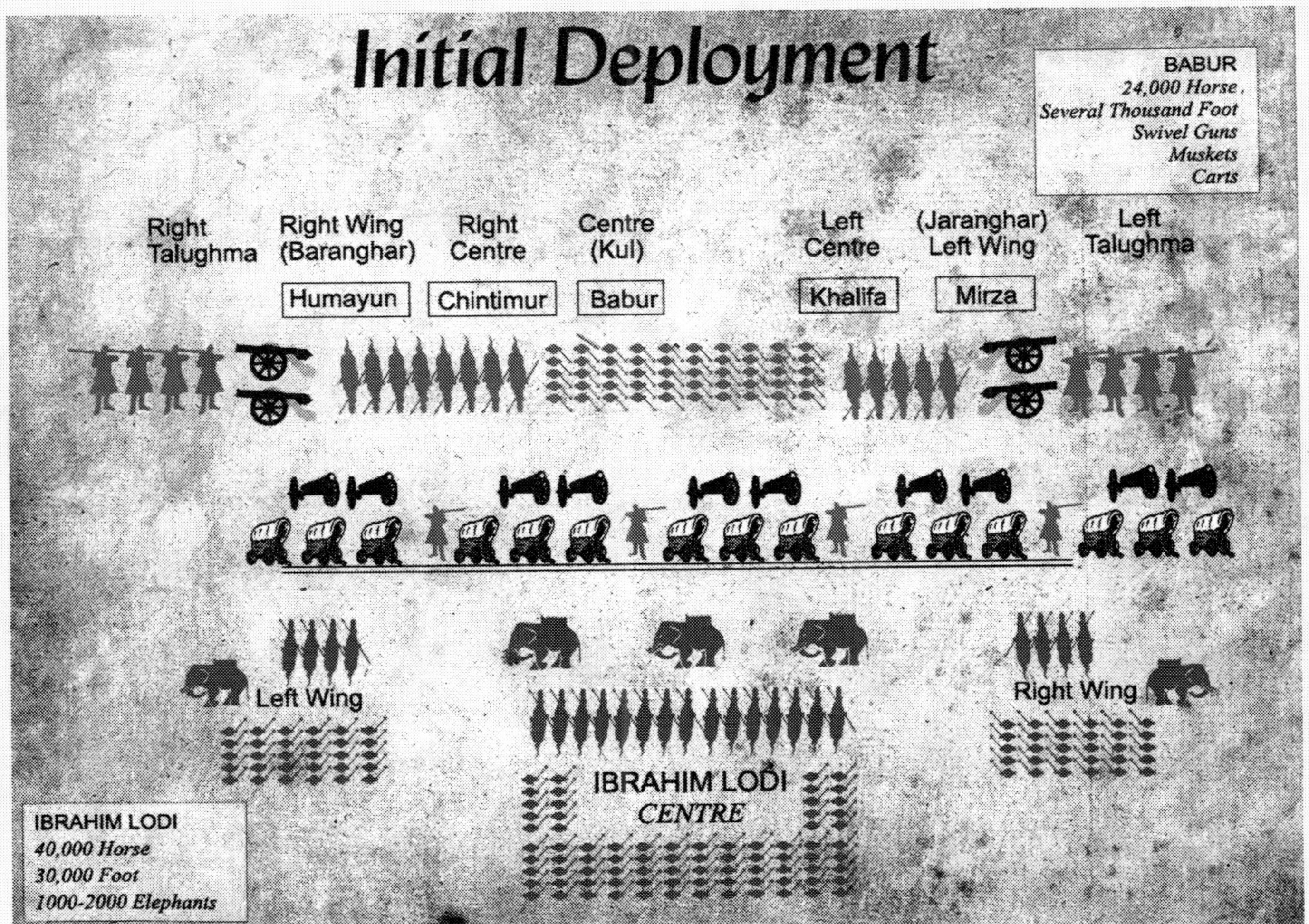
Initial Deployment
BABUR
24,000 Horse,
Several Thousand Foot
Swivel Guns
Muskets
Carts
Right Talughma
Right Wing (Baranghar)
Right Centre
Centre (Kul)
Left Centre
(Jaranghar) Left Wing
Left Talughma
Humayun
Chintimur
Babur
Khalifa
Mirza
Left Wing
Right Wing
IBRAHIM LODI
CENTRE
IBRAHIM LODI
40,000 Horse
30,000 Foot
1000-2000 Elephants

The First Battle of Panipat

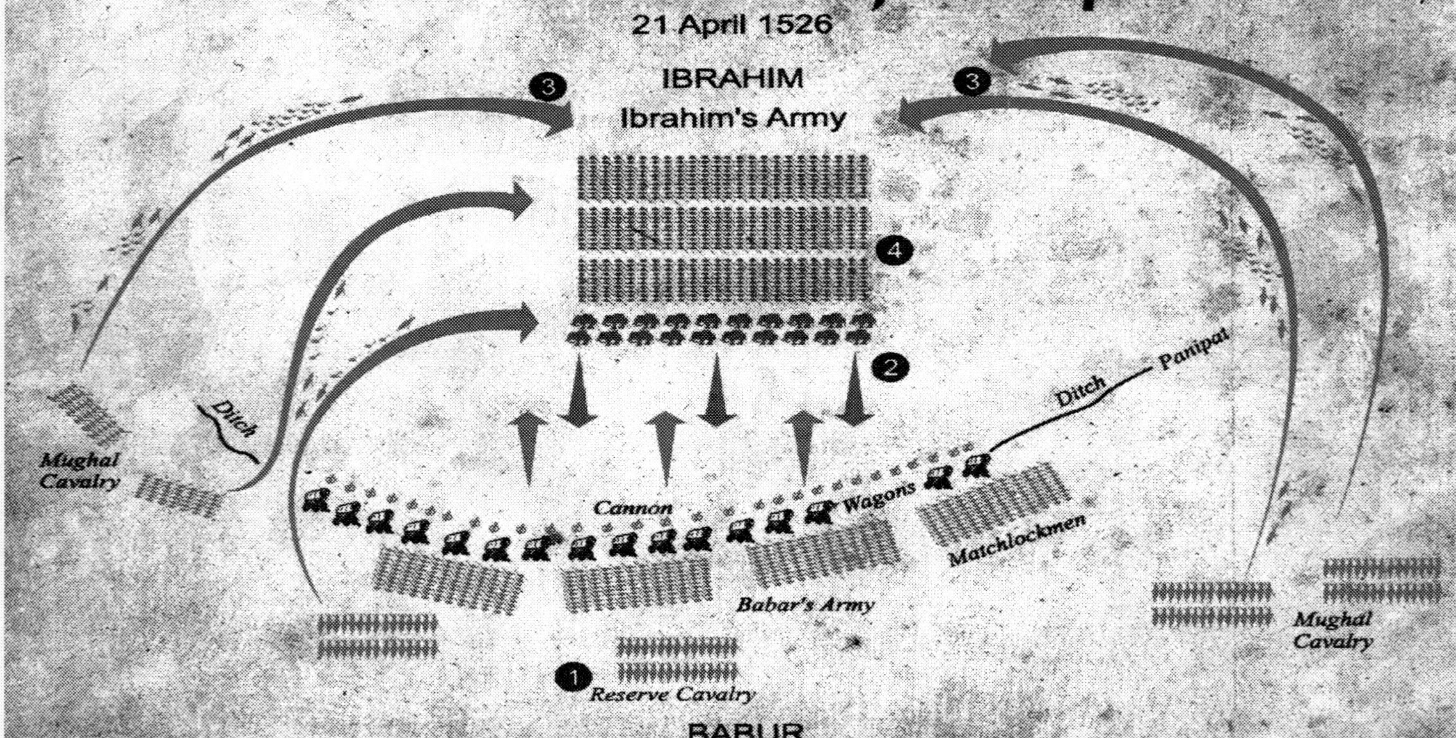

1. Babur prepared his positions with his right flank extending upto Panipat town, a ditch in front and a line of defensive works based on wagons, cannons and musketmen.
2. Ibrahim advanced towards Babur's defensive line without reconnaissance. His attacks flounder against the line of fortifications.
3. As Ibrahim's men concentrate against his defenses, Babur's launches his cavalry from the flanks.
4. Hemmed in from the flanks and unable to manuevre with the ditch in front, the Afghans are easy prey and slaughtered. Ibrahim is killed on the field with his men.

In November 1525 Babur set from Kabul – moving out well before the snows closed the mountain passes. He had built his army to around 20,000 men and reinforced it with troops and levies provided by the local chieftains he subdued en-route. He prudently sent ahead an advance guard under one of his best generals, Jehangir Kuli Khan with two thousand of his best Mughal troops to secure roads and passes and the ferries on the rivers which he would have to cross. His main force followed a few days march behind moving at an unhurried pace interspersed with many skirmishes along the way. He reached Sialkot by end December, Lahore a month later and after affecting a major crossing on the Satluj River in January 1526 reached Ambala by March. He was now within striking range of Delhi at the site near Panipat where the most notable battles in India's history had always been fought. This stretch of open land which extended between the Yamuna River in the South and the Shivalik Mountains to the North was the traditional gateway to Delhi. On this arena India's destiny had been often decided in the past. Now in the hot, dry summer of 1526 this battlefield would shape the history of India for the next 400 years.

Ibrahim Lodhi, the Afghan ruler of Delhi had received reports of Babur's move but was not unduly perturbed. Perhaps he too imagined that it would be another foray which would come and go without posing a direct threat to his rule. But as the threat grew closer and came within striking distance of Delhi he realized that he had option but to counter it. With an army of almost 100000 Afghan troops comprising of 40,000 Cavalry, 60,000 *paidgam* (infantry) and his *piece-do-main;* over 1000 war elephants he set out towards Panipat. But the large strength of his army hid its weaknesses. Only around half the strength were regular fighting troops. The others were a conglomeration of ill-mounted and poorly equipped levies hastily assembled from local chieftains. The army had not trained together and their equipment was out-dated. Even amongst the regular Afghan army, a sense of decadence had arisen due to years of easy, luxurious living. Ibrahim Lodhi himself was no military leader, nor did he have any capable generals or skilled advisors. Babur scornfully referred to him as "an unproved brave – one who had seen neither war nor hardship". He sized up Ibrahim as "An inexperienced man, negligent in all his movements, who marched without order, halted or retired without plan and engaged in battle without foresight." His assessment was right. The glaring difference in the quality of generalship would make all the difference in the outcome of the battle, in spite of Ibrahim's numerical superiority.

In spite of the numerical inferiority Babur held three major aces. The first was his leadership and the quality of his generals. They had been bought up in a diet of war for over two decades and were proved and tested veterans. The other was the quality of his Cavalry, whose tactics had been honed and tested in many a bitter battle. With the invention of the stirrup, his horsemen had perfected the art of firing arrows on the move and were equipped with specially designed composite bows which could be used while on horseback. According to an historian "His horsemen could fire six times before a musketeer could even load his weapon. Their arrows could pierce elephant hide and even on the move they could hit a teacup at over 60 yards." Their favorite tactic was to disorganize an enemy formation with a shower of arrows fired on the move and then

THE WEAPONS

Artillery – Used for the first time on the Indian battlefield. The piece de resistance of their equipment was the *Kazan*, a heavy mortar, and the *zarbzams*, light cannon along with 4000 matchlocks. During the initial battles when Babur's musket men fired, the opponents laughed thinking they were suffering from flatulence.

The composite bow. A small, light bow specially designed to enable the horseman to fire while on the move.

The Afghans relied heavily on the traditional heavy weaponry. This slowed them down and made them virtually unusable when they were hemmed in during the battle.

1000 elephants were the piece de resistance. These heavy armored pachyderms were disoriented by cannon fire and the sound and flash of matchlocks and ran amok in their own ranks.

follow up with a thunderous change. If the opposition held, they would simply wheel away and charge again from another direction. The Mughal horsemen had perfected the knack of making sweeping attacks from the flanks and their maneuvers were closely integrated with the actions of the infantry and the use of fire-power. The concept of using his cavalry in an integrated manner would help tilt the scales in the battle that lay ahead.

There was a third and the most important ace. His artillery and firepower. Gunpowder had just come to India and Siege guns had been seen on the Indian battlefield. But Babur would be the first to use them in close support on the battlefield. Babur's artillery arm had been honed under the watchful eyes of 'Master' Ali Quli, a Turkish artillery expert whose family had over three generations of experience in fire craft. Exact estimates of his artillery are not available, but sources refer to it as *Atish-bazi-e-bisyar or* numerous. His three major weapons were the *kazan*, heavy mortar on a four wheeled cart, a *zarbzan*, a light cannon on a two-wheeled cart and around 4000 matchlocks. From all accounts he could not have held more than two or three dozen pieces of heavy artillery. He had however developed the art of integrated their fire effectively with the maneuvers of his cavalry and the actions of his infantry and that would act as a tremendous force multiplier.

Yet, in terms of numerical and materiel superiority the odds favored Ibrahim. His army was at least four times as large and they were fighting on a ground of their own choosing. Yet Ibrahim's actions when they reached Panipat were not of an army preparing for battle. He assembled his nobles and soldiers and gave a weak, conciliatory address which was unlikely to inspire any confidence. He said that he could not predict the outcome of the coming battle but promised to be a better ruler if they came out successful. He then distributed his wealth amongst them in a weak attempt to gain popular favor. No tactics were developed nor was any attempt made to discern Babur's strength or intentions. No detailed reconnaissance of Babur's positions was made. His strategy was simple. He would play a waiting game and block the route of Babur's army and then force him to attack. His passive tactics, had they been allowed to work may have actually helped him use his superiority optimally. But Babur had no such ideas. His plans hinged on making Ibrahim attack him, hold him and then use the mobility of his cavalry to simply scythe through the vast army.

In spite of the aces that he held, Babur had reasons to feel apprehensive. Yet, one event before the main battle carried a welcome augury. The advance guard of his army led by his 18 year old son Humayun with some 150 horsemen encountered the contingent of the 4000 Afghan cavalry who were on their way to join Ibrahim Lodhi. Though outnumbered, Humayun's advance guard held its nerve and their positions. They pinned down the much larger force till additional troops from Babur's camp arrived and delivered the coup-de-grace. The first contact with the enemy was a triumph. The Afghan contingent was completely routed and over 100 of the enemy were killed and another 100 captured, including six of their prized war-elephants. This was Humayun's first victory in his maiden battle and it proved to be a tremendous tonic for the morale of the army.

Armed with the augury, Babur approached Panipat. Unlike his previous battles, which were usually fought in hilly terrain, the ground here was flat and open. The vast open country was more suited for the numerical superiority of his opponent as it would permit him to expand and simply sweep like a torrent over Babur's smaller force. Babur ordered a council of war and with the advice of his battle-tested generals evolved the strategy that they would adopt with telling success. The essence was to create a narrow front and force the Afghan Army to advance into a restricted space. This would hem in the much larger adversary and enable the cavalry to maneuver to the flanks and rear. The constricted space would also provide a killing ground for his cannon and musket which would be able to extract a heavy toll. Yet how could they create a narrow front with enough depth to withstand the initial Afghan onslaught and hold them long enough to launch the flanking cavalry attacks?

After a long and careful reconnaissance, Babur sited his defensive position. He deployed around three kilometers east of the town with a dry channel of the Yamuna River protecting his left flank. He reinforced this by creating another obstacle belt of fallen trees and ditches. His right flank was protected by the town of Panipat whose huts and buildings would prevent an adversary from launching any maneuver from that direction. The enemy had no option but to attack along the front between these two obstacles where Babur had prepared another surprise.

To give added protection to his frontlines and absorb the shock of the Afghan assault, Babur set up an obstacle belt of over seven hundred carts yoked together in pairs across his entire front. Each pair had a gap of around four meters between them which was covered with stretched rawhide and ropes to act as a tripwire in case the line was breached. In breastworks behind these gaps were firing positions in which six to seven musket men were concealed – suitably deployed to fire through the gaps. In the centre and around the flanks, the heavier cannon had been deployed in larger gaps of around fifteen to twenty feet through which they could fire their lethal volleys. As an added measure, Babur cleverly left a gap of around one hundred and fifty meters on the flanks through which his cavalry could maneuver and sally forth. These gaps were concealed with shrub wood and covered by the fire of his archers and musket men. With his skillfully sited defenses in place, Babur now pondered over the key question. How could he get Ibrahim Lodhi to attack?

In fact Ibrahim should have attacked much earlier; even before Babur reached Panipat and definitely before he could prepare and consolidate his defenses. After all, Babur had invaded his territory, he knew his ground over which he would be fighting and most significantly, he was fresh and waiting while Babur's army was fatigued after three months of marching and constant skirmishing. He was initially better deployed and had he attacked before Babur stabilized in is defenses, he would have been able to use his numerical strength to advantage. Yet he waited for Babur to make the first move and that proved fatal.

From 12–19 April in the hot Indian summer of 1526 the two armies waited just a few kilometers apart, sizing each other. Each waited for the other to make the first move; each was apprehensive of attacking first. In an attempt to provoke his enemy, Babur sent his archers and cavalry on a series of raids on the enemy camp, to hurl abuses and fire ineffective salvoes of arrows, but to no effect. The Afghans played the waiting game and simply refused to respond. In his camp, the quivering tension of the wait began to tell and morale wilted in the heat. Then Babur decided to act.

Babur ordered a large scale raid with over 4000 men (almost a fourth of his army) to attack the enemy camp at night. What he hoped to achieve is unclear. Perhaps it was to be an act of provocation, or perhaps it was just a measure to alleviate the tension of the wait. Whatever it was the result was a disaster. The raiding party did not assemble in time, the different groups made a shaky and uncoordinated start and many of the parties lost their way in the intervening ground. By dawn they succeeded in making the way to the Afghan camp only to find the enemy alert and waiting. In the breaking light the movements of the raiding parties were clearly visible and they were greeted with showers of arrows from the Afghan camp. The Afghans inflicted heavy causalities on the raiding parties and chased them back into their own camp. It was only Humayun's skillful covering fire that allowed the remnants to creep back into the sanctuary of their own defenses chastened, bloodied and quite demoralized.

Babur, in his memoirs, states that it was all according to plan but in all probability it was just a botched-up raid that went horribly wrong. But it achieved the desired result. It convinced Ibrahim that his Afghans were more than a match for Babur's rag-tag army and finally provoked him into attack.

The day of 20th April, immediately after the raid was an edgy one for Babur's camp. They anticipated an Afghan attack any moment. A false alarm at night added to the confusion and as dawn broke on the 21st April, one of the most fateful day in India's history, Mughal scouts confirmed their fears. Ibrahim's army was on the move and heading towards their defenses.

Even as the Afghan advanced, Babur fine-tuned his deployment. He placed himself in the centre of the defenses (*Kul/ghol*) where he could control the flow of events. The right flank (*Baranghar*) was under command of Prince Humayun and the left flank (*Jaranghar*) under Mohammed Mirza. Ahead of his main defenses he had deployed a small covering force which fed back information of the enemy approach. To the rear he deployed his reserve (*Iltimish*), a

THE TACTICS

Babur used ground skillfully to from a narrow defensive position in which the much larger Afghan army would be constricted.

Babur's offensive tactics were a hallmark of his ingenuity. He lined up his oxen carts in pairs and formed a defensive layout ahead of his main positions. Gaps were strategically placed through which cannon and matchlocks could fire. He used his defensive layout to hold initial Afghan assaults and then sent his cavalry to the rear to surround and cut down the enemy.

Ibrahim relied purely on the conventional tactics of the time. Decided to use the brute force of his superior army to overwhelm Babur's smaller force.

Had implicit faith in the 1000 war elephants without considering the effect of gunpowder on them.

He flouted the most fundamental principle of war. He attacked Babur's defensive layout without reconnaissance, without even forming up for the attack and blundered into the well sited defenses. Although he had a large cavalry arm, he did not use its mobility, preferring instead to launch frontal attacks on the well entrenched enemy.

large force of his best cavalry. This was a classical defensive deployment of the time and to this he added another element, squadrons of cavalry (*tulaqmas*) on the right and left flanks which would sweep in from both flanks after the enemy was held by the centre. Ditches and other obstacles were prepared and were cleverly camouflaged just ahead of the defenses. A withering torrent of cannon and musket fire would pour out from the gaps between the defensive lay-out of oxen carts. As Ibrahim's ponderous army approached Babur was ready with his defenses.

The Afghan attacked, supremely confident after their easy victory of the previous night. They marched straight from their camp, a distance of around 10 kilometers, and without even waiting to form up went headlong into the attack. The result was carnage. Without any scouts to lead them and with no information of Babur's defensive layout, the assault line simply blundered into the waiting barrage of carts Hemmed in by the obstacles created on both flanks, the attackers bunched up providing an easy target for the cannon and musketeers. As the leading waves wilted, the following echelons simply crashed into them hurtling forward by the momentum of their charge. In the chaos, the cannons and muskets opened up. It was not a charge any longer. The entire assaulting waves were a seething mass of confused disoriented warriors, trapped in a confined space, unable to advance and hemmed in from both flanks. They were no longer an army. They were merely cannon folder for the archers and muskets who continued their carnage at standoff ranges.

At the moment when the bulk of the Afghan army was virtually trapped in the ground ahead of his defenses, Babur launched his two *talugmas* towards the rear of the floundering Afghan army. Simultaneously he ordered both his right and left wing to attack from the flanks. The attacking wings now hemmed in the bottled up enemy. The Afghans tried repeatedly to fight their way out of the closing trap and one column almost succeeding in breaking out though the right flank. Had that column managed to break out, it would have created space for the following forces and perhaps posed a threat to Babur's

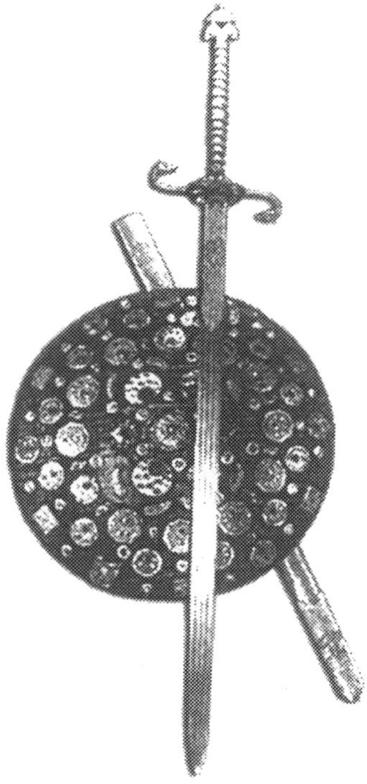

own flank. Yet, like all great generals, Babur had the instinct to understand the implication of each action of the battlefield. Just as the desperate Afghan attacks seemed to be on the verge of breaking through, Babur's pulled out reinforcements from his reserves in the centre to seal the breach and prevent the Afghans from breaking through his defensive line. The attacking Afghans were now pinned down on the obstacles ahead of his defenses and from the flanks and the rear, the jaws of the trap were closing in inexorably.

With the *talugmas* sweeping from the rear and the two wings closing in from the flanks the trapped attackers were sitting ducks for the torrent of arrows, bullets and cannon shot that poured on to them. As they tried to withdraw, Babur's two *talugmas* linked up in the rear, effectively bottling them within their pincers. The cavalry resorted to their time-tested tactic of unleashing shower after shower of arrows onto the enemy before launching their main change. The two wings of his army also began closing from both sides, gradually sealing the beleaguered army between them. With no space to maneuver, or even use their weapons effectively the Afghans become a disjointed, immobile force and it was literally every man for himself. Dozens of futile local counter-attacks failed and the Mughal wings slowly closed in. What followed was a massacre. By noon, hundreds of dead Afghan lay on the field where it was impossible to walk a step without stepping on a dead or dying enemy. Sultan Ibrahim realizing the gravity of the situation launched one last assault with his remaining cavalry, but it was too late to save the day. He himself fell leading a futile change (The first Muslim ruler of Delhi ever to fall in battle) and was amongst the 20,000 odd Afghan soldiers who were slaughtered on the battlefield. When the Mughals found the body, as was customary amongst them, they severed the head and carried to grisly memento to Babur. Babur treated the remains with respect and ordered the body be washed, covered with a shroud and had it buried with military honors at the spot where he fell.

The others were not accorded the same privilege. A pyramid of heads was made and the Mughals settled down to strip the bodies of any valuables and then systematically loot their camp. The remnants of the shattered army and a few camp followers managed to find their way back to Delhi but by the time the sun set, Afghan rule had been virtually erased in just five hours of battle. Babur himself wrote "The battle had commenced when the sun was spear high and lasted till midday when the enemy was completely broken and routed. By the grace and mercy of Almighty God, this arduous undertaking was rendered easy for me and this mighty army, in the space of half a day, lay in the dust."

Babur did not wait long after the battle. That very day be ordered Humayun to set out to occupy Agra (the Lodhi Capital) while he moved to Delhi and ordered a *Khusthah*, a formal prayer for a reigning monarch, to be read out in the main mosque to commensurate his victory. Two weeks later, on the 16th May, he ceremonially entered Agra and rode into the palace of Ibrahim Lodhi to take up his residence as the new Emperor of India.

Emperor of India? No not yet. Panipat had merely given him

THE MOMENT

Ibrahim had almost a month when he could have attacked Babur's army at any time before it could even arrive at the battlefield. Instead he allowed it to consolidate and prepare its defensive layout. He attacked at a time when the Mughals were ready and waiting and squandered the advantage.

Babur revealed his sense of timing at two crucial junctures of the battle. He reinforced his right flank with his reserves just in time to prevent an Afghan break in to his defenses. He launched his cavalry at the precise moment when the Afghan army was hemmed in ahead of his defenses and unable to maneuver. This helped trap it and seal its fate.

the foothold on the throne. To consolidate his rule, there would be more battles against even more powerful enemies. But Panipat marked the beginning. This battle was perhaps the most crucial in Indian history and had shaped it more than any other. A four month campaign culminating in a five hour battle had brought a new dynasty into India and would define its course for the next four hundred years. The geography, the psyche, the culture, the architecture, the dress, the cuisine and the very history of India would now change. Panipat changed India irrevocably, though this was but the start point of Mughal rule in India. There would be more battles, some even more bitter and close fought than this, which to follow which would define the shape and chisel the contours of the new Mughal empire.

Fierce hand-to-hand fighting in the closing stages of the Battle of Khanua

4

Consolidating the Empire – The Battle of Khanua

"How much better it is to die with honor, than to live with infamy" – Babur, addressing his troops on the eve of battle.

❖ ❖ ❖

Panipat merely gave a foothold to the Mughal Empire in India. There were other even more difficult battles to be fought against even more formidable adversaries, before the empire could be consolidated. Just eight months after the victory at Panipat, Babur would fight an even more decisive battle at Khanua against the powerful Rajput confederacy under Rana Sangram Singh, or Rana Sanga. This battle, even more then Panipat, would decide the destiny of Mughal rule in India.

Many in the Mughal army expected Babur to return to Kabul, laden with booty, as they had done in their previous expeditions. Yet Babur's ambitions called for more than just a raid. After almost thirty years of continual strife he had won for himself one of the greatest empires of the time and now Ferghana, Samarkhand and even Kabul could not match the sheer glory of the throne of India. He hated the heat, disliked the local population and missed with all his heart the sounds and smells of Kabul. Yet, in spite of his home-sickness, he decided to stay and make India his home. It was a decision which would not go down well with his men. Like him, they longed for their homes and found the environment of India to be hostile and forbidding. They hated the heat and dust of India and the summer of 1526 was one of the worst in living memory. They were friendless in an alien land and felt the palpable resentment from the local population. Ominously, war clouds were rolling in from all directions as the Rajputs and the Afghans marshaled their forces against the outsiders.

Rana Sanga – the battle scarred veteran of over a hundred battles

Babur set about harnessing his forces with his usual dynamism. He first quelled the discontentment amongst the men with a stirring address to his sullen and glum troops, in which he praised their battles and their conquests, their struggles and the victories and the glories of the Empire that awaited them in India. He himself would not leave but permitted all those who wished to depart with grace and honor. Some of his men, including his most trusted general Khwaja Kalan, accepted the offer to leave and they were allowed to do so, laden with gifts and bounties and with every mark of respect. Amongst the remainder, he distributed all the wealth and plunder that he had collected, but more than that he infused in them his vision of a rising Mughal empire in India and the determination to achieve it.

Yet securing the empire would be far more difficult than he imagined. The very vastness of India would suck in virtually all his troops and everywhere voices rose in revolt. The Afghan chieftains were still a power to reckon with in the East. Though they shared little love for Ibrahim Lodi they were definitely not going to acquiesce to an outsider. After securing Delhi and Agra he now set out to quell the Afghan emirs rising in revolt in the adjoining districts of Sambhal, Bayana, Mewat, Dholpur and Gwalior. Further to the east, the Afghans held sway over the entire area east of the Ganges and if they united they could prove to be a formidable foe and thwart his future ambitions. He sent Humayun with a powerful

THE MAN

Babur – General *par excellence*. He understood technology and tactics. Physically very strong. He could run a mile with a man under each arm and boasted of having swum across each river in India. He had a deep insight into the psyche of his soldiers. His oratory and vow of renunciation on the eve of the Battle of Khanua transformed his dejected army into a frenzied, excited horde

Rana Sangram Singh – Ruled the powerful Mewar kingdom from 1508-1528. Managed to unite the Rajput princes under the banner of a Hindu kingdom.

While his courage and skill matched that of his adversary, he lacked a sense of technology. He refused to innovate or change tactics even when confronted with gunpowder and cannon on the battlefield.

His concept of chivalry and a fair fight made him negate his advantage of numbers. He plunged into head-long frontal assaults on Babur's well prepared defenses with disastrous results.

Did not realize the treachery of Taur Silhadi, the Chief of Raisen even through he knew that his loyalties were suspect. He instead appointed him as the head of the vanguard which allowed him to defect at the most critical juncture of the battle.

expeditionary force to quell them and bring the outlying areas under Mughal control. Humayun had matured into a seasoned war-veteran even though he had "not as yet put razor to cheek". He soon secured control of Jaunpur, the major Afghan kingdom in the East and defeated the Afghan emirs in a brutal battle. Many of the Afghan Chiefs, realizing that Babur intended to stay, now turned sides and pledged allegiance to him in return for concessions to keep their land and titles. But while the fragmented Afghan emirs were easily quelled, the Rajputs were more formidable opponents. The major adversary was in the figure of Rana Sanga, the powerful ruler of Mewar who had assembled together virtually all the ruling chiefs of Rajasthan along with several Afghan chieftains (including Mohammed Lodi, the brother of Ibrahim Lodi) and formed a confederacy to throw out the invader. After many years, India had found a Hindu ruler who was now in a position to claim the throne of Delhi.

The Rana himself was a formidable adversary. Unlike Ibrahim Lodi, he was a veteran of over a hundred battles and his body carried the scars and wounds of an intrepid and ferocious warrior. He has been described as "being of middle stature, but of great muscular strength, fair in complexion with unusually large eyes. He exhibited but the fragments of a warrior. One eye was lost in a broil with his brother, one arm in action with the Lodi King of Delhi. He himself was lame with a limb being broken by a cannon ball and by the sword and lance he counted eighty wounds on various parts of his body". Yet for all his ferocity and great skill in battle he was reputed to be a chivalrous and noble foe.

Rana Sanga's star was on the ascendant. Already adored and widely respected for his manly qualities and noted chivalry he was the one man who could get the squabbling chieftains to unite. Over the years he had build up the Rajput kingdom of Mewar from Mandu (near Indore) in the south towards Agra and Bayana in the North and East. As his kindom expanded he came virtually to the doorstep of Delh. He had fought eighteen pitched battles with the kings of Delhi. In the last battle he had defeated Ibrahim Lodi in person, captured his son and routed the Afghan army. His eyes too were on the throne of Delhi and the prospects of finally establishing a Hindu Empire in India. He had got together most of the kings of Rajputana, including seven *Rajahs* of the highest rank, nine *Raos* and one hundred and four chieftains. Two Afghan chiefs, Hasan Khan Mewati, and Mahmud Khan, the son of Ibrahim Lodi had also come together under his banner. His banner depicting the sun god, began being seen as a symbol of victory; after all he had not lost a single battle before this. Now his banner became the rallying point for the campaign against the invader. According to Babur, he had assembled a force of over 200000 warriors, but that seems to be an exaggeration. A figure of around 80,000 fighters seems to be the more plausible estimate.

From some accounts, the Rana and Babur were in touch even before his invasion of India. According to Babur in his autobiography *Babur-Nama*, he was amongst the Indian chiefs who had sent an envoy to Kabul, inviting Babur to attack Ibrahim Lodi. He had also reportedly promised to launch a diversionary attack on Agra as Babur approached Delhi to divide Ibrahim's reaction and divert his troops. Babur, in fact accuses him of not keeping his part of the bargain. However, Rajput versions claim that it was Babur who approached Rana Sanga with a promise to accept Rana's kingdom up to the *peela-khar* (the Gambhar River). He even agreed to pay an annual tribute to the Rana if accepted these boundaries. There must be some truth in both versions. It is likely that Rana's tacit support at Babur's invasion against the unpopular and tottering Afghan rule at Delhi may have been conveyed to Babur. It is also likely that the Rana may have foreseen a long and protracted struggle between Babur and Ibrahim which would weaken both sufficiently for him to establish a Hindu Kingdom in India.

Babur on the other hand, did not want to fight an adversary as powerful and dangerous as the Rajputs whose courage and ferocity in battle were quite renowned. Nor did he want to clash with the most powerful ruler of India at a time when he had not fully consolidated his position. Emissaries had been making rounds of each others camps with proposals and counter-proposals even as preparations for war were building up. Negotiations had been continuing under Taur Silhadi, the Rajput chief of Raisen, who had recently converted to Islam, and used his newly acquired stature to gain access to Babur. The negotiations inevitably broke down, but it gave Raisen the opportunity to strike his own deal with Babur – one which would have disastrous consequences. It was but inevitable that the two most powerful rulers of India would clash

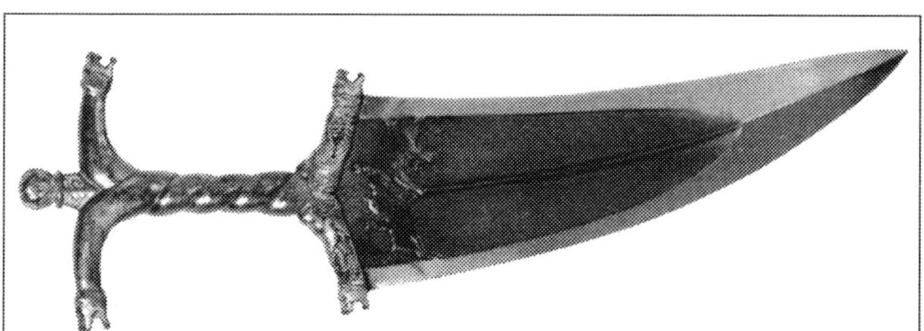

Short Khanjar – traditionally used by Rajput soldiers

for the throne of Delhi. And on the outcome of that clash would hinge the destiny of India.

The Build-up to Battle

Babur had almost eight months to prepare before the clash. The hot summer of 1526 gave way to a torrential monsoon making any campaigning impossible. Babur used this period to consolidate his position and re-build the strength of his army. His generosity in sharing the booty after the battle of Panipat had drawn many volunteers from Uzbekistan, Afghanistan and his captured territories, who swelled his ranks and made up for the numbers that had fallen in battle. Many Indian chiefs expected him to depart after the battle and chose to merely keep a neutral distance. But when they realized that he was here to stay, they allied themselves to him and hitched their stars to his rising fortune. Babur had used this time to also pursue his other interests, namely his writing and love for gardening. He wrote extensively on his biography the *Babur-nama* and used the monsoon period to layout a beautiful garden on the left bank of the Yamuna, with well-laid out, symmetrical rows of flowers-beds, shrubs and lawns. This garden retreat, designed on the lines of Kabul, soon became an affluent suburb of Agra and was prosaically named Kabul by the local inhabitants. This was the first infusion of Mughal culture into India, and over the next four hundred years, the impact of this

Mughal body armour and greaves

culture would touch every thing; its architecture, its music, clothes, dance even its cuisine.

In this Babur narrowly survived an abortive attempt on his life. He had inherited the staff of Ibrahim Lodi and four of his former cooks were still in the palaces. One of these was bribed by Ibrahim's mother to poison Babur and he managed to sprinkle a considerable amount of poison on the hare meat which Babur was to have for dinner. Babur was fortunate. He was hit by a violent attack of nausea and retching after the first few morsels and gave up the rest of the meal. His staffs were not so fortunate. The cook was flayed alive; two slaves were trampled under elephants and the *bekawal* was hewn to pieces. In a few days, Babur had recovered and was none the worse for the episode.

The brief interlude which the monsoon brought, soon came to a close and Babur turned his attention on more important issues. Humayun's campaign in the East had brought most of the rebellious Afghan chief to this knees, but this preoccupation with the Eastern flanks allowed Rana Sanga to consolidate his large confederacy and prepare for his campaign against Babur.

Mughal helmet – the chain flaps around the neck and ears provided additional protection

Rana Sanga began his move against Babur in early 1527. By all accounts he advanced Eastwards at a leisurely pace, subduing his rivals and swelling his armies with allies en route. By end January, he occupied Kalpi and Dholpur and shifted his attention to Bayana. It was here that the two armies first skirmished and tested each other. Babur had seized the fort in the previous autumn and it formed the outlying Mughal outpost on its South Western boundaries. Rana Sanga advanced towards it confidently and in February 1527, laid siege to the fort. He advanced on the fort from all four directions and slowly closed the noose to prevent it from being reinforced. Babur sent Mohammed Sultan Mirza, one of his most trusted Generals with a light force to reinforce the fort but the relieving force was ambushed en route and forced to retreat with heavy casualties. On 21th February the fort surrendered and the ease with which Rana Sanga managed to capture Bayana and the prowess which the Rajputs revealed in each skirmish with the Mughals merely helped demoralize Babur's army further.

By now Babur had managed to concentrate his army considerably by pulling in troops from his outlying garrisons and recalling Humayun from his expeditions east of the Ganges. On 11 February 1527, Babur was strong enough to march out of Agra for his most decisive battle. This time the auguries were ominous. Even before the battle was joined, news of Rajput valor, their skill and chivalry had percolated down to the men. In each skirmish the Mughals invariably came out mangled and bruised. The first major encounter with the Rajput army was also a disaster. Babur invariably gave the role of his advance guard to different generals in rotation. As they advanced from Agra to Khanua, the Mughal vanguard of around 1500 cavalry led by Abdul Aziz, one of his young and impetuous commanders blundered into a strong force of 5000 Rajput horsemen around eight to ten kilometers away from Fatehpur Sikri. The advance guard was virtually annihilated and the

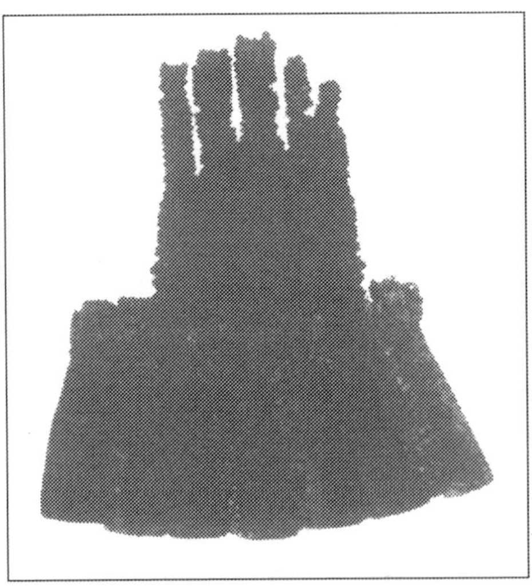

Mughal gauntlet used for additional protection to the sword arm

contingents which Babur sent to relieve them were beaten back and forced to withdraw. Most were killed or taken prisoner and Abdul Aziz's horse tail standard was captured and taken as a valuable war-trophy. The Rajputs chased the few survivors virtually up to the gates of their camp, but did not follow up their attack and withdrew in good order leaving the Mughals in a state of consternation and disarray.

The sense of defeatism that crept in the army was reinforced by the arrival of Mohammed Sharif, a reputed astrologer from Kabul, who pessimistically proclaimed that since Mars was now aligned in the West whoever engaged it from the opposite direction would be defeated. His gloomy predictions demoralized the troops even further.

Yet Babur preferred to let actions, rather than the alignment of the stars, decide his destiny. In the wake of the defeat of his vanguard he halted his army and decided to take up a defensive position just ahead of Sikri (Now Fatehpur Sikri) with a deployment similar to that at Panipat. One of his flanks was protected by a large lake and the entire defensive layout was fortified by ditches and trenches. As in Panipat, he linked together a line of around 1000 carts, each set-up in pairs and joined by chains. In between each pair was a gap of 60 to 70 meters which was covered by the fire of his artillery and muskets. He also created a new innovation, wooden tripods on wheels with movable shields affixed to them. His musketeers could fire behind the shields, safe from the fire of enemy archers and the tripods could be wheeled to any part of the battlefield thus providing an effective mobile defensive position. This simple innovation would be one of the deciding factors of the battle. He followed the same time-tested defensive layout using his artillery and infantry deployed behind the line of carts, his cavalry in a reserve in the rear and the two *talugmas* deployed along the flanks. This deployment would now withstand any immediate attack, provided the men held it with the same resoluteness that they had shown at Panipat.

In the one month during which the Mughal army remained

Helmet worn by ordinary foot soldiers

deployed in their camp, the Rajputs regularly sent skirmish parties to launch raids right up till the line of his guns. A column of reinforcements coming to join Babur from Kabul were intercepted and decimated. Morale plummeted even further and the dejection spread like a contagion. Many of his most loyal followers openly declared that they should merely call it a day and leave back for Kabul. While out riding Babur mulled over the problem and his agile mind found the perfect solution to raise the morale of his men. Over the years he had been a heavy drinker (and quite fond of opium too), a common failing in most of his army. He now assembled his army in full battle order and addressed his troops. He gathered all the wine casks and poured the precious wine into a shallow well. His gold and silver goblets were smashed and the fragments distributed amongst the poor. In an emotional oratory he took a solemn vow of reconciliation, vowing to abjure from wine forever (a vow that he would break later in his years). He exhorted his men once again with promises of glory and fame as he roused them for the coming battle. "Whoever sits down to the feast of life must drink the cup of death' he intoned. "How much better then it is, to die with honor than to live with infamy". He also declared a *jihad* and vowed, Quran in hand, to fight a holy war against the infidels.

The result was electric. In one moment, he turned his glum and demoralized army into an exhilarated, frenetic horde who took their own vows of renunciation, smashed their wine-cups and pledged to fight the holy war. Like all true leaders Babur had identified the one chord of emotion which would unify his army. This was the first instance of *jihad* being invoked in the sub-continent and it produced the desired results.

With the morale of the army rejuvenated once again, Babur set about consolidating his position with his usual energy. Additional reinforcements managed to join him and the mood of the camp gradually shifted to one of confidence. In that month long period when Babur was static and deployed, it was surprising that the Rana did not act more forcefully. Barring a few raids by the Rajput cavalry, there was virtual inactivity by the Rana. A forceful attack at this juncture when the Mughals were unbalanced and still a little shaken by their early defeats could have been perhaps sealed the issue once and for all. However, rather than attack, he chose instead to continue negotiations with Babur using Tuar Silhad; the Chief of Raisen as an emissary. According to Rajput sources, Babur had accepted the demand that the Rajput Kingdom would extend up to *Peela-Khal* (Gambher River). In return, Babur wanted be allowed to retain the throne of Delhi and even agreed to pay an annual tribute. Though the negotiations broke down, the long-terms effects were dramatic. Firstly, it enabled Tuar Silhadi to enter his own agreement in which he was promised territory and security if he defected to Babur at the right time. (An action he would perform, with telling results at a critical stage of the battle). The negotiations also created a sense of discord in the Rajput camp amongst the many rulers and chieftains – each powerful in their own right – whose opinions could not be discounted. Slowly an imperceptible split began to appear in the fragile Rajput confederacy, as the internal dissensions and personal egos came to the fore.

THE MOMENT

The turning moment of the battle came when Tuar Silhadi deserted just as Rana Sanga's attacks seemed to be making some headway. His defection left a yawing gap in the battle array which was exploited by Babur. He also provided him valuable information about the state of the Rajput army, the deployment and even of the wounds suffered by the Rana. This gave Babur the insight to plan his subsequent moves and the precise moment to launch his counter attack.

While the Rajput camp inexplicably gave way to inertia, Babur consolidated his position. On the 12th of March, he moved out of his camp into a previously reconnoitered, well-sited defensible location around three kilometers ahead. As always he chose his ground well. One side was protected by a small lake and the deployment itself was based around a small hill which gave him the advantage of height. He formed the same layout that had served so well at Panipat, protecting his forward line with 1000 carts yoked in pairs with gaps between them. In these gaps he deployed his musketeers behind his newly created movable tripods. His trump card, the cannons were deployed behind an artificial ditch, which would prevent the charging Rajput cavalry from reaching them even if they managed to cross the initial defense line. His master gunner Ustad Ali Quli had recently cast a large mortar which formed the piece-de-main of his artillery deployment. The line of guns was further covered by his archers deployed on their flanks. He positioned himself in the centre, where his skilled eye could follow the battle unfolding and retained 10,000 cavalry under his direct command as a mobile reserve and the final ace up his sleeve. The right flank was placed under Chin Timor Sultan with a strong cavalry component of around 5,000 horsemen under Prince Humayun. Mahdi Khwaja and Mohammed Sultan Mirza, two of his trusted and experienced generals were in charge of the left wing with an equally strong mobile reserve of 3000 cavalry. He placed two out flanking columns of around 1000 Mughal horsemen who formed the right and left *talugmas* and would be used to sweep along the flanks in the critical stages of the battle. Babur based his deployment and his plan of battle on the time-tested tactics of Panipat. And as in Panipat, events unfolded in virtually the same manner and with the same results.

At dawn on the 16th of March, again a Saturday as it was at Panipat, Babur's scouts reported that the Rajput army was on the move. During the period of redeploying his defenses, Rajput horsemen had attacked his camp, but unlike their previous forays this time they had been badly defeated and driven off. The chasing force returned with heads tied on to their saddlebags, a barbaric Mughal custom of the time and this victory after weeks of initial reverses had helped reinforce the morale of the Mughal camp. Babur himself rode around his defensive layout, picking out each wrongly sited position and fine-tuning each detail of his defenses with the eye of a skilled, experienced general. At around nine-thirty, the Rajputs launched their first assault on the right wing of the Mughal and proceeded by the beating of drums and clamor of *ran-bankuras*. The charge was as furious and valiant as it was futile. The Rajput horsemen in close formation were mowed down by the fire of cannon and matchlocks that cut down both horse and rider and broke the momentum of the charge. Babur's recently cast mortar added to the hail of fire but before it could truly make its mark, it shattered due to a misfire killing its crew. The waves of Rajput horsemen came in relentlessly almost piercing the defenses but were unable to reach the line of cannon and matchlock men and halt their withering fire. It seemed that the right flank would finally give way in the face of sustained, determined assaults, but with his usual acumen, Babur reinforced it in time and the increased resistance finally broke the ranks of the Rajput cavalry. The elephant squadrons which were to be the battering rams of the initial charge simply ran amok when confronted by the flash and roar of cannon fire. By mid-day repeated charges had been beaten back and not withstanding some great feats of heroism and chivalry the Rajput attacks simply ground to a halt under the fusillade of fire.

Rana Sanga now decided to shift the weight of the attack on the relatively unaddressed left wing. The charges were as courageous as before but as futile. By noon, the flower of Rajput chivalry lay dead and bleeding on the battlefield. Rana Sanga himself led the attacks from the front, suffering injury after injury as he tried to push forward the attacks and finally collapsed in his *howdah* due to loss of blood. The loss of their leader would have broken the morale of the army and it was decided to conceal his injuries, for the time being at least. He was carried away and his place taken by Raja Ajja Jhala of Halwad who bore a strong resemblance to him.

The royal emblems of the *Chhatra* (umbrella) and *Chanwar* (ceremonial whisk) were raised over his head to convince the soldiers that the Rana was still directing operations from the front. Yet, chivalry and valor were not enough. Eventually it was better generalship and tactics which decided the day. As the attacks slowly faltered and the Rajput army floundered, Babur moved his cannons and mobile musketeers forward, compressing the attackers into a constricted mass which was unable to move or maneuver.

According to historians, it was the treachery of Taur Silhadi of Raisen, which tilted the scales. Sensing that the balance of the battle was about to turn, he defected to the Mughal camp with his followers. Unfortunately, the Rana had selected him to be in the vanguard and his defection exposed the main body of the following troops to Mughal fire. Silhadi also conveyed the entire array of battle to Babur and more importantly informed him of Rana's injuries and his absence from the battlefield. This information and the yawing gap that appeared in the Rajput lines after the defection changed the complexion of the battle.

Babur now sensed that the moment was ripe to unleash his mobile reserves. His *taluqmas*, still fresh and uncommitted, streaked into the rear of the Rajput lines effectively cutting off their retreat and hemming them even closer. Babur led the final attack with his reserve of 10,000 cavalry which scythed their way into the centre of the Rajput lines, now weakened by hours of fighting. As the cavalry charged, the Mughal cannon and match-lock men advanced forward to give close fire support. The use of fire and move tactics was a new innovation of the time and the results were telling. The cannons brought down a withering fire on to the packed ranks. Unable to maneuver or use their own weapons effectively, the Rajput ranks gradually collapsed, as the Mughal cavalry swept over them to completed the carnage.

By evening it was all over. Isolated pockets broke out of the Mughal encirclement and fought their way out, but the flower of Rajput nobility lay on the battlefield. The Rana was carried away

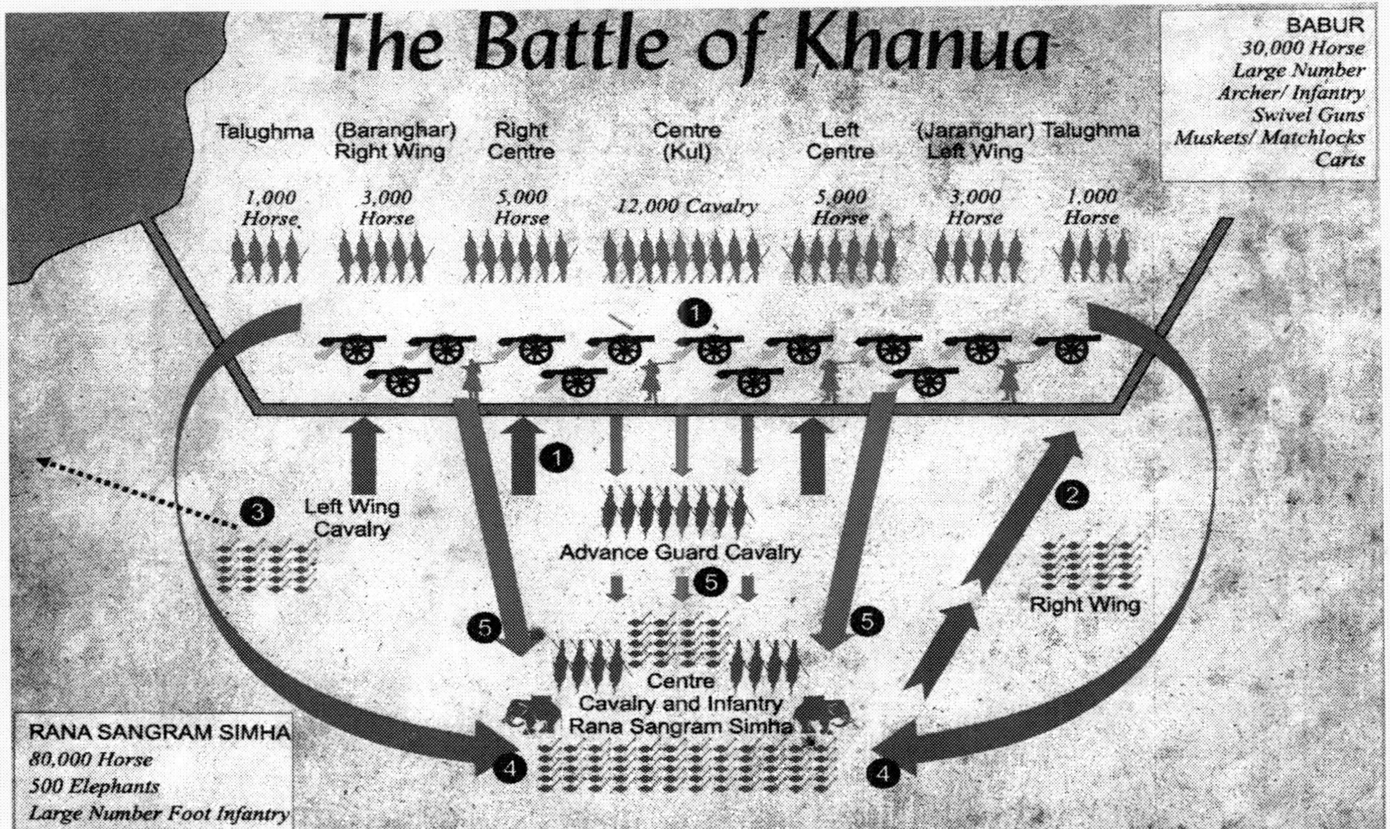

1. Initial Rajput attacks on centre fail against Baber's defensive deployment and cannon fire.
2. Rajput attacks shifts to flanks. Beaten back by Mughal fire. Rana Sanga wounded leading the attack.
3. Taur Silhadi, the traitor leaves the field of battle and defects to Babur. Rajput left flanks exposed.
4. Babur launches 'Talugmas', mobile reserves which cut off rear of Rajput lines.
5. Main attack launched from centre under covering fire of cannons. Rajput army surrounded and destroyed.

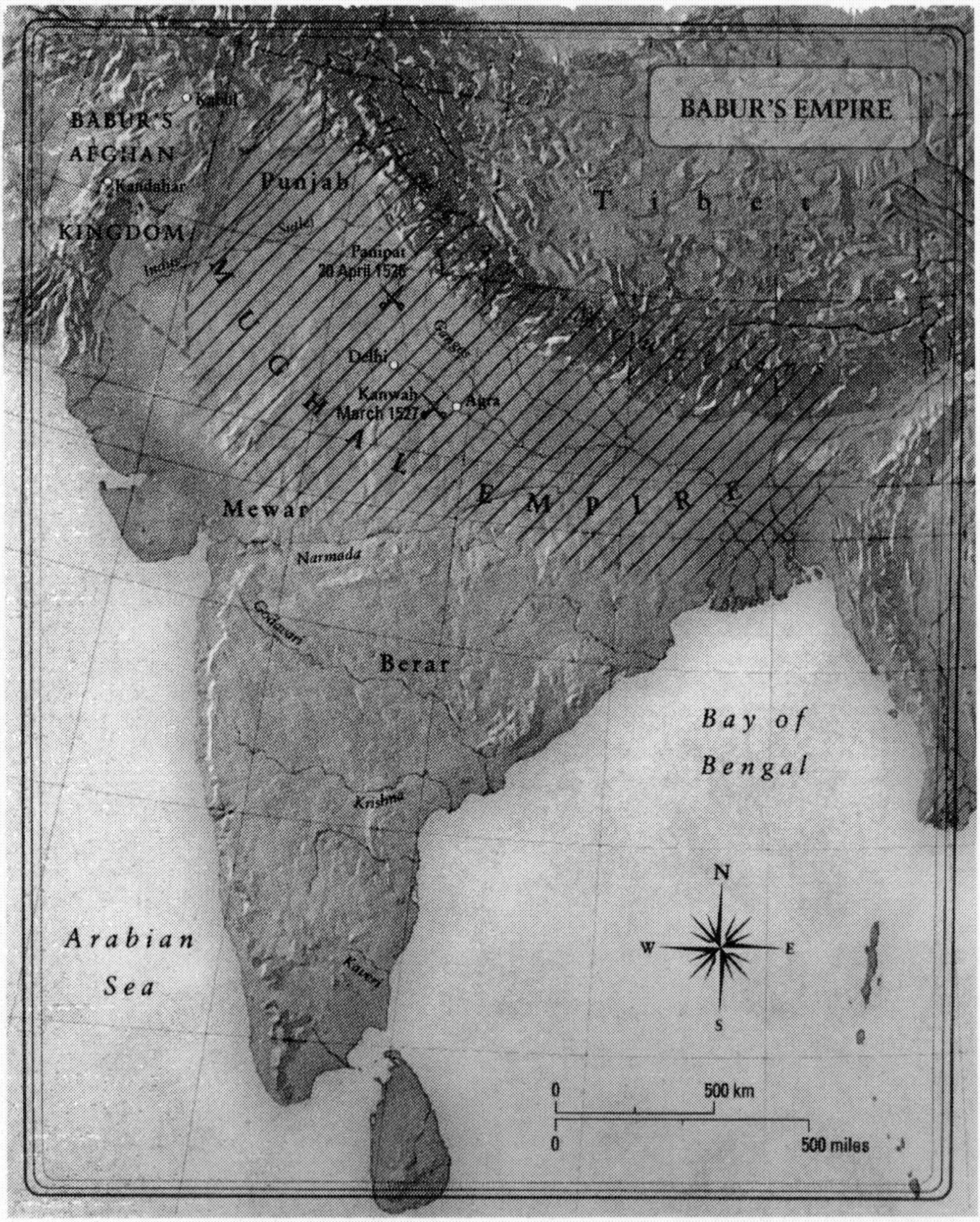
BABUR'S EMPIRE
Kabul
BABUR'S
AFGHAN
Kandahar
KINGDOM
Punjab
Sutlej
Indus
Panipat
30 April 1526
Tibet
MUGHAL EMPIRE
Ganges
Delhi
Kanwah
March 1527
Agra
Mewar
Narmada
Godavari
Berar
Bay of
Bengal
Krishna
Arabian
Sea
Kaveri
N
W
E
S
0
500 km
0
500 miles

by his loyal followers to a nearby site called Baswa, injured and semi-conscious. On the field, the line of the fallen was long. Rawal Udai Singh of Dungarpur, Ratan Singh Chandrawat of Salumbar, Raimal Rathore of Marwar, the Metia Rathore chiefs, scions of the Chauhans of Mewar, Hussein Khan of Mewar and the son of Ibrahim Lodi fell along with their followers on the blood-streaked battlefield. It is estimated that twenty to thirty thousand were killed or captured in this battle, which broke the backbone of Rajput military power.

The Rana himself, his spirit still unbroken, had regained consciousness and wanted to return to the battlefield immediately, but was dissuaded from doing so. Babur chased the Rana and his retinue for three or four kilometers but wisely abandoned the chase as they approached the Rajput camp. Rajput historians say that when the Rana was informed of the tragedy that had befallen his army he replaced his royal turban with a length of simple cloth, and vowed never to enter Chittor again till he had avenged this defeat.

It was a pledge he could not keep. The fragile Rajput confederacy soon fell apart as the weakened Rana was unable to maintain their hold on them. The smaller chiefs were content with their small kingdoms and comfortable lives and did not fancy a long and perhaps ineffectual campaign against Babur. The internal dissensions took their toll. Within a year the Rana was dead. On the 30th January 1528, the survivor of innumerable battles succumbed to the effects of a slow poison that in all probability was administered to him by his own companions. He was never to enter Chittor again, and was cremated besides a small rivulet near Mandalgarh, defeated but unbowed till the very end.

Babur meanwhile had followed up his victory with the barbaric celebratory custom of erecting a pyramid of human heads on a hill near the battlefield. This was a Mughal military rite performed after each victorious battle to strike fear in potential adversaries. Be moved back to Agra in triumph and took on the title of *Ghazi*; a holy warrior, a title which was then passed down to his descendents.

Babur the Emperor of India had arrived. As the sun set on the blood-soaked fields of Khanua on the 16 March 1527, it rose again the next morning to shine on the Mughal Empire in India. It would shine on the empire for another 400 years.

Analysis of the Battle

The Battle for Khanua shaped India's destiny, perhaps even more than Panipat. At Panipat, Babur secured the throne of Delhi from a weak, unpopular monarch who in any case would have been soon removed from his throne. The Afghan Empire was weak and ripe for defeat and Babur merely hastened its downfall. On the other hand, the Rajput Kingdom was on the ascendant. In Rana Sanga they had the ruler of stature who managed to combine the fractious, egoistic princes of Rajputana under a Hindu banner. If Babur had not come along, Rana Sanga's confederation would have soon swept Ibrahim Lodi and established a Hindu leadership on the throne of Delhi. With Babur on the coveted throne, the enemy was different but the stakes were the same.

In a sense both Panipat and Khanua were interconnected. Had Babur lost at Panipat, India may have never come under Mughal Rule. Even if the battle had been more evenly contested and the price higher, Babur may have never stayed on to form an Empire but would have returned to Kabul with his loot. A longer battle, or a protracted struggle between Babur and Ibrahim would here weakened both and induced Babur to leave Hindustan and would have drained Ibrahim's will and resources and make him too weak to withstand the rising power of the Rajput Kingdom.

As it was both battles were lost in a day and a new kingdom carved in a total of just over eighteen hours of battle. But what was it that went so wrong? The Rajput army was about twice as large as the Mughals, they had around eighty thousand fighters against the forty thousand strong army which Babur had fielded. They were brave warriors, well-trained and ably led. Yet they chose to fight a war of a century ago. They just did not adapt to the changing battlefield or the impact of firepower and the newer tactics evolved by Babur.

For one, in spite of their strength, the army was not a cohesive unit. It was a conglomeration of different clans and their armies, each loyal only to their leader, each following their own tactics and with no central unity of command or control. When they operated in small cohesive detachments, usually comprising of the same clan and under their own leader, they were superb, as was seen in their victories over the Mughal van guard and their successful skirmishes against the Mughal camp. When they came together, they still retained the tendency to operate as bodies of independent groups without any joint doctrine or tactics and just a loose thread of command holding them together.

THE WEAPONS

As at Panipat it was gunpowder that decided the issue. Although the Rajputs were aware of Babur's cannons and matchlocks, they ignored the threat. Their traditional weapons, especially elephants had little effect when confronted with this technology.

Another innovation prepared by Babur was the crafting of wooden movable tripods protected by shields on three sides. It allowed his matchlock men to fire behind mobile defensive positions. It enabled Babur to move his line of guns forward and provide intimate fire support to his cavalry.

Their very concept of bravery and chivalry mitigated their skill and courage. Rajput cavalry was superb in raids but they did not raid Babur's camp often enough. They allowed him to move and change camp without harassing him or cutting his supply lines. They did not even resort to night raids since it went against their concept of a fair fight. When they attacked, they resorted to a futile, frontal charges against an entrenched enemy armed with guns and their attacks were usually announced with much drumbeats and bugles which gave away surprise. Had they used their own mobility better to come from the rear of the Mughal dispositions, Babur's deployment and the fire power of his cannons would have been negated.

On the other hand, Babur had revolutionized the concepts of firepower by the incorporation of fire and move tactics. His artillery was deployed to cover the move of his cavalry and the actions of his infantry, archers, artillery and cavalry were closely integrated. Babur had mounted his guns on carts and had them moved forward during the crucial stages of the battle to provide intimate fine support to his cavalry. His matchlock men too operated from mobile fire positions based on heavily-protected wheeled tripods which allowed them to fire under protection and also move rapidly to any part of the battlefield. Yet what clinched the issue was the employment of cavalry. Rajput cavalry was perhaps the best in the country, but they were heavily armed with sword, spear and long bows. The riders rode in full armor, which slowed down the movement of both rider and mount. Their heavy spears and swords were very effective at the end of a thundering cavalry charge, but it was actually a disadvantage in one-to-one combat; especially when the enemy preferred to merely fire from light composite bows at stand-off ranges. And then, all the skill and individual courage could not negate the flying cannon ball or the whizzing bullets. Babur's

Babur hunting with his men as depicted in this Mughal painting

use of artillery and muskets sealed the day just as it did at Panipat. It is not that the Rajputs did not know better. Babur's tactics, his defensive deployment, his use of artillery would have been studied by the Rajput leadership and the lessons of Panipat should have been better understood. After all Rana Sanga had many in his army who had fought at Panipat. The futility of charging an entrenched enemy armed with firepower should have been realized and the frontal attack should never have been resorted to. The Rajputs were also familiar with gunpowder. Although cannons and muskets were still a new concept, siege guns were in existence in India for over a hundred years now and even Rana Sanga had used them in his campaigns. Yet they chose to discount the threat of cannons and matchlock and preferred to believe that raw courage and human valor would overcome it. Technology is always ignored at one's peril and in this case their ignorance of the prevailing technology of gunpowder helped rewrite India's history.

Generalship also helped seal the day. There is no doubt that Rana Sanga was a man of immense courage and an excellent warrior. Like all courageous generals, he believed that his place was at the head of his army and personally led the attacks with great skill and vigor. Yet, in his position at the head of the assault, he lost track of the bigger picture and did not realize what was happening to the other flanks or his reserves. He was in no position to control the flow of the battle. Babur, on the other hand positioned himself in the centre of his defensive layout and coordinated the actions of each element of his enemy. His razor-sharp instinct and the practiced general's eye told him the exact moment when to reinforce his right flank, when to move his reserves, the precise moment when to launch his *talugmas*. He himself moved into the attack during the last charge of his cavalry reserve to deliver the *coup-de-grace.* His positioning and sense of timing were superb.

There is another reason which is attributed to the shock defeat. The ugly specter of Indian power politics raised its head once again. Tuar Silhadi's defection at the most critical stage of the battle shifted the scales decisively in Babur's favor, giving him a large gap which he could exploit and also detailed information of his attackers plans and weaknesses. It was not the first time that treachery would hand over the nation to an outsider and it would not be the last. But, this defection has consequences that were more telling and far-reaching than any other in India's history.

Conclusion

The Battle of Khanua marked the supremacy of the Mughal Empire over the hot-bed of squabbling states which was then India. With the Lodhi dynasty dethroned and the Rajput confederacy disbanded, the two most powerful elements of the India's political scene had been effectively neutralized. But Babur's campaigns were not yet over. They would continue till he subdued the rebellious states of Central India and more importantly, the Afghan chiefs who were still a power to reckon with in Bihar and Bengal. The Afghans had combined under the Lodi chief, Nusrat Shah, who had assembled an army of over 100,000 troops and had even managed to procure some cannons from the Portuguese. The rising Afghan power would be a potential source of rivalry and in 1529 Babur set out to quell this threat.

Babur would fight his last major battle on the east bank of the Gogra River in a manner which was very similar to Alexander's Battle of the Jhelum River over a millennium ago. Nusrat Lodhi's army was deployed on the East bank of the Gogra denying Babur any crossing place. As Babur thrust and parried with his adversary from the opposite bank, he sent five divisions of his army to force a crossing around twenty kilometers upstream. Around 40,000 men got across the Gogra, using boats that were assembled and pre-positioned there. Nusrat Lodhi rushed upstream to counter them. This was the moment Babur was waiting for. With the enemy off balance he crossed the Gogra with over twenty thousand troops under a hail of covering fire from his cannon and matchlocks deployed on the west side of the river. The Afghan army tried to halt the crossing but a bridge head was soon established. Babur advanced rapidly from the bridgehead, attacking Nusrat Lodi from the rear. Surrounded from two sides with a river on one flank, Lodi was effectively encircled and in the closed space Babur's cavalry completed the carnage with their usual flanking attacks. In just two days, on the 2nd and 3rd of May 1529, he crushed the rising Afghan power and established his control over all of Northern India. His sovereignty now extended from the Amur Durya (The Oxus River) in Uzbekistan up to Bihar in the East and from the foothills of the Himalayas to the Malwa Plateau in the South.

Panipat, Khanua and Gogra were the three major battles that decided the fate of India. If Panipat gave Babur the entry, Khanua enabled him to consolidate his position and Gogra established the extremities of his Empire. Each of these battles were fought over an interval of little less than a year and decided in just a day or so. Panipat on 21 April 1526 was decided in just five hours of battle; Khanua on 16 March 1527 was won in just around 10 to 12 hours of intense battle and Gogra was sealed in two days of maneuver battle on 2nd and 3rd May 1529. It took just four days of battle for the map of India to be redrawn and its future to be irrevocably shaped. In four days of battle the Mughal Empire established itself in India for the next four hundred years and changed the very history of India.

5

The Flight of a Fateful Arrow – The Second Battle of Panipat

"It is not the creed of a warrior to kill an already defeated enemy" – Akbar, when asked to behead a wounded Himu.

❖ ❖ ❖

It is rare, if ever, that the destiny of a nation is decided by a single arrow. Yet one arrow, fired on the afternoon of 5th November 1556 did just that. This simple missile changed the outcome of the Second Battle of Panipat and in a single stroke altered the history of India. If the First Battle of Panipat gave Babur and the Mughal Empire a foothold into India, the Second Battle, fought between his grandson Akbar and Hem Chandra (or Himu as he was popularly known) firmly established the Mughal Empire in India for the next 300 years.

When Babur wrested the throne of Delhi in 1526 he was not destined to enjoy his new kingdom for long. In 1530, after just four years of rule, he was dead, leaving his kingdom to his son Humayun, who lived the same life of strife as his father. Humayun fought a constant battle for survival with the Afghan rulers of India and was defeated soundly by Sher Shah Suri in the Battles of Chaunsa in 1539 and at Bilgram the following year, which established the Suri dynasty on the throne of Delhi. The two defeats forced Humayun out of India and back to Kabul when he remained in a state of exile for almost five years.

Yet, with the death of Sher Shah Suri in 1545, the usual fratricidal war and struggle for succession began. The Empire of the Suri dynasty was divided amongst his three sons. The eldest, Mohammed Adil Shah, occupied the throne of Delhi, but remained constantly in a state of war with his brothers and the rising Rajput powers of Western India. In this state of turmoil, Humayun saw the moment to re-enter India and once again stake his claim. He advanced up to Delhi and Agra in 1555 and managed to re-occupy both cities. A fragile Mughal rule re-established itself on the throne of Delhi, but it was to be short-lived. Humayun died an untimely death on 26 January 1556, after a freak fall from a flight of stairs and once again the Mughal kingdom fell into disarray. His son, the 13 year old Akbar ascended the throne, and like his ancestors was hurled immediately into battle to hold the fragile empire that he had inherited.

Akbar had to contend with one of the most charismatic and brilliant characters of Indian history in the form Himu, the *Wazir* of Mohammed Adil Shah, the son of Sher Shah Suri. Himu was the son of a small shopkeeper from Rewari, who, by sheer merit and hard work rose to become the Superintendent of Delhi market, then the head of the Department of Posts and finally the *Wazir* or Prime Minister in the court of Adil Shah. The very fact that though he was a Hindu, he still rose to a position of such pre-eminence speaks volumes for his capabilities. Himu helped Adil Shah stave off the many contenders to the throne and had fought 22 battles against his enemies without once being defeated. His brilliance and military acumen were legendary and he had established himself as the dominant figure of the Afghan court and the actual power behind the throne. Himu's skill had helped Adil Shah maintain a tenuous hold on power. This hold was to be challenged once again by the rising power of the Mughals as they advanced from Kabul into Punjab and reoccupied Delhi and Agra. As the Mughals came closer, Adil Shah, weakened by constant fratricidal wars, was in no position to counter them and withdrew to Gwalior. The Suri and the Mughal kingdoms co-existed in an uneasy state of no-war-no-peace and then Humayun died suddenly and Himu saw the opportunity to make his move.

The Opening Foray

After Humayun's death, his son Akbar was taken under charge by Bairam Khan, one of his father's most trusted advisors. In actuality, the 13 year old Akbar was just a figurehead and the powerful figure of Bairam Khan was the real power behind the throne. The recently recaptured Mughal dominions of Delhi and Agra were in the hands of trusted generals, with Tardi Beg Khan as the governor of Delhi and Iskandar Khan Uzbek in charge of Agra. At the time of Humayun's death, Akbar was in Punjab along with Bairam Khan, who hastily coroneted the young prince at a site called Kalanaur (around 80 kilometers from Amritsar). The Mughal kingdom was barely holding together, the army was demoralized and the nobility acutely divided amongst themselves. In this disarray, Hemchandra realized that the time was ripe to eliminate the Mughal threat once and for all and advised Adil Shah to march out against them. But, as was his wont, Adil Shah withdrew to the safety of Gwalior and tasked Himu to confront the Mughals and recapture the lost territories on his behalf. Granted complete freedom to act, Himu slowly consolidated his power. He rallied the Afghan nobility and Rajput chieftains to his cause and by the end of the monsoon had gathered a large army of around 50,000 troops, 1000 elephant, 51 cannons and around 500 musketeers. By end September he was strong enough to commence his campaign and marched out towards Agra. The Mughal Governor fled without a fight and Himu soon occupied this prestigious city. After consolidating himself in Agra, he marched out towards Delhi and reached the outskirts of the capital by end October. Here he encamped and planned his subsequent moves.

Indian War Elephant – The prime used by Himu

Mughal Art depiction of the battle

Tardi Beg Khan, the Mughal Governor of Delhi was preparing for the inevitable battle as well. He had gathered a large force to counter Himu, but was no match either in terms of skill or generalship. When news of Himu's arrival reached him, he marched out to Tughlaqabad to meet him without waiting for the reinforcements which were to arrive from the outlying dominions. It was a hasty, unplanned move and similar actions would be repeated in the course of the coming battle. The Mughal army deployed on the battlefield in its usual formations based on the Advance guard, the Main Body, the two flanking wings and a large reserve of cavalry. The Mughals resorted to their time-tested tactics of launching furious cavalry attacks from the flanks while holding firm with the centre. One of the attacks tore through Himu's right flank, killed its commander and captured 40 of the prized elephants. This initial success may have tilted the scales in their favor, when the Mughals made the fatal mistake of pursuing the withdrawing right flank away from the field of battle. Their pursuit carried them away from the battlefield and they were unable to influence the subsequent course of the main battle. Himu saw his opportunity and launched a furious charge with his left wing and his centre with 300 elephants and around 3000 of his best troops under his personal command. The momentum of the charge broke the Mughal Centre and brought him towards Tardi Beg Khan who realized that the day was lost and fled the battlefield. Seeing their commander flee, the troops gave way and the Mughal army fled the battlefield in complete disarray.

Himu should have followed up his initial gains with a determined pursuit and a complete annihilation of the fleeing enemy. But he realized that the Mughal cavalry was still undefeated and could return any moment. He considered the withdrawal to be a ruse and decided to halt his troops and consolidate rather than pursue the fleeing enemy. The defeated Mughal army was allowed to withdraw and he himself rode into Delhi in triumph. Flushed with victory, he now shook off his services to the ineffectual Adil Shah and proclaimed himself as Raja Vikramaditya or Bikramjit. Himu was the last Hindu ruler to sit on the throne of Delhi – albeit for a very brief time and he hoped to re-establish a Hindu kingdom in India. After all, his credentials were impeccable. He was the most brilliant general of that time who had never lost a battle, his army was battle-hardened and seasoned and he himself was widely respected. The Afghans officers and troops of Adil Shah were won over by liberal distribution of plunder and the Rajput rulers willingly joined him in the battle to throw out a foreign invader. The Mughals had been thrown out of Delhi, but the threat of Akbar (or more appropriately of Bairam Khan, Akbar's guardian) still remained. The bulk of the Mughal Army itself was undefeated and coiled and waiting in the Punjab. The clash of the two armies would come a month later at the battlefield of Panipat, just seven kilometers North-west of the site where Babur had fought the first battle. On the outcome of this battle the destiny of both Himu and Akbar would be decided and with it the destiny of all of India.

Deployment and Preparations

After the relatively easy victory at Tuglaquabad and the occupation of Delhi, Himu had every reason to be confident. Virtually all the Afghan nobles and the Rajput princes of Western India had accepted his sovereignty and he had assembled a large army of over 50,000 cavalry, 500 war-elephants and an artillery park of 51 guns. Himu's organization and tactics reveal an amalgamation of Indian and Afghan influence. Following the Indian concepts, he still relied primarily on his elephants as the arm of decision but cavalry and artillery were effectively incorporated in his army. Yet his use of artillery had not been adequately refined as subsequent events revealed. His army was almost twice as large as his opponent and he was confident that he would be able to comprehensively defeat the remnants of the Mughal forces and drive them back to Kabul.

In the Mughal camp it was not the 13 year-old Akbar, but his loyal, if over-bearing guardian Bairam Khan, whose force of personality decided the issue. Bairam and Akbar were encamped at Jullandhar when Tardi Beg Khan and the remnants of his force reached him. The army was a de-motivated force, devoid of effective leadership and demoralized by the string of defeats they had suffered. A council of war was held and the general consensus was that they should withdraw from India and go back to Kabul. This defeatist idea was violently overruled by Bairam Khan who not only discounted any notions of a withdrawal but insisted on returning to Delhi to give battle. To reinforce his point he had Tardi Beg executed for his failure to hold Delhi (an action he carried out in Akbar's absence and later obtained his reluctant post-facto sanction). The execution had a salutary effect on the army. It imposed the writ of Akbar and *de facto* Bairam Khan and provided a single point leadership. The squabbling nobles

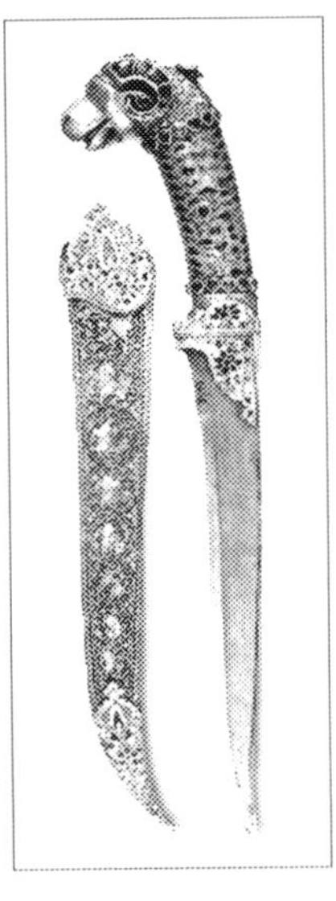

stopped their bickering, the men stopped giving vent to defeatist notions and discipline was almost instantly restored. A rejuvenated and unified army marched out towards Panipat with the knowledge that there would be no withdrawal from India and their only hope of salvation lay in victory.

In early November, just three weeks after entering Delhi, Himu marched towards Panipat for the decisive confrontation with the Mughal Army. But during the approach march itself, he made a crucial error. He sent forward an advance guard of around 2000 troops under the command of Mubarak Khan, yet inexplicably he grouped his entire contingent of artillery with them. Mubarak's own move was tardy. He did not take adequate measures for security or even bother to reconnoiter the areas ahead. On 4th November as he approached Thanesar, around 30 kilometers short of Panipat, he was violently attacked by a Mughal force of around 10,000 cavalry who routed them and captured all the precious artillery. Even before the battle was joined Himu had suffered a grievous loss. The capture of his artillery left him bereft of his fire support means and almost doubled the Mughal resources, besides providing a tremendous moral victory. The loss of his artillery would play a significant role in the outcome of the battle.

Yet, Himu shrugged off this setback and continued his march to Panipat which he reached the next day on 5th November. Here he found the Mughal army, under command of Ali Quli Khan, who had been appointed *Sar-e-Lashkar*, or Commander-in-Chief, already deployed and waiting. The Mughal army was deployed in the traditional Turkish manner with a screen of archers and skirmishers placed ahead to harass the enemy and fall back when engaged. Behind the screen was a covering position occupied by an Advance Guard of around 5000 men and behind them, the main positions. Quli Khan had deployed the bulk of the artillery ahead of his main positions, just behind the Advance Guard, to get the advantage of additional range. He could well afford the luxury of doing so, secure in the knowledge that Himu had no artillery of his own to provide retaliatory fire. Quli had chosen his ground well. The entire frontage was covered by a deep, dry *nullah* over which cavalry could maneuver, but would prove to be a formidable obstacle for elephants. Behind the Advance guard and the line of guns was the centre, commanded by Ali Quli himself with a strong reserve of around 6000 cavalry behind it. The right and left wings of around 4000 troops each were commanded by Sikander Khan Uzbek and Abdullah Khan Uzbek; both veterans of proven worth. The deployment and plan of attack was based on holding firm with the infantry and artillery and using the cavalry to launch their *Talughmas* or wide, wheeling maneuvers to attack the enemy positions from the flanks and rear. Akbar himself did not play any role in the battle. He had placed himself at a vantage point in the rear along with Bairam Khan and wisely left the conduct of operations to his more experienced generals.

Himu's too deployed in the traditional battle array. His deployment hinged around the use of his war-elephants. He placed himself in the centre with a strong contingent of around 30,000 Afghan and Rajput Cavalry and 500 war elephants. The two wings of the army with around 10,000 troops each were commanded by Shadi Khan Kakkar – an Afghan general of repute, on his right and Rammaya, his own nephew, on the left flank. It was a conventional deployment, which was based largely on being able to launch massive frontal attacks using elephants and cavalry. Yet Himu deployed in haste and attacked even more hastily. On the 4th November, his advance guard had been defeated, on the 5th he reached Panipat and the very next day launched himself into battle. Also by deploying directly opposite Quli he played into his hands by entering battle on the ground of his opponents choosing. Perhaps a little more deliberate build-up and careful reconnaissance would have revealed the presence of the ditch and allowed him to deploy in a ground more suited to his own strengths. Now the advantage of two critical factors, ground and fire support was firmly on the Mughal side.

Painting depicting the Battle of Panipat

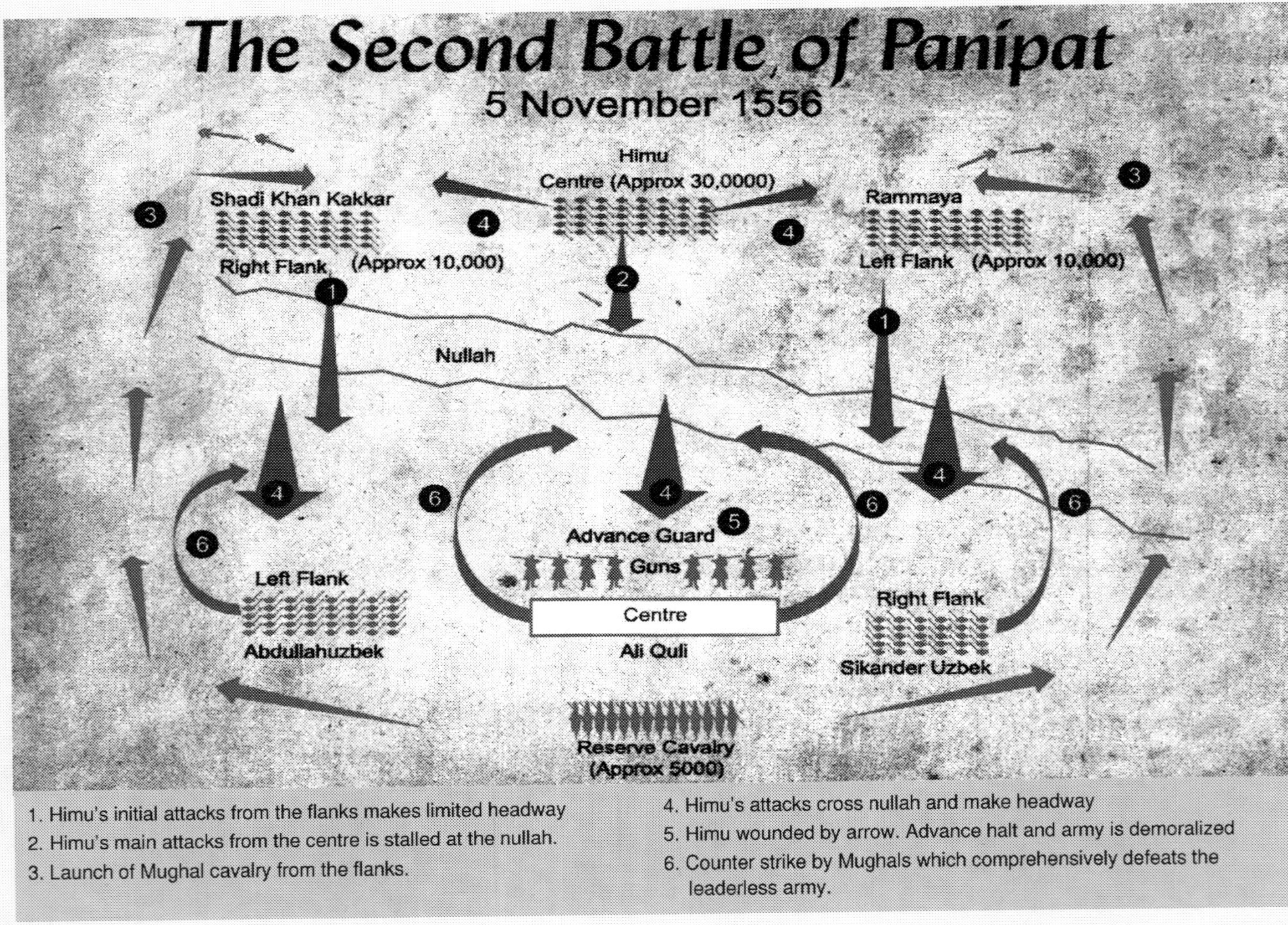

1. Himu's initial attacks from the flanks makes limited headway
2. Himu's main attacks from the centre is stalled at the nullah.
3. Launch of Mughal cavalry from the flanks.
4. Himu's attacks cross nullah and make headway
5. Himu wounded by arrow. Advance halt and army is demoralized
6. Counter strike by Mughals which comprehensively defeats the leaderless army.

The Battle

Quli Ali hoped to play a watch-and wait game, but he did not have to wait long. As it is the Mughal Army had reached the battleground well in time and were well deployed and rested. Himu made the first move. At dawn of 6th November 1556, almost immediately after completing the deployment, both wings of Himu's army launched a near simultaneous attack on both Mughal flanks. The flanks gave way under pressure, but retained their cohesion and withdrew in good order. Himu hoped to wrap up one of the flanks and from there converge on to the centre using tactics similar to what he had followed at Tuglaqabad. Yet, in this case the Mughal flanks held and their superior artillery brought down a withering torrent of fire which broke up the momentum of the attack. With the defensive line holding firm, the Mughals launched their own counter-attack and unleashed their cavalry in a wide outflanking move which crossed the *nullah*, wheeled around the flanks and attacked from the rear. The Mughal cavalry raced in at high speed, fired showers of arrows and closed in with their swords and lances causing heavy casualties and managed to penetrate into the right flank. Ali Quli now launched his reserve of 6000 heavy cavalry and the heavily-armed and mailed Turkish cavalry tore through the weakened right flank and managed to kill the commander Shadi Khan Kakkar. Himu meanwhile had been trying to launch an attack towards the centre of the Mughal deployment but his assault was stalled by the *nullah* ahead of their lines which the elephants could not cross. He sent his cavalry to reconnoiter a crossing place and he himself turned back towards his threatened rear and flanks. His counter-attack succeeded in throwing back the Mughal cavalry and stabilized the situation and now the battle held in balance. The Mughal lines still held and Himu ordered the final assault on the Mughal positions whose outcome would decide the day.

Himu's centre and left flank attacked simultaneously. The right flank had still not reformed after the Mughal attacks and was unable to reinforce this attack. Himu led the assault himself, mounted on *Hawai*, a tall, imposing war-elephant. Ali Quli meanwhile had advanced forward towards the edge of the ditch and from this protected position fired salvo after salvo of deadly artillery fire, many from the cannons captured from Himu's advance guard. His archers joined the fray and the covering fire took a heavy toll on the attacking army. Yet the very force of numbers and the dynamism of Himu's personal leadership gradually turned the tide in their favor as the attack gained momentum and the Mughal lines crumbled under the force of the assault. A breakthrough seemed imminent now as the Mughal lines wilted and began withdrawing, exposing their centre. Then tragedy struck.

Himu's presence atop his heavily armored and bejeweled elephant, *Hawai* was the rallying point for his men. His figure battling valiantly beneath the ornamented *howdah* was the inspiration which urged his Rajput and Afghan troops forward. As he closed in to the Mughal ranks shower after shower of arrows sped in his direction, one of them striking him in the eye. Himu yanked out the arrow, bandaged his wound with a scarf and continued his

THE MAN

Himu – The last Hindu king to sit on the throne of Delhi.

Son of a small shopkeeper who rose to become Prime Minster of the Shah dynasty by sheer merit. In those days it was unprecedented for a Hindu to rise to such a high position in the aristocracy

He has been under rated as a general but had won 22 battles consecutively prior to his defeat at Panipat.

However his generalship of Panipat was not of high order. He deployed his artillery wrongly, thus losing them in the initial foray. He did not reconnoiter the area and was not aware of the ditch in his line of assault. He laid too much emphasis on his war elephants instead of cavalry.

Akbar – Was only 13 years old at the time of battle.

His leadership lay in understanding who were the best men for the job and utilizing their services optimally. Wisely left the conduct of the battle to his generals and remained in the rear with his guardian, Bairam Khan.

Akbar in his court

valiant battle. But the shock and loss of blood proved too much for him and he slowly collapsed and fell semi-conscious in his *howdah*. Seeing the fall of their leader and the empty *howdah*, the army lost heart and the attack ground to a halt. His forces which were on the verge of victory now halted in confusion and began withdrawing. Quli seized the moment and launched his final counter-stroke. His cavalry reserves which had regrouped by then, once again swept from the flanks and into the packed ranks of Himu's forces, cutting and slashing. The leaderless army fled the battlefield with the Mughal cavalry in hot pursuit and the withdrawal turned into a rout. Himu's *mahout* tried to guide his elephant away from the battlefield and take his unconscious master to safety, but was intercepted, captured and led to Akbar with Himu still lying in the howdah. Here, Bairam Khan urged Akbar to kill his enemy, but Akbar refused. (Though some accounts say that Akbar killed him after further urging) An enraged Bairam decapitated Himu with his own sword and with it India lost one of its most brilliant and charismatic personalities. He was the last Hindu ruler to have sat on the throne of Delhi even if only for around three weeks or so, and his meteoric rise and fall marked a pivotal stage in Indian history. With his passing there was no central authority now left to counter Mughal rule.

An estimated five to ten thousand Afghan and Rajput soldiers were killed on that fateful day – most of them during the pursuit after the battle. Mughal losses have not been formally recorded and vary from a ludicrously low figure of 200 to around 2000. But it was not the casualty figure that mattered but the impact of the battle. Akbar realized the significance of the victory and did not tarry long. On the very next day, he made a formal entry into Delhi along with his army and proclaimed himself as king. Delhi and India were now firmly in Mughal hands.

Analysis of the Battle

What was it that decided the outcome of this fateful battle? Was it really just a fluke arrow or were there other military reasons for Himu's defeat. The arrow did play its role by striking not only Himu, but the very psyche of Indian soldiers who traditionally followed only their leader in battle. The loss of a leader, as had happened before and would happen many times again, simply broke up the morale of the army and converted a definite victory into ignoble defeat.

The Afghan and Rajput soldiers who had gathered around Himu's banner were held together by the force of his personality. There was no second-in-command, that concept simply did not exist in Indian armies. Thus when Himu fell, his troops had no rallying point and there was no one to take over command. On hindsight, had Himu conducted operations from the rear, his safety could have

THE MOMENT

The turning moment of the battle came when arrow struck Himu in the eye, wounding him.

He had not designated any second in command and seeing Himu fall, his leaderless army turned and fled- even through their attacks has gained momentum by then. The fall of Himu turned a likely victory into a rout.

been ensured and the battle itself would have been better coordinated. Even if the assaulting troops had simply pressed forward with their attack, the issue might have still been decided in their favor. But with Himu's fall and the absence of the visible presence of a leader the army simply disintegrated.

There were other major strategic and tactical reasons for the defeat. After the defeat of Tardi Beg at the Battle of Tughlaquabad, Himu should have followed up the pursuit and decimated the Mughal army. Instead he halted the pursuit and allowed them to withdraw. The Mughal army fled from Tuglaquabad to Jullundhar in complete disarray but not even harassing attacks were launched during its 200 kilometer long retreat. Himu then spent the next month at Delhi, allowing Akbar (or more appropriately, Bairam Khan) to consolidate his forces and restore their flagging morale. Even if he had marched out immediately and attacked the Mughal army while it was still in Punjab, he would have taken them unprepared and at a time when their morale was at its lowest ebb.

When Himu marched out against the Mughal Army, he made the cardinal error of sending **ALL** his guns with the advance guard, where they were unprotected. This action defies military logic. Even

THE EQUIPMENT AND TACTICS

Both sides followed the conventional tactics of the time.

However, the Mughals deployed their forces on the battlefield well in time. Himu arrived late on the battlefield and was forced to deploy in haste. He was thus only reacting to his opponent's deployment.

The Mughals adopted an offensive defense, holding the bulk of their infantry to block Himu's attacks and using their cavalry in wide outflanking sweeps. Himu on the other hand, attacked conventionally, mainly with war-elephants and did not employ his cavalry effectively. His elephants were halted by a large obstacle between the forces.

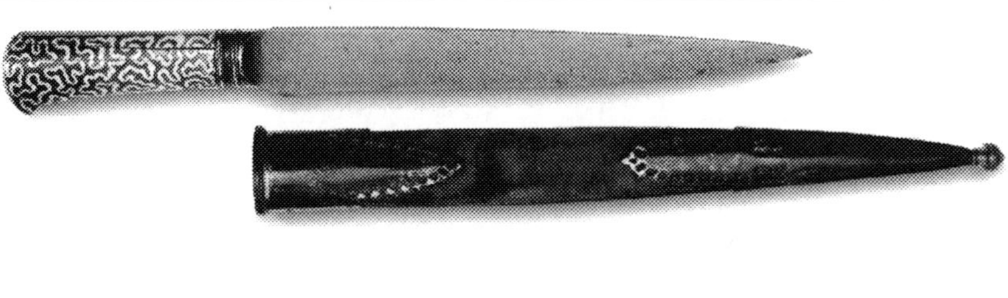

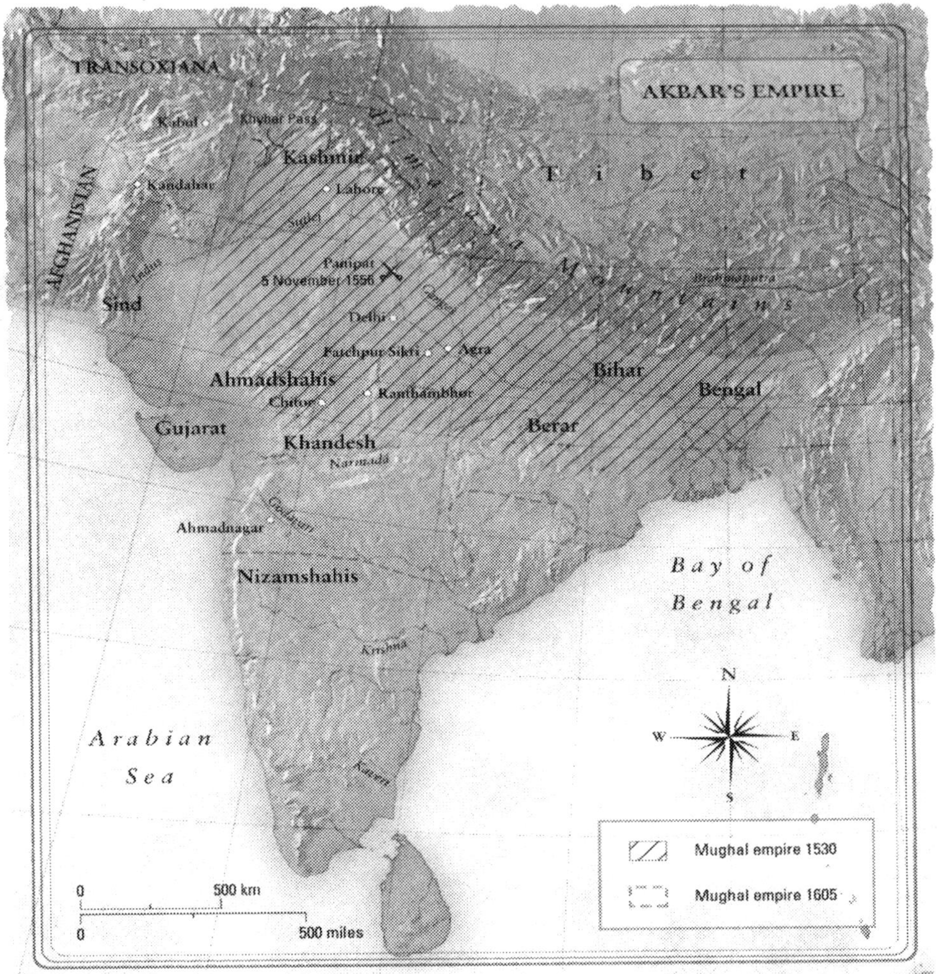

for fire support, a battery or so could have been grouped with the advance guard while the bulk of the guns should have been with the main body. The actions of the advance guard spoke of poor military sense and they allowed the precious guns to be captured. The loss of all his artillery and the manner in which they were used to reinforce Akbar's own fire support, was a major cause of the defeat.

Even the selection of ground did not live up to Himu's reputation for tactical genius. Firstly, he allowed the Mughal army to reach, encamp and deploy at Panipat. Then he chose to attack them when they were already deployed on the ground of their own choosing. Also he showed undue haste in attacking immediately after deploying without resting his men, without correctly assessing the enemy and without proper reconnaissance. Thus when he launched his main attacks, he was taken by surprise by the presence of the deep *nullah* ahead of the Mughal lines which the elephants could not cross. Like in the First Battle of Panipat, the Mughals had selected ground superbly and created a defensive layout for their infantry and artillery while the cavalry maneuvered around the flanks. The presence of the ditch nullified the advantage of the formidable elephants and blunted even the most resolute of assaults.

Yet, with all this, Himu's military skill and the very strength of numbers would have still carried the day. He himself had reacted rapidly to the Mughal cavalry which attacked from the flanks and personally led the counter-attack which drove them off. Akbar paid tribute to his skill and courage in his memoirs, the *Akbar Namah* where he describes his actions as "leaving no strategy or heroic deed that his mind could conceive un-attempted". After the threat to the rear was stabilized and the final assault was launched by Himu, the Mughal had already fired their bolt and their last reserves had already been committed. The assault was well poised and on the verge of victory. Perhaps just a few more hours of battle would have decided the issue in Himu's favor and changed the destiny of India. But then, the fateful arrow came.

6

Victory in Defeat – The Battles of Chittor and Haldi Ghati

"The warriors gave up their lives, but preserved their honor" – Akbar, after the battle.

❖ ❖ ❖

Mewar Valour versus Mughal Might

After the hard fought victory at Panipat, Akbar set about expanding and consolidating the Mughal Empire. His empire would eventually encompass virtually all of India from Gujarat in the West to Bengal in the East with the Himalayas and the Vindhyas forming its Northern and Southern extremities. His struggle for expansion would bring him into direct conflict with the Rajput rulers of Mewar, the most powerful force in Western India and pit him against Maharana Pratap – one of the greatest sons of India.

Akbar's expansion took him to Malwa up to the banks of the Narmada River. However to expand his empire southwards he would first have to subjugate the powerful Mewar kingdom. Although the rest of India slowly came under his yoke, the Rajput kingdom maintained its sovereignty and remained not only a threat but a beacon of resistance. Akbar realized that if he had to obtain complete sway over India, the Mewar kingdom had to be either conquered or won over to his side. His attempts to subjugate it saw the bitter siege of Chittor in 1567 which culminated in the heroic death of all its defenders and subsequent massacre of over 30,000 innocent villagers, women and children. Yet the loss of its capital did not dilute Rajput resistance. Under the proud, defiant figure of Rana Pratap, the struggle continued and reached its pinnacle in the Battle of Haldi Ghati, also called the "Thermopylae of Mewar". These battles did not have the same impact of the battles of Panipat or even Tarain, but stand out as sagas of heroism and courage against insurmountable odds which have been imprinted in the Indian psyche.

The Seige of Chittor

By 1567, a decade after Panipat, Akbar had subjugated or won over most of the Rajput Chiefs. In his policy of amalgamation, he had married Jodha Bai, the daughter of the Kushwaha Rajput chief,

The siege of Chittor – Akbar can be seen directing the attackers

Raja Bihari Mal of Amber and his nephew, Man Singh was now one of his most trusted and capable generals. Most of Rajasthan came under his sway, but the Sisodiyas of Mewar continued to defy him. To assert his moral and psychological ascendancy, Mewar had to be subjugated, or at least won over. Mewar lay on the strategic routes astride his lines of communication to Gujarat and the Deccan and if he was to hold on to these newly conquered territories, Mewar had to be under his control. In the dynamics of power politics of that time, its capital Chittor stood as a symbol of resistance and Akbar realized that once it fell, it would enhance his standing and automatically reduce resistance amongst the few kingdoms that still withstood Mughal rule.

Akbar began his campaign on 30 August 1567. The importance he gave to the campaign can be gauged by the fact that he led it himself, rather than entrust the task to one of his generals. To maintain secrecy about his move, he announced that he was going hunting, but actually moved towards Chittor. On the way he besieged and captured the fortresses of Mandalgarh and Rampura and by 30 October had reached the vicinity of Chittor at the head of his large army. In Chittor, the ruler of Mewar, Udai Singh was forced by his advisors to leave and take refuge in the inaccessible hills of Southern Rajasthan, leaving the defense of the fort to the gallant chieftain, Jaimal Rathore and Patta, the young chief of Kailwa. It was a politically wise decision. Chittor though formidable was not really a match for the combined might of the Mughal regime and the loss of their ruler would have permanently destroyed the Mewar dynasty. Around 8000 die-hard warriors and about a thousand expert musketeers were sworn to its defense and the fortress was stocked for a prolonged siege. The adjoining countryside was laid bare to prevent the Mughals from utilizing any local resources and the fortifications were reinforced to withstand the impending assaults. The fortress would not be easy to breach. The fort was almost five kilometers long and a kilometer wide, based on a huge hill almost 500 feet high, with sheer escarpments on three sides. It was only from the Southern face, that the fort could be assaulted and this side was further reinforced by double ramparts, high towers and battlements. An attacker would have to go through seven gates before even reaching the walls and at each step of his advance the defender could pour down a rain of arrows, bullets and boulders. Chittor was a difficult target and the formidable valor of the Rajputs would first have to be breached before any attacker could cross its walls.

Akbar systematically encircled the fort by establishing camps in all directions. He cut off all routes of entry or exit and then inched his way forward. In mid November, he ordered his first attack. Several assaults were launched, each one repulsed with heavy casualties without even coming close to the gates. Akbar then changed tactics and decided to wear down the defenders through constant bombardments. Three batteries of guns were stationed on high mounds on three sides of the fort. The earthen mounds, erected to provide a high platform for the guns to fire more effectively into the fort were called *Mohur Magri*, since Akbar gifted one gold coin to each soldier for each basket of earth placed on it. A large siege mortar capable of hurling a cannon ball half a mile deep into the fort was especially constructed. The artillery barrage continued to pour in to the fort and its battlements causing casualties and gradually wearing down the defenders. Akbar also ordered the construction of two *sabats,* large covered passages which began just beyond gunshot range and zigzagged their way towards the walls of the fort. The *sabat* was not a tunnel. Rather it was a trench with overhead protection which was covered by walls of packed mud on both sides and protected from the top by layers of buffalo hide and timber. Constructing the *sabat* was a slow and tedious process. Almost 200 laborers, miners and carpenters were killed daily during the construction and their bodies entombed in the wall to further reinforce them. By December, two such *sabats* 'had inched their way to the base of the fort. The larger one, named *Morcha-e-Badshahi* (Or, trench of the Emperor) was wide enough to permit ten horses to move abreast and high enough to permit a elephant to pass through. On the roof of this *sabat,* a specially protected gallery was made from where Akbar could conduct operations.

By mid-December, with the *sabats* at the base of the fort walls, Akbar decided on another sustained assault. His cannon continued to launch a relentless barrage inside the fort, as the assaulting troops assembled beyond the gunfire range of the ramparts. From inside the *sabats,* two large mines filled with 120 and 80 kilograms of gunpowder were to be placed beneath the walls to blow up the main bastions of the Southern walls. The engineers prepared the mines and detonated the first one which exploded with an ear-shattering blast. The force of the explosion succeeded in creating a breach in the massive walls. As the Mughal forces and Rajput defenders rushed towards the breach, the second mine exploded prematurely, perhaps by the shock of the previous detonation. Almost two hundred of the assaulting party, most of them officers, were instantly killed and their corpses hurled over a mile away by the force of the explosion. The Rajput defenders rapidly sealed their

The sabat snakes towards the ramparts of Chittor during the siege. The premature explosion of the mine is depicted on left

breach, filled it up with cotton, wood and oil to be ignited if the Mughals reached there again and once again the formidable integrity of its walls was restored.

Akbar now played a wait-and-watch game, hoping to exhaust the defenders into submission. By February, the battle had degenerated into a stalemate. His batteries repeatedly shelled the town and the constant bombardment had weakened the walls, but the Rajputs repaired each breach before the attackers could come close. Many determined attacks were launched and repulsed with equal determination. The Mughal cannon fire caused numerous casualties within the fort, but the fort held on. The Mughal re-supply caravans and camps were attacked by Rajput raiding parties operating outside the fort. Yet, after four months of siege, provisions inside the fort were running out and the fabled walls were dangerously close to crumbling.

During the battle, Akbar usually positioned himself on the gallery of the *sabat,* shooting at anything that moved inside the fort. His marksmanship was legendary and he rarely missed, causing over a hundred casualties during the long siege. It was during one of his nightly forays that his unwavering aim changed the course of the battle.

Around midnight on 23 Feb 1568, Akbar was on his usual position in the gallery, picking up Rajput soldiers on the walls with his favorite gun '*Sangram*'. The Mughals had launched

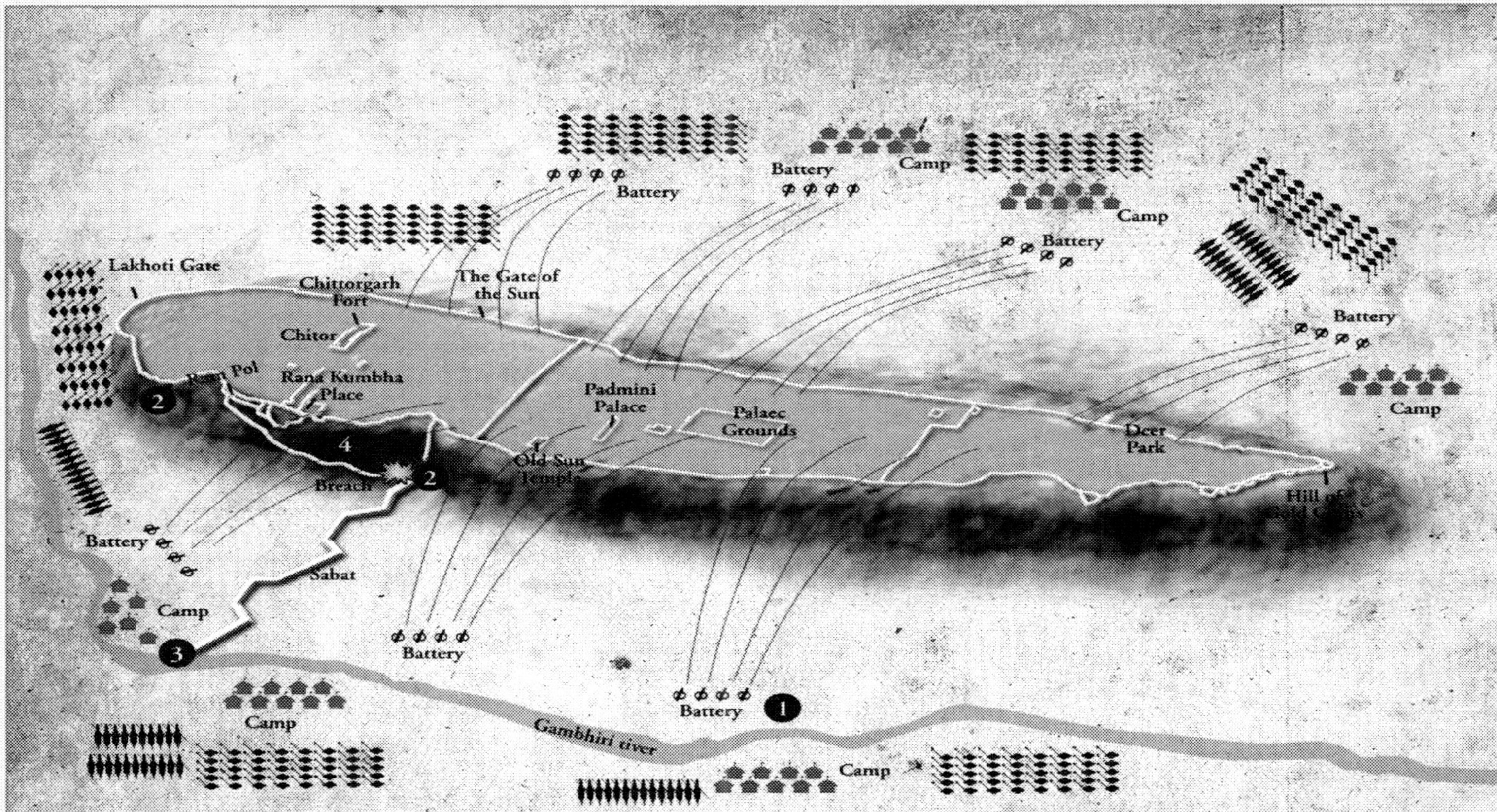

1. Akbar located batteries all around Chitor, wirh major emplacements to the north and west of the city.
2. Mines are dug under the northwest walls and filled with explosives, breaching the wall but also killing many of Akbar's men in a secondary explosion. An attack finally makes it through but is defeated.
3. A *sabat* (coverd way) is builf from near the river towards the city in December 1567. It reaches the wall the followign February.
4. Akbar's men charge through breach at the end of the sabat and slaughter those within.

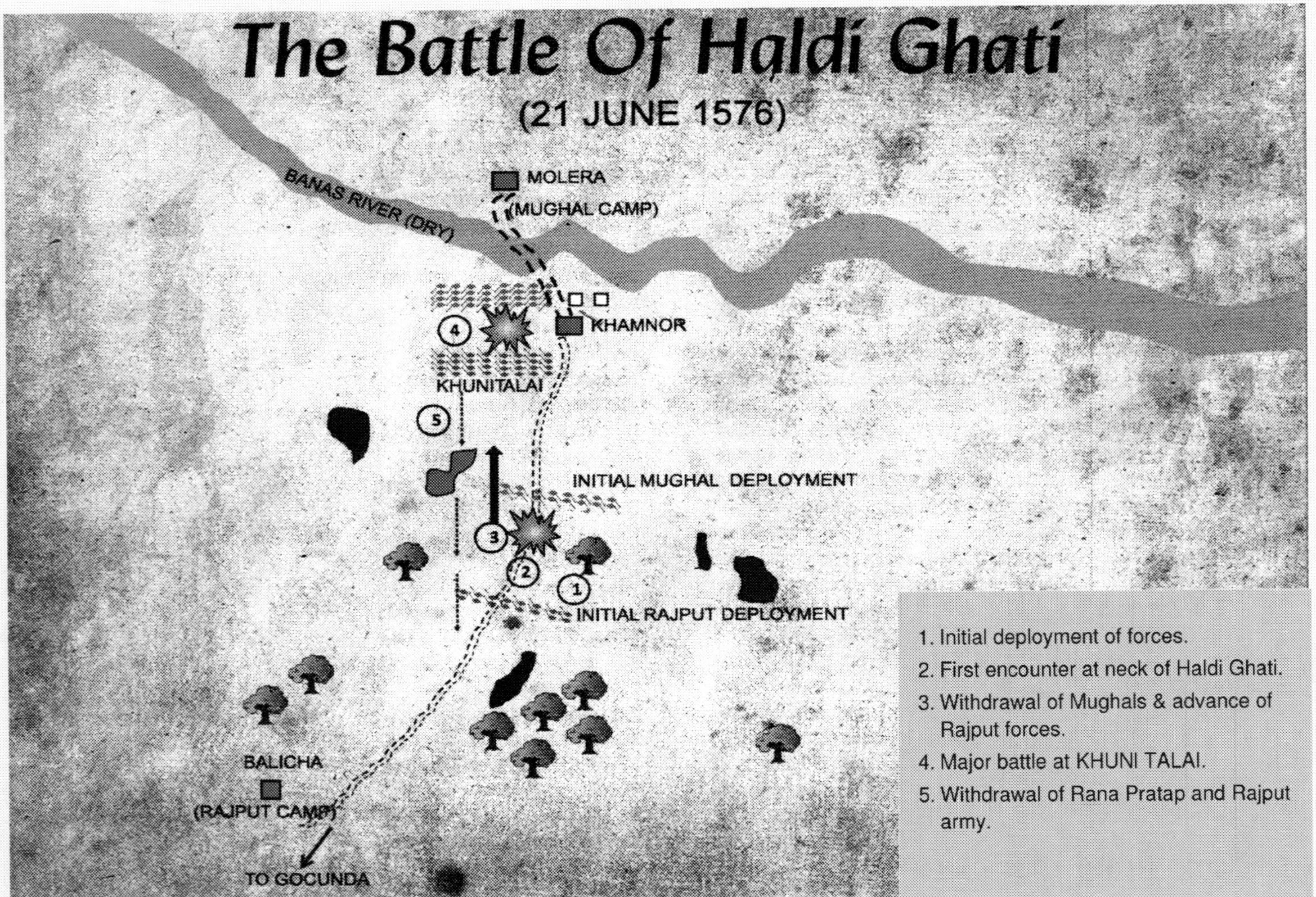

The Battle Of Haldi Ghati
(21 JUNE 1576)
MOLERA
(MUGHAL CAMP)
BANAS RIVER (DRY)
KHAMNOR
KHUNITALAI
INITIAL MUGHAL DEPLOYMENT
INITIAL RAJPUT DEPLOYMENT
BALICHA
(RAJPUT CAMP)
TO GOCUNDA
1. Initial deployment of forces.
2. First encounter at neck of Haldi Ghati.
3. Withdrawal of Mughals & advance of Rajput forces.
4. Major battle at KHUNI TALAI.
5. Withdrawal of Rana Pratap and Rajput army.

an all-out attack the night before and the Rajputs were energetically repairing the damage, directed by a tall, commanding figure in a shining cuirass. Akbar fired; the bullet sped to its target and hit Jaimal, the valiant, inspiring commander, wounding him mortally. The Rajput defenders left their bastions and a sudden silence filled the fort. As the gloomy night made way to day, the flickers of large fires dotting the areas of the imperial palaces could be discerned within the fort. The Rajputs, convinced that the end was near, had chosen death before dishonor. For the third time in the history of the fort, the grisly rite of *Jauhar* was performed as over 300 women and children embraced fire and burnt themselves alive rather than succumb to an enemy.

The next morning the remaining defenders donned saffron robes over their chain armor, embraced each other, placed a sacramental *tulsi* seed in their mouth and launched the final *'Shaka'*, the fight to the finish. They hurled open the gates of the fort and led by Patta, the sixteen year old nephew of Jaimal, launched their final charge. Akbar was waiting and his troops were already arrayed behind a line of three hundred war elephants. The result was inevitable. By mid-day each of the Rajput warriors had been killed in a final blaze of glory and the fort lay open and exposed.

What followed was carnage. Over 30,000 inhabitants, including women and children were massacred in a wild orgy of revenge. This senseless slaughter has been a major blot on Akbar's reputation although he did try to make amends by erecting statues of Jaimal and Patta at the gates of Agra Fort. Yet, even though Chittor fell, Rajput valor and defiance remained abated. The Mewar rulers, although deprived of their Capital and the prosperous Eastern regions continued the struggle from the wooded hills and forests of South Western Rajasthan. They founded a new capital, the beautiful city of Udaipur, named after their king, Udai Singh. The struggle against Mughal domination continued, a two-decade long struggle which was best symbolized by the Battle of Haldi Ghati.

The Battle of Haldi Ghati

With the fall of Chittor on 25 February 1568, most of Mewar came under Akbar's sway. The Mewar Kingdom gradually receded towards the interiors of South Western Rajasthan and moved deeper into the Aravalli Hills. But in spite of the destruction of their capital and the massacre of its population, Mewar remained unbowed and the struggle continued.

With the death of Udai Singh in 1572, his eldest son Rana Pratap ascended the throne (but not without the usual intrigues and power play that characterized Indian politics). Rana Pratap (also known affectionately as Rana Kika, or younger brother) has been venerated as one of India's greatest heroes and his two decade long struggle against the Mughals is one of the most endearing stories of Indian history. When he ascended the throne, most of Mewar was under Mughal occupation and his beleaguered state was surrounded from the North, East and West by the Mughal Empire. But even in its truncated form, his kingdom still posed a threat to the Mughal Empire as it stood astride the lines of communication to Akbar's newly-conquered dominion of Gujarat. Rana Pratap realized the futility of waging a pitched battle against his powerful adversary and wisely chose to fight a guerilla war in the hills and forests of South Rajasthan. Mughal outposts were attacked,

Rana Pratap

the forces traveling towards Gujarat were harassed and caravans coming from Western ports headed for Agra and Delhi were repeatedly raided. In areas occupied by the Mughals, entire villages were burnt; wells were blocked with rubble and masonry and standing crops destroyed to deprive the Mughals of any local resource. From the hills and forests of the Aravalli Hills and the Kumbhalgarh Range, Rana Pratap waged his lone battle against the expanding Mughal Empire.

Akbar tried to win over the recalcitrant ruler of Mewar by first isolating him and then through diplomacy. Three emissaries were sent to persuade Pratap to accept Mughal sovereignty, including Raja Man Singh, the Khushwaha Prince of Ambar. The emissaries failed. Pratap was not willing to enter Akbar's court or accept his sovereignty unless Chittor was first returned to him. From some accounts, Man Singh, the nephew of Jodha Bai, Akbar's Rajput wife, was rudely insulted during his visit to Rana's palace and taunted for taking up sides with the Mughals. With no hope of a political solution, Akbar now decided to use force to settle the issue.

In the spring of 1576, Akbar launched his campaign against Rana Pratap, appointing Man Singh as the Commander-in-Chief of the

Rana Pratap addressing the 'Bhils' prior to battle

Build up to Battle

expedition. It was an astute political decision of pitting one Rajput against another. Man Singh's army was a mixed force of around 5000 of his own Khushwaha Rajputs and around 5000 Mughal troops. As always, the army was well equipped and organized around its cavalry. A large number of muskets were also carried and over a hundred elephants, the traditional strengths of Indian armies. Man Singh had initially tried to carry some of his artillery, but the heavy cannon could not be transported over the difficult country and had to be left behind. The numbers were definitely on the Mughal side.

The Rajputs on the other hand had mustered a force of around 3000 cavalry, including a contingent of 500 Afghan horsemen under Hakim Khan Suri. One thousand Bhils, local tribesmen of the area, also joined the Rana's cause. Their intimate knowledge of ground and their skill with traditional bows and arrows made them ideally suited to operate in that difficult country. His army held no muskets or fire arms which placed them at a tremendous disadvantage and his only ace was a force of about one hundred elephants which Rana held as a final reserve. Yet this outnumbered army was motivated, skilled and fighting for their very survival. Many were kinsmen of the warriors of Chittor and its embers still reflected in their eyes. They knew the area backwards and for this decisive confrontation, Rana Pratap decided to take on the powerful Mughal army in the area of Haldi Ghati, a pass which would acquire a special significance in Indian history.

The Flow of Battle

Haldi Ghati was a narrow pass around two kilometers long, formed by a spur of the Arravalis hills. It lay astride the only track leading to Gogunda, Mewar's principle city and had high hills on both sides. In those days not more than one or two horseman could cross the pass at a time and it was ideal for a defensive battle. The area within and around the pass was broken and uneven but as one emerged from the neck of the pass the country became flat and level.

Fierce hand-to-hand combat characterised the battle

Around three kilometers to the West, the Banas River, dry at this time of the year, flowed and the riverbed and the areas adjoining it provided a flat, open ground. On the bank of the river was the village of Khamnor. The pass drew its name from its powdery rocks, which when crumbled revealed bright yellow sand which looked just like turmeric or *Haldi* powder. The yellow sand would soon turn a deeper shade of red and the pass itself would acquire fame as the site of one of India's most famous battlefields.

Rana had chosen his site well. Man Singh had to cross Haldi Ghati, on his route to Gogunda and here his Bhil bowmen and light, hardy cavalry were in their element. Just a few men could hold the pass indefinitely and the nimble ponies could negotiate the difficult broken ground with ease. Man Singh instead did not want to enter the pass but preferred to fight in the comparatively level ground between the Banas River and the Khamnor village where his numerical superiority could be better applied. He reached the vicinity of the pass through a slow, gradual march interspersed with long halts and eventually reached Molena on the far bank of the Manas River by the mid-June. Here he halted, without entering the pass and simply waited for Rana Pratap to make the next move.

Man Singh had calculated on the impetuosity of Rana Pratap and he was proved right. On 21st June, the Rana left his well-defended positions on Haldi Ghati and moved out of the pass to engage his enemy. It is not clear what drew the Rana out. After all, he was deployed and waiting in a ground which was best suited for his kind of warfare. Why did he leave the safety of the pass and attack a force almost two and a half times his size? Some historians say, his foray began as a raid on the Mughal camp which developed into a full-fledged battle. Others state that he was provoked into attacking by his Rajput chieftains who were tired of waiting and wanted to decide the issue with the weight of their swords. At around eight in the morning, accompanied by the sound of trumpets, drumbeats and battle songs, the Rajput army moved out and arrayed itself in the neck of the pass in the traditional order of *Harawal* (Van Guard) *Chandawal* (Rear Guard), *Vam Parshwa* and *Dakshin Parshwa* – the left and right wings. In the centre was the Rana himself, in a distinctive white tunic over his mail armor, atop his favorite horse – Chetak – who would also acquire a sort of immortality in the battle. The Bhils under Rana Punja, were deployed at the edge of the pass armed with their traditional bows, arrows and short swords. With his limited strength, he did not have the luxury of a cavalry reserve and his only reserve was a small complement of war elephants that were to be used as his final card.

When his scouts informed him of the news of Rana Pratap's move, Man Singh was elated. By drawing out the Rana, events were unfolding in just the manner that he had hoped. He moved forward and arrayed his forces just beyond the neck of the pass. In his front line was a force of eighty skirmishers and archers, also called the *Chuza-i-harawal* or "Chickens of the front line." They were to act as the screen and early warning force and fall back after the initial contact. Behind them, a composite mounted force of Khushwaha Rajputs and Mughal horsemen formed the advance guard which was to absorb the main weight of the attack. In the centre was a composite force of 6000 Khushwaha Rajputs and Mughal horsemen commanded by Man Singh himself. He deployed two strong wings of around 1500 on each flank. He also had the luxury of maintaining a rear guard and an *iltimish*; or immediate reserve of 1000 horsemen and around 100 elephants which would be the final trump card. It was a sound defensive layout and more importantly, Man Singh was able to fight the battle away from the pass on a ground which was better suited to him.

As the sounds of drum beats and trumpets reached a crescendo, the Rajputs launched their first, furious attack. The Afghan

The Rana's final attack on Man Singh. Chetak has a leather extension resembling a trunk. The near sighted elephants mistook this for a young elephant and did not attack them

contingent under Hakim Khan Sur and 500 Rajput horsemen hurled themselves from the left flank, simply tore apart the *Chuza-i-Harawal* and slammed into the van guard. Here at the neck of the pass, the terrain still favored the Rajputs and their light nimble ponies. The Mughal Advance Guard collapsed under their frenzied attack and fell back in disorder. Encouraged by this swift success the Rajput Right Wing (under command of Ram Singh; the son of Jaimal – the gallant defender of Chittor), charged down on the Mughal Left Wing. The combined force of the assault smashed the van guard, advance guard and both wings and in the uneven ground, the Mughal army was unable to maneuver and slowly withdrew. Yet, in spite of heavy casualties, the Mughal Right flank, held by the

Sayyids of Barha – who were themselves famed fighters, held their nerve and their positions and prevented the withdrawal from turning into a rout. Man Singh realized the gravity of the situation and knew that if the wings collapsed, the centre would be exposed to the full force of the Rajput attack. He ordered his *iltimish* (immediate reserve) of 1000 horsemen to move to the threatened Right flank and help stabilize the situation. It seemed that the very ferocity of the Rajput charge would win the day, even against their numerically superior opponents. As the flanks trembled, Mihtar Khan, the commander of the reserve rushed forward shouting loudly that the Emperor himself had arrived with reinforcements to the battle site. The false proclamation had the desired effect. The withdrawing Mughal flanks re-formed and held together to beat back the repeated charges of Rajput cavalry. What would have become a panicked rout gradually became an orderly withdrawal and Man Singh succeeding in moving his forces back in to the open wide plain near the banks of the Banas river, a open area better suited for his heavier forces.

THE MAN

Rana Pratap

One of India's greatest sons. Became a legendary figure due to his heroic resistance to Akbar.

Waged a successful guerrilla war for many years. However, was enticed into fighting a pitched battle at Haldi Ghati.

Was physically very courageous and a skillful fighter. Was able to personally inspire his men to fight against superior odds. Led the final charge himself on Man Singh's elephant which almost succeeded in killing him.

Man Singh

The nephew of Jodha Bai, Akbar's Rajput wife who Akbar astutely appointed as Commander-in-Chief in the campaign against Rana Pratap. Led a mixed force of Khushwaha Rajputs and Mughals.

Chivalrous and loyal, he won a major victory against his Rajput kinsman. He was however derided by Akbar for not pursuing the wounded Rana Pratap and allowing him to escape.

Rana Pratap now advanced from the neck of Haldi Ghati towards the open ground between the Banas River and the village Khamnor. The two armies clashed in a bloody conflict that soon degenerated into individual hand-to-hand combat. The Rajputs fought their way through the centre of Man Singh's Khushwaha Rajputs, taunting them and insulting them for joining ranks with the enemy. As the saffron-clad Rajputs waged their bitter, fratricidal war, acts of incredible valor were displayed on both sides. Akbar would write later "the warriors of both sides yielded up their lives, but preserved their honor". In the melee of fierce hand-to-hand combat, the Mughal Cavalry was free to gallop around the seething, fighting mass in the centre, pouring arrows and musket shot in the packed ranks. They could not distinguish between their own Rajputs or Rana's Pratap's forces and the firing was indiscriminate and injudicious causing casualties on both sides. Not that they attempted to differentiate much. Asif Khan one of their more bigoted generals remarked "It does not matter on whichever side they be killed, it will be a gain to Islam".

By now it was nearly 11 am and the Rajputs had been battling nonstop for almost three hours. The cruel mid-day heat and the injuries that most of the warriors suffered added to their exhaustion

The death of Chetak – His cenotaph still stands at the site where he fell

and slowly the tide turned in favor of the Mughals. The Rana realized that the only way to decide the issue was to bring in his last reserve to break Mughal ranks and ordered the elephants to be moved forward. The famed rank breaking elephant "Lona" charged the Mughal positions, creating havoc in their battle formation and almost breaking their lines. The Mughals countered by sending forward "Gajmukta" (Pearl amongst Elephants) and the two heavily armored mammoths slammed into each other. "Gajmukta" was badly injured in this titanic clash and began withdrawing when a bullet struck "Lona's" mahout, killing him and forcing him to withdraw. The Chief Elephant of the Rana's stables "Ram Prasad" was now brought forward and his own furious charge was countered by the imperial elephant Gajraj. The elephants crashed into one another with a combined force of over ten tons and the ground shook with the power and fury of their charges. Ram Prasad succeeded in goring Gajraj with his powerful tusks and accompanied by the cheers of the fighting Rajput warriors, began pushing him back towards the Mughal lines. At that crucial juncture, Ram Prasad's mahout was killed by an arrow. His rival mahout, leaped onto Ram Prasad's back, captured him and took him away as a prized trophy to be presented to Akbar after the battle.

With the last reserves gone, the Rana realized that his only hope lay in killing Man Singh, knowing full well the effect that the loss of a leader had on Indian armies. In a final, desperate attack, he charged full tilt towards his opponent's position. He was wounded repeatedly and his body guards virtually decimated as he cut his way through the Khushwaha Rajput ranks and approached within striking distance of Man Singh's elephant. Chetak reared upwards, his front legs resting on the trunk of Man Singh's elephant and gave his master the opportunity for one perfect shot. Rana Pratap hurled his spear which smashed into Man Singh's protected *howdah* almost penetrating it. (The damaged howdah is now on display in the museum at Jaipur). Man Singh ducked into the safety of his *howdah* and before Rana Pratap could strike again, Man Singh's bodyguards converged upon him. Cut off and surrounded, the Rana slashed his way through insurmountable odds and at that point it seemed that the end was near.

Seeing Rana's critical predicament, Bida Mana, a Jhala chieftain, raced towards his beleaguered leader and snatched the Royal *Chattari* (Umbrella) which hung over Rana's Pratap's head. Placing it over his own person, he shouted loudly that he was the Rana and challenged any one to come close to him. His ruse was successful. The Khushwaha and Mughal soldiers rushed towards him and in the diversion, a severely wounded Rana Pratap was led away towards the safety of the pass. It was here that Chetak earned his

THE MOMENT

The decisive moment of the battle was Rana Pratap's attack on Man Singh. Had he succeeded in killing or injuring him the outcome would have changed.

With the failure of the attack, the course of the battle shifted to the side of the Mughals.

reputation as the "Flying Horse". Chetak himself had been wounded during the attack on Man Singh, when a sword on the trunk of the elephant slashed through his forelegs. Limping, he carried his wounded master to safety, through the pockets of battling soldiers across the frenzied, bloodstained battleground. With Mughal officers in hot pursuit, they reached a wide rocky stream and here he made his final, heroic leap across the chasm that none of his pursuers could emulate. Chetak died after this final effort but Rana Pratap was saved. A grateful Rana later erected a cenotaph which still marks the spot where he fell.

Rana was carried away to safety and the remnants of his army slowly withdrew towards the safety of the pass. The Bhil tribesmen gave effective covering fire with their arrows and Man Singh, perhaps out of deference to Rajput tradition, did not follow up the pursuit. This act earned him a censure from his emperor, who felt that he had allowed a fellow Rajput to escape. With Rana's escape, the battle was not conclusive and no strategic gains had been achieved. Tactically, yes, it was a victory. A blood-soaked victory, which saw over five hundred Rajput warriors fall on this "Thermopylae of Mewar" as it has been described by the historian, James Todd. Twice as many were wounded and almost half the fighting force became casualties in just around five hours of intense battle. The Mughal Army too suffered with over two hundred killed and three hundred and fifty or so wounded; most of them from Man Singh's Khushwaha Rajputs. For years thereafter, locals spoke of hearing sounds of battle and the moans of the dying in the area between the Banas River and the village Khamnor, an area that soon came to be called *Rakta Talai ;* or the lake of blood. Today a school stands on the site of battleground with a worn, weather-beaten sign heralding it as the site of one of India's most memorable battles.

THE TACTICS

Both sides used similar tactics and equipment. Both relied heavily on elephants and both fought traditionally. There was little maneuver.

The superior utilization of terrain decided the day. Rana Pratap was in a strong defensible position at Haldi Ghati. However he was enticed ahead into open country, where Man Singh's superior strength was more effective.

Man Singh's skillful use of reserves prevented the Rajputs from breaking through their lines after the initial charge. This helped contain the Rajputs who had no reserves of their own to exploit their initial success.

The Mughals followed their success with a rapid advance towards to Gogunda and captured it without a fight (though Rana Pratap recovered it soon after Man Singh's departure). The Rana moved deeper into the difficult hills of Kumbalgarh and his new capital Udaipur continued to be under his control. He had learnt from the lessons of this battle. Never again did he fight a pitched battle, but continued with his low intensity guerilla war, continuously attacking the Mughal lines of communication through his territory. In the years that followed, Akbar launched three expeditions to subjugate him, each of which achieved temporary gains but were eventually forced to withdraw. Rana Pratap's struggle continued and in spite of immense difficulties he managed to recover most of his lost territories. Yet his life-long dream of recapturing Chittor could never be realized.

When Rana Pratap died in January 1597, due to an internal injury sustained while hunting, India lost one of her greatest sons. When news of his death reached Akbar's court, the Emperor did not rejoice but fell into a deep silence. A Rajastani bard, who was present, recited a couplet, praising Rana Pratap as one who never bowed to 'Dilli' and was victorious even in death. Akbar's response was reportedly to reward the poet; his own noble mind understanding the nobility and courage of his opponent. Rana Pratap was a great leader and a brave general. His stand at Haldi Ghati and the two decade long struggle which he waged against the mightiest empire of that time has earned him a heroic fame perhaps unmatched by any other son of India.

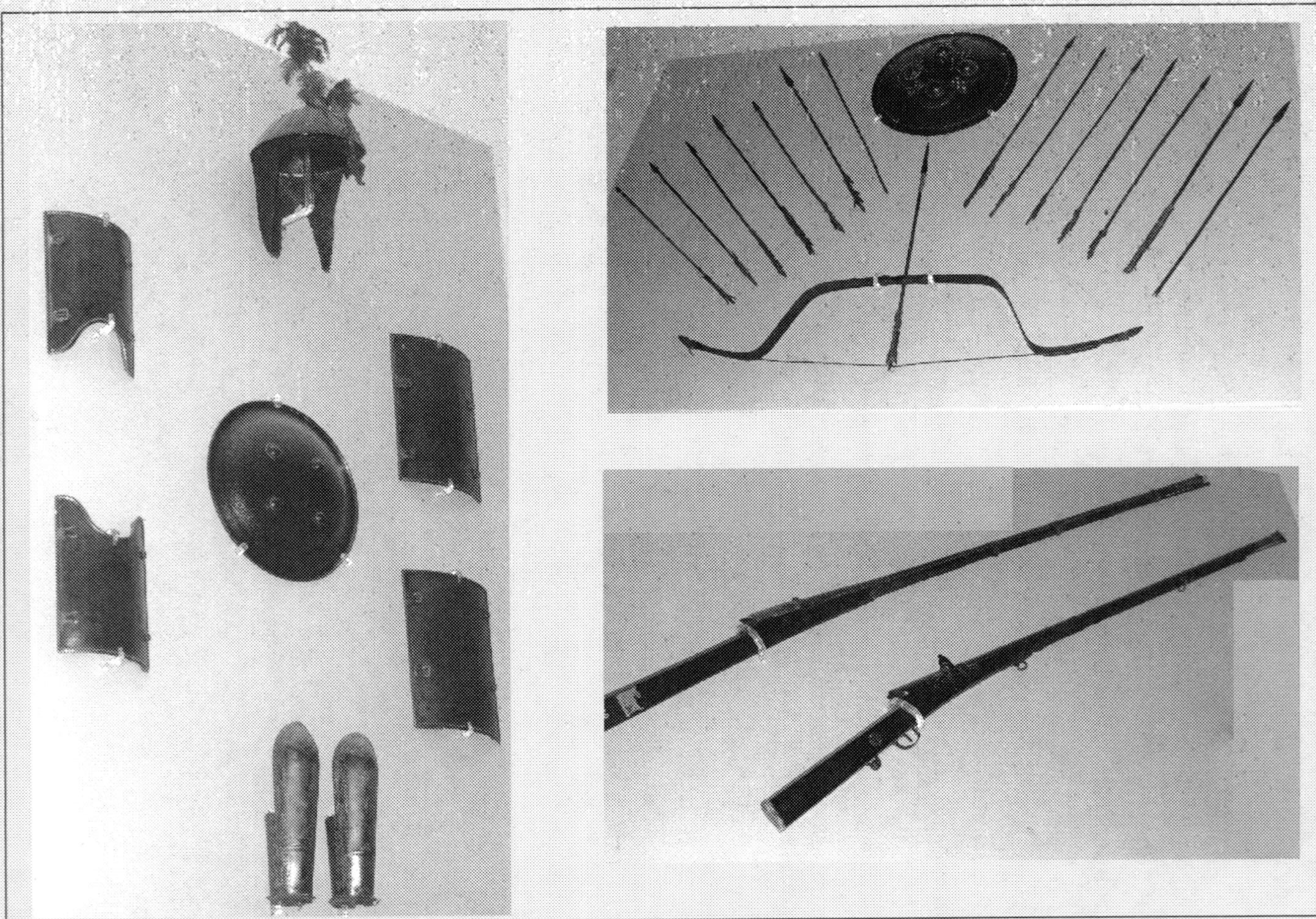

Maratha weapons used during the battle now displayed at the Gwalior Museum

7

Carnage – Disaster at Panipat

"Two pearls have been dissolved, twenty seven gold mohurs have been lost and of the silver and copper, the total quantity cannot be cast up"

❖ ❖ ❖

In the "Cockpit of Indian History", the tract of land between Panipat, Kurukshetra and Tarain, the history of India has been repeatedly decided. Located around a 100 kilometers North West of Delhi, this flat open area lay astride the direct route from the Punjab to Delhi, traditionally used by every invader to reach the seat and symbol of power in North India. Here the epic war of the Mahabharat etched itself in the Indian sub-conscious; Allaudin Khilji was defeated and then emerged victorious in these same battlefields; Babur laid the foundations of the Mughal Empire and Akbar firmly established it here. Panipat has been synonymous with the fate of India since recorded history and in the year 1761 it would witness its bloodiest battle ever. The Third Battle of Panipat between the Afghan invader Ahmad Shah Abdali and the Marathas under Sadashiv Rao Bhau, would once again see the invader emerge victorious and inflict a crippling defeat of Indian forces. In terms of sheer casualties and losses, this battle was far bloodier than any of the previous wars and has impacted itself indelibly on the Indian psyche.

But how did these two widely separated antagonists, one from the lofty mountains of Afghanistan the other from Peninsular India meet in this distant battlefield? Why were their fates and the future of their empires decided here? The answer to that lies in the turbulence that existed in India in the bleak political landscape of the 18th Century. The Mughal Empire had begun a slow decline since the death of Aurangzeb in 1707. His sons battled amongst themselves and in the absence of any central authority the country was once again exposed to the cupidity of foreign invaders. Nadir Shah ravaged Delhi in 1739, plundered the city and returned with the fabled *Koh-i-noor* diamond and the Peacock throne. Nadir's invasion was the final body blow to the already weakened Mughal Empire. It was now powerless to halt the rise of the Sikhs in Punjab or the expansion of the Maratha Empire in the Deccan. With Nadir's assassination in 1747, one of his chief lieutenants, Ahmad Shah Abdali; or Durr-i-Durrani' (the Pearl amongst Pearls) succeeded him. He was fired by the same rapacity and ambition of his predecessor and would lead five invasions into India – the last of which culminated in the fateful Third Battle of Panipat.

Ahmad Shah first invasion in 1748 led to his defeat at Manpur. Undeterred he followed up with three other invasions in 1750, 1751 and 1756, capturing the Punjab and eventually reaching Delhi in his last expedition. He returned to Kabul but installed his son, Timur Shah at Lahore as the titular ruler and his representative in the country. Timur's regency was marked by chaos and misrule. He maltreated the local population, levied unacceptable taxes, antagonized the Sikh rulers of Punjab and plunged all of North India into chaos. In this turmoil, Adina Beg Khan, the Governor of Punjab Province, invited the Marathas to conquer the Punjab and reestablish an Indian power in North India.

At the time of these momentous events in North India Maratha power had been gradually expanding in the Deccan and Peninsular India. Since the start of the 18th Century, their empire had gradually extended beyond the Narmada and up to the Chambal River. By 1755 they were the dominant power of India. The Mughals, though occupying the throne of Delhi, were ineffective and in a state of decline. The Rajputs were confined to their kingdoms in Rajasthan and too busy battling each other to pose any serious claims. The Sikhs in Punjab were on the rise but were seriously weakened by the repeated invasions of Nadir Shah and Ahmad Shah. The Jat rulers were largely neutral, content to live and let live. Other notable powers were the Nawab of Oudh, Shuja-ud-Daula, who ruled the Awadh kingdom in the Indo-Gangetic plains, the Rohilla Chief Najib-ud-Daula and Indian Afghan chiefs who reigned over their own small kingdoms. The Marathas had been following a policy of expansion under Peshwa Balaji Baji Rao and used this fragmented state of affairs to extend their influence northwards. They readily accepted Adina Beg's invitation to invade Punjab (sweetened as it was by an offer of Rupees one lakh for each day of marching and fifty thousand Rupees for each day's halt) and in February 1758, the Grand Maratha army under Raghunath Rao, set out to extend their influence into Punjab and beyond.

In April 1758, the Marathas along with Adina Beg and their Sikh allies reached Delhi and soundly defeated Najib-ud-Daula, Abdali's representative in India. The triumphant Marathas then marched across Punjab and onto Lahore. Here they inflicted a crushing defeat on Abdali's son, Timur Shah, wiping out the entire Afghan garrison and forcing him to flee to Kabul. The Marathas rapidly captured Attock, Peshawar and Multan and established their authority over all of undivided Punjab. This was the high water mark of Maratha rule. In this period the Maratha Empire extended from Peninsular India virtually up to the Afghan frontier. A letter written by Raghunath Rao to the Peshwa dated 4th May 1758 states, "We have already brought Lahore, Multan, Kashmir and other *subahs* on this side of Attock under our rule. ... Ahmad Khan's son Taimur Sultan and his general Jahan Khan have been pursued and their troops completely looted. We have decided to extend our rule up to Kandahar." But the Maratha plans for further expansion were abruptly shelved when the Peshwa Balaji Rao recalled Raghunath Rao to Pune in May 1758. He departed leaving behind a strong force in Lahore and appointed Adina Beg as the Governor of Punjab. By that stage in mid-1758, it seemed that the Marathas had succeeded in establishing their writ over all of North India. But it proved to be a temporary phase.

Just four months later in September 1758, Adina Beg the able administrator of Punjab died and once again Punjab plunged into a state of disorientation. The Maratha presence in Punjab was too weak and they were too far away to directly influence matters. In this state of affairs, Najib-ud-Daula, the Rohilla Pathan chief appealed to Ahmad Shah Abdali to return to India and re-establish his authority. Abdali smarting under the defeat of his son and keen to re-assert himself, seized the moment and launched his fifth and most fateful invasion of India.

Abdali initially sent an army under Jahan Khan to re-occupy the Punjab, but this army was defeated by the Marathas and forced to retreat to Peshawar. Abdali now built up a strong, well equipped army of over 60,000 Persians, Afghans, Uzbeks and Turks and marched at its head into the Punjab in October 1759. He managed to secure vital alliances amongst the Rohilla Pathan rulers including Najib-ud-Daula, Hafiz Rahmat Khan and other Muslim rulers which reinforced his strength greatly. His advance was rapid. He crossed the Indus and overwhelmed the small Maratha garrison at Lahore. Abdali continued his rapid march and in the first serious encounter defeated the Maratha Advance Guard near Tarain. He followed this up with a decisive victory over the main body of the Maratha army in January 1760 near Delhi. The Maratha's short-lived domination of Punjab and Delhi was over and their influence receded to the area south of the Chambal River. Abdali was poised to return to Kabul when Najib-ud-Daula and the other Rohilla Pathan chiefs urged him to remain in India and prevent any resurgence of Marathas power. With the promise of ample tribute, Abdali agreed to stay and established himself in the area of Koil – (present day Aligarh)– where he spent the year of 1760 consolidating his strength, securing allies and preparing for a decisive confrontation which loomed large on the horizon.

The Build-Up to Battle

The Marathas had watched their influence in North India crumble in the wake of Abdali's invasion and the rude ouster of their forces in Punjab. Though they themselves were responsible for this state of affairs. They had not left a large enough force to adequately defend Punjab, nor had they secured alliances amongst the Sikhs and Rajput rulers. With Abdali back in India, the Peshwa decided to send another large expedition to recapture the Punjab and re-assert his authority in North India.

The Maratha army left the Deccan around February 1760, under the command of his cousin Sadashiv Rao Bhau, a brave and capable general, though one who could be impetuous and avaricious. The Peshwa's seventeen year old son, Vishwas Rao was appointed as the nominal head with the Bhau as his guardian and executive manager of all his affairs. It was a large, well-trained army, though not very cohesive. It consisted of troops under different chiefs, each with their own styles and concepts of war-fighting. En route, its strength increased as the important Maratha Chiefs of Holkar, Scindia, Gaikwars joined them during their northward march, boosting its strength to around 45,000 combatants. Yet, for all its impressive size, the army did not have proper equipment or finances. The Bhau had been given just around 8000 cannon balls, 160 mounds of lead, 800 mounds of gunpowder and around 85 sheets of paper to charge their muskets, which was just around half of what was bid for and would not suffice for a sustained campaign. The Peshwa did not even provide the necessary finances for his army, giving only Rupees 22 Lakhs against the 72 Lakhs required for the campaign, declaring that "a Maratha army should be able to sustain itself on its plunder". The Marathas earlier campaigns had seen it achieve spectacular successes in capturing vast enemy stocks, but one cannot base a campaign on that premise. Ultimately, the disastrous policy of plunder and foraging for their resources would make the Maratha army lose all good will amongst the population and deny it the local support which was needed to fight a campaign far from their own lands and homes.

The strength of the army lay in its artillery. The Maratha artillery had been assiduously developed by Ibrahim Khan Gardi, a Muslim chief who rose to become one of the premier generals of Peshwa's army. He had been trained under the French General Busse and under his guidance the Maratha *'Top-Khana'* became its strongest arm. It had 200 pieces of excellent French made, rifled cannons which gave them a tremendous advantage of range. But the guns were heavy and the gun carriages were weak and tended to break down especially when carried over difficult terrain. Once deployed, they were difficult to shift and their cannon balls too were not perfected calibrated resulting in misfires and accidents. They also possessed around a thousand rockets but these were unpredictable and inaccurate and often did little more than scare the horses. The army was armed with the traditional swords, spears, shields, bows and arrows. Matchlocks had been recently introduced, but their barrels were short and they fired light bullets which had relatively short ranges and were notoriously inaccurate. The uniforms were light and flimsy more suited for the warm climes of the Deccan. The

Maratha Horsemen. They were lightly armed and protected, mounted on small nimble ponies which were suited for guerilla warfare but no match for the heavy cavalry of Abdali

officers wore light garments without any protective armor, while the men usually fought with nothing but a dhoti wrapped around their loins- which made Abdali derisively call them "naked-backed". This was an army steeped in the traditions of Shivaji's fast, nimble guerilla tactics and was clothed and equipped accordingly. Yet, the campaign they were embarking upon was a different one. In a conventional battle which they would have to fight in the cold North Indian winters, heavy clothing and protective armor would have been literally life-saving.

The bulk of the officers seemed to have forgotten Shivaji's Spartan code. Their tents were elaborate and luxurious, "The lofty and spacious tents, lined with silks and brocade, were surmounted by gilded ornaments.... It was an imitation of the Mughal in the zenith of their glory," wrote the historian Grant Duff, in his description of the Maratha army. Each officer had a retinue of personal servants and many of their families traveled with them. This large army was also encumbered by around 100,000 civilians, mostly middle class Maharastrians who had accompanied it on a pilgrimage to the holy sites of Mathura, Prayag, Kashi and to see the *Aryan Desh* of North India. These presence of these non-combatants slowed the progress of the army as they were forced to halt at the various pilgrimage sites en route. The encumbered army crawled slowly northwards without any sense of urgency or any premonition of what lay ahead.

There was another major handicap. Their courageous but rigid leader himself. The Bhau had never seen North India. He did not know the people, the climatic conditions, the local rulers or the political situation. His only knowledge was that Abdali was sitting on the Yamuna awaiting his arrival. He did not develop an intelligence network nor try to build up alliances as he advanced to meet his enemy. In June 1760, he crossed the Chambal and from now on he was in unfriendly territory. He halted in the vicinity of Gwalior where he was well looked after by Suraj Mal, the powerful Jat ruler of Central India. Suraj Mal was a shrewd and experienced campaigner who advised Bhau to leave his women folk, camp followers and heavy baggage behind in the sanctuary of his forts at Jhansi and Gwalior and move forward lightly. He knew of the powerful army Abdali had built up and advised Bhau not to engage him in a pitched battle but to resort to the guerilla tactics which were the traditional forte of the Marathas. It was sound advice. A sustained guerilla campaign would have slowly worn out Abdali and forced him to return to Kabul. But the Bhau, supremely confident of his own army, derisively ignored it saying "I do not take advice from *zamindars* and goat-herds". In doing so he antagonized the sensible and knowledgeable Suraj Mal who later withdrew from the campaign.

He was not the only one whom the Marathas alienated. The Rajput chiefs of Kota, Bundi, Udaipur and Bundelkhand were approached for help in this battle against a Muslim invader, but religion did not prove a strong enough glue. They too had been repeated antagonized by the high handed conduct of the Marathas and now chose to remain aloof even as the destiny of India was about to unravel in the coming months.

While the Maratha army made its slow move northwards, Abdali was busy securing his own alliances. He won over the Rohilla Pathan chiefs, including Shuja-ud-Daula, the powerful ruler of Awadh. Shuja was swaying towards joining the Marathas but was won over at the last minute by astute diplomacy. Most of the Muslim chiefs of North India also sided with Abdali. The Sikhs, under coercion, agreed to remain neutral. The war of diplomacy which precedes all battles was clearly won by Abdali.

The Maratha army reached Delhi in end July and entered the Imperial capital on 01 August 1760. But for all the pomp of their arrival they were already in a precarious state. They had been marching for over six months, their supplies were running out and their finances were exhausted. The Bhau now ordered the gold and silver ornaments within the palace of the capital to be seized and its silver-lined walls and roofs were stripped in an effort to raise some funds. Supplies, already scanty in war-ravaged Delhi, were forcibly seized. These actions got him a paltry sum of Rupees Seventeen Lakhs but it turned the population of the entire city and those of the adjoining areas against the Marathas. It also led to many of his North Indian allies, including the powerful Suraj Mal, leaving him at the most critical stage. By now the Bhau had "not a single friend left, north of the Narmada". He was in alien territory – friendless, short of supplies and disoriented; and the battle was just about to be joined.

The Preparatory Period

For two months, till October 1760, the Maratha Army remained in the vicinity of Delhi. Abdali continued to be encamped on the East bank of the Yamuna and made no attempt to contest them. The Marathas were slowly running out of supplies, since the vast army and its followers had to buy each item in hard cash and their finances were slowly dwindling. By their foraging and plundering they had antagonized the villages all around and no local help was forthcoming. Abdali's army too was equally hard-pressed for supplies but in a slightly better position due to the help of his local allies. Both sides made a last minute attempt for a truce but Abdali insisted that the terms would be that the boundary between the Maratha and the Durrani Empire should be considered as the Chambal River while the Bhau wanted it to be along the line of the Indus. The talks failed and as October arrived, the first chill of winter began setting in. The effects of the shortage of supplies now began telling on both sides. Both adversaries realized that the matter would be decided by the army that out-lasted the other and began maneuvering to positions where they would be able to cut off the supply lines of their opponent. As the two sides jostled and skirmished the stage was being inexorably set for the final, violent showdown.

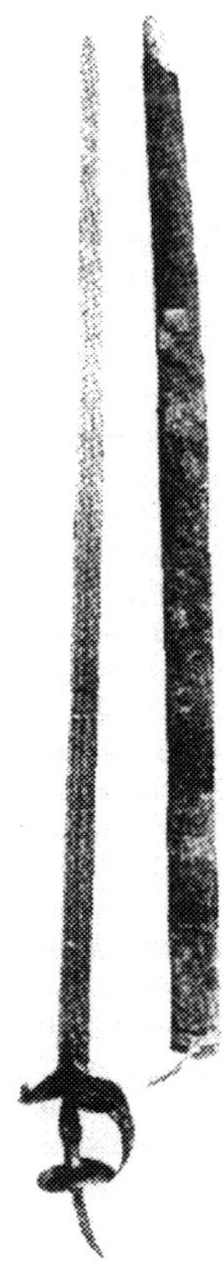

In mid October, the Maratha army moved towards Kunjpura, an Afghan strong point on the West bank of the Yamuna; around 150 kilometers from Delhi. This was Abdali's logistic hub where money and supplies were collected from all over Punjab and sent to the Durrani camp. Kunjpura was well fortified and strongly held by around 10,000 determined Afghans. On 17 October the Marathas launched a violent attack preceded by heavy cannon fire and forced their way inside. The garrison was slaughtered and over 4000 Afghans taken prisoner. Abdali was encamped on the Eastern bank of the river and could see the fighting and hear the cries of his dying soldiers but was unable to do anything since the Yamuna was in flood and could not be crossed. Kunjpura and its vast stock of supplies came in Maratha hands and with it their position improved considerably in term of morale and logistics. This was a major success and from the letters Bhau wrote to the Peshwa, he seemed confident that he would soon oust Abdali. The Maratha camp celebrated Dushhera and Divali joyously and even undertook a pilgrimage to the temples around Kurukshetra. But their optimism was to be short lived.

With Kunjpura captured, Abdali was in danger of being cut off from his lines of supply which were all based west of the Yamuna. The rains stopped; the waters began receding and Abdali took a calculated risk to cross the River. Aided by a native guide his army forded the still swollen Yamuna over three days and nights, losing almost a thousand men but finally getting across to the Western bank around 25 October in the vicinity of Baghpat, South of the Maratha positions. The Bhau had left posts of around a thousand men to guard the river crossings but they were surprised, overwhelmed and massacred – in one case surrounded and slaughtered as they slept. With Abdali across the river and sitting behind the Maratha positions the tables were turned. The Maratha lines of supply from Delhi were now cut off and the Bhau was forced to move towards Panipat on 29 October from where he could block Abdali's access back to Afghanistan just as he had blocked his to Delhi. Here he carefully selected his positions along a strong defensive line extending from the village of Nimbdi in the North West to the village of Ugra Kheri, South West of the town. The Panipat Hill flanked their Eastern extremities and the 'Shah Nahr' or the Imperial canal protected their Western flank. All the non-combatants were placed in the town of Panipat and its adjoining villages. The entire camp was fortified and protected by a 10 kilometer long ditch which was 20 meters broad and 4 meters deep- a virtually insurmountable barrier. The prized field artillery of around 200 French made cannon was equally distributed along the perimeter. The Maratha camp gave the appearance of a well-defended fortress – but it was a fortress which was cut off and isolated and very much under siege.

Abdali too set up camp in the vicinity of Panipat sitting astride the road to Delhi, thus cutting off the Maratha communication to the capital and their sources of supply. For almost two and a half months the armies remained in this posture, with violent skirmishes taking place almost every day. Both sides tried to intercept each other's supply trains. A major loss took place when Govind Pant Bundela with around 10,000 light Cavalry, who were on a foraging mission near Meerut, were ambushed and decimated by a strong Afghan force. Bundela's head was cut off and sent to the Bhau as a grisly token and it had a telling effect on morale. The Marathas suffered another major loss when a force of 2000 soldiers arriving from Delhi, laden with salaries for their troops inadvertently strayed into the Afghan camp. They were ruthlessly slaughtered and the much needed money captured. The lack of finances and resources was now telling on the Marathas. Almost daily, foraging parties moved out of the Maratha camp, but the Afghans burnt all the

Afghan troopers were heavily armed and well protected. This gave them an edge in hand-to-hand combat

villages in the vicinity and supplies were nowhere to be found. The foraging parties were repeatedly ambushed and gradually morale plummeted.

By December, the Afghans also recaptured Kunjpura with its precious hoard of grain and fodder. With this the only remaining line of supply to the Marathas – that from Patiala was blocked. The Maratha camp was now effectively isolated and cut off from every source of supply or reinforcements.

It was not just starvation that weakened the Marathas. In the congested conditions of the camp, sanitation was non-existent and virulent epidemics broke out which killed most of the horses and cattle. All around the camp, the air was heavy with the moldy stench of decaying bodies and horses, victims of the almost daily skirmishes of the past two months. The army was tired, hungry and demoralized and finally on 13 January, the officers and men approached the Bhau and pleaded with him to give the order to attack and decide the issue on the strength of their swords. It was preferable to die in battle than continue in the abysmal conditions that they now endured. The only hope lay in breaking the siege which Abdali had enforced and withdraw to Delhi where provisions were available and the army could rest till reinforcements arrived from the south. The bhau acquiesced to their request. He ordered the distribution of all available grain in the Quarter Master stores, gave his men the first- and for many the final – full meal that they had eaten in weeks and ceremonially distributed *paan* and betel nut – the symbol of departure. The Marathas spent the night preparing for their final battle and on 14 January 1761 began moving out of the camp arrayed in full battle order. On this cold, fog-shrouded morning Panipat would witness its bloodiest battle ever.

Plan of Deployment of Forces

Third Battle of Panipat (14 January 1761)

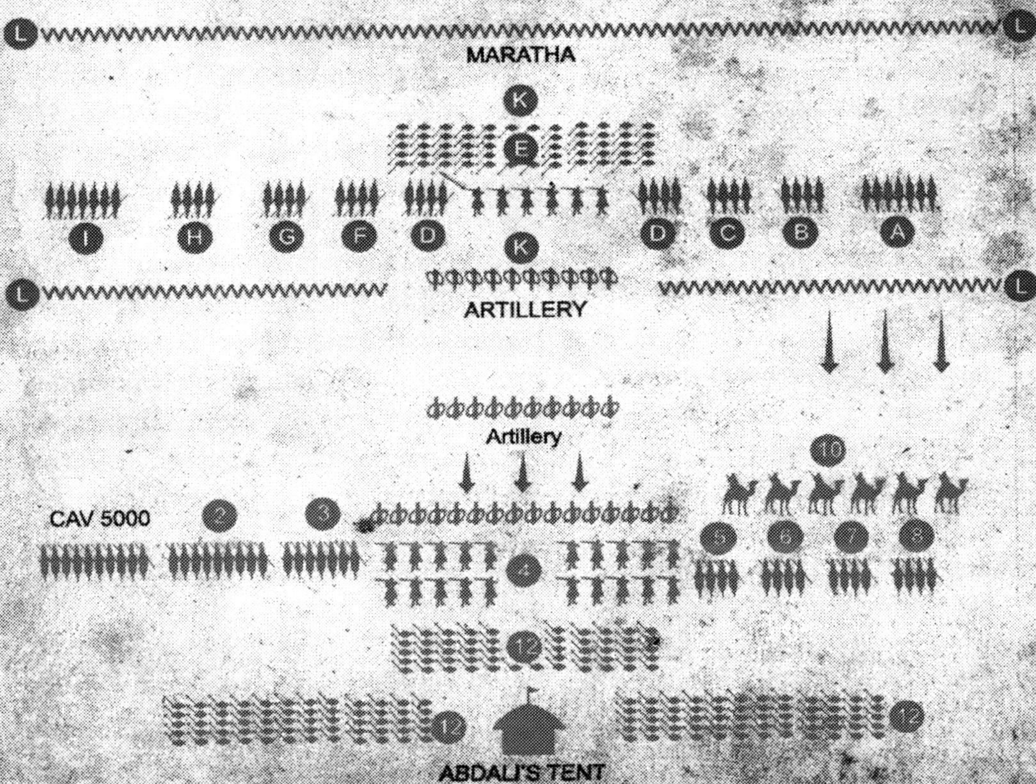

MARATHAS

A. Ibrahim Khan Gardi (9000).
B. Damaji Gaekwad (3000).
C. Shic Deo Patel (1000).
D. Minor Captains.
E. Centre.
F. Jaswant Rao Puar
G. Minor Captains.
H. Mlhar Rao Holkar (5000).
I. Jankoji Sindhia (10,000).
J. Artillery.
K. Bahua's position.
L. 12 feet deep and 50 feet wide trench around Maratha position.

AFGHANS

1. Shah Pasand Khan (5000-mainly Cavalry)
2. Najib.
3. Shuja.
4. Grand Wazir Shah Wali Khan.
5. Ahmad Khan Bangash.
6. Hafiz Rahmat Khan.
7. Dundy Khan.
8. Amir Beg and others.
9. Barkhurdar Khan (5000-mainly Cavalry).
10. Camel mounted with musketeers armed with Zamburaks and a force of Kabuli Infantry.
11. Artillery.
12. Slave squadrons of bodyguards (3000).
13. Abdali's tent.

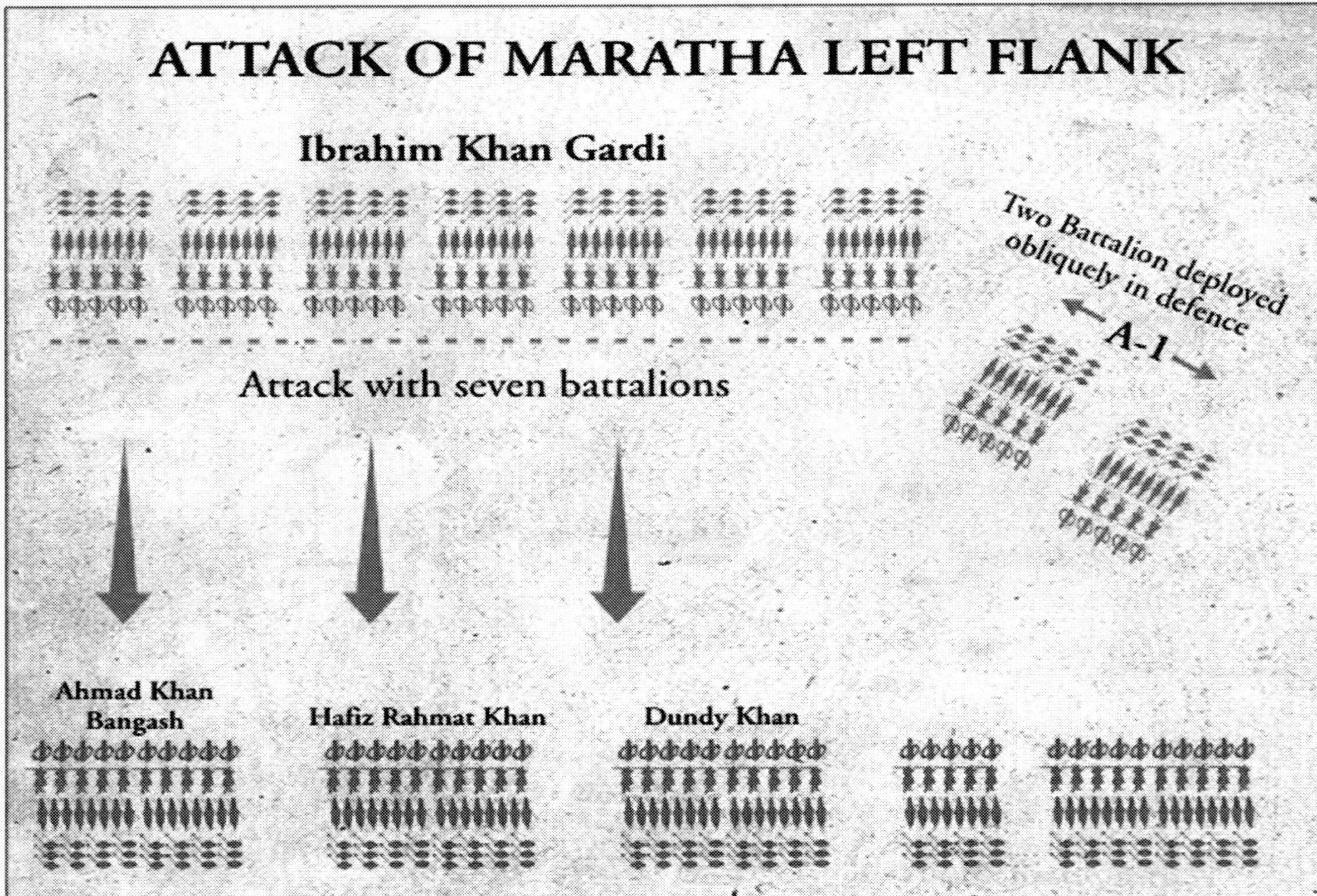
ATTACK OF MARATHA LEFT FLANK
Ibrahim Khan Gardi
Attack with seven battalions
Two Battalion deployed obliquely in defence
A-1
Ahmad Khan Bangash
Hafiz Rahmat Khan
Dundy Khan

Deployment

It is not clear what exactly the Bhau had in mind before he embarked on this battle. From some accounts the discussions in his camp went on till around midnight with many advising him to adhere to the successful guerilla tactics of the past, others insisting on a conventional attack to break out through the Afghan lines. Bhau was eventually been convinced to attempt a break-out. His plan revolved around using his artillery to first soften the Afghan positions and then break through their lines using the full force of his infantry and cavalry. He based his deployment around his existing fortification in Panipat. On his left flank, which he hoped to utilize as the flank of decision, he placed Ibrahim Khan Gardi. Gardi was deployed in the South West of Panipat near the village of Nimbdi with nine of his excellent, French trained battalions – a force of around 8000 foot soldiers. The heavy cannon, which Gardi personally commanded were placed in front of the line so that their fire would not be blocked by his own men. Behind Gardi's infantry, the Bhau had deployed Damaji Gaikwar and Vittal Shivdeo with around 4000 cavalry. The role of Gardi's left flank was simple. His long range artillery would first wear down the Afghan lines with a heavy bombardment and then Gardi would attack with his infantry

THE MAN

Sadashiv Rao Bhau – A bold and capable general who however was impetuous and prone to temper. His high handedness alienated most of the Rajput and Jat rulers of Northern india. He had no experience of the terrain and environment of North India.

Although physically courageous he lacked the strategic vision for a sustained campaign against Abdali.

Ahmad Shah Abdali – A very skilled general. Attended to each detail of tactics and administration. Was cool and composed even during the initial reverses.

A good diplomat who succeeded in winning over all Muslim rulers to his side and stitched a strong alliance of diverse chiefs whom he held together by sheer force.

battalions on the Afghan right flank. When they had broken through the Afghan lines the Maratha cavalry would charge and consolidate their gains. The Bhau was located in the Centre with Vishwas Rao and around 13,000, *Huzurat,* personal troops which he himself commanded. He was positioned beneath a Black Mango tree near the site of the village of Ugrakhedi. In that site, today stands the village of *Kala Amb*, with a historic war memorial commemorating the battle. The Maratha Centre under the Bhau's command was to attack in conjunction with the Left Flank. When the combined attack had broken the crust of the Afghan lines, the Right Wing would attack on orders of the Bhau to complete the break through.

The right wing was located around two kilometers south of Panipat, under Jankoji Scindia, Malhar Rao Holkar and a force of almost 17000 men. It was a strong force but as events would prove, it did very little in the battle and eventually was instrumental in losing the day. The Maratha deployment with its force of over 45,000 men extended 12 kilometers wide. But short of troops, the Bhau had kept no reserves to exploit an opening or reinforce a contingency. His lack of reserves was a telling weakness. But, he had one more fear. Behind him, in the camp were around 30-40,000 civilians and pilgrims – unarmed and defenseless – who would become easy prey if their attack failed.

Around eight kilometers opposite them, the 60,000 strong Afghan army arrayed itself in a similar extended formation. Its numerical superiority allowed it to expand its frontage to almost 14 kilometers, two kilometers more then the Marathas. This prevented them from being out-flanked and also gave it the flexibility to out-flank their opponent. Abdali's forces were a mix of his own Afghans and his Indian allies namely Najib-ud-Daula; Shuja-ud-Daula, the Nawab of Oudh, Hafiz Rahmat Khan along with a host of

Maratha cannon

other chieftains. His Right Wing (facing the Maratha Left under Ibrahim Gardi) had around 15000 foot soldiers and 3000 excellent Persian Cavalry commanded by Hafiz Rahmat Khan and Ahmad Khan Bangash. In the centre, was the Wazir, Shah Wali Khan with around 15000 troops supported by 2000 Camel mounted swivel guns called *Zamburaks* and around 1000 Kabuli infantry. The Left Wing was held by Shah Pasand Khan with around 5000 Persian Cavalry, Najib-ud-Daula with around 15,000 foot soldiers and Shuja-ud-Daula with his contingent of 5000 soldiers. Abdali himself positioned himself behind the battle lines on a high ground where with a pair of excellent binoculars and a contingent of fast messengers he could monitor and control each activity on the battle-field. He had placed his slave squadrons and Personal Body Guards of around 10,000 heavy Cavalry as an immediate reserve under his personal command. This sound deployment and his skillful use of reserves would eventually help decide the day.

The Day of Doom

On the wintry dawn of 14 January 1761 – one of the blackest days in Indian history – the Marathas wheeled their heavy guns forwards and began forming up for the battle. In the mist of the North Indian morning, the actions of the opposing sides could be barely discernable across the five kilometers that separated them. Yet eyewitnesses state that the body language of the once invincible Maratha army did not speak of confidence. Their turbans were untied and disheveled. Their hands and faces were smeared with turmeric as if in preparation for a final rite (although the tumeric could have been applied as an immediate antiseptic for any wounds sustained in the coming battle) and their actions seemed to reflect a futility and not the confidence of an army determined to wrest victory. As the saffron flag of the Marathas and the green and white standard of the Afghans went up, cries of "*Har Har Mahadeo*" and "*Allah-O-Akbar*" reverberated through the air. Even with the sounds of battle cries, the clamor of drums and trumpets and the trampling of feet on the march, a strange stillness seemed to envelop the area and the air hung heavy with tension.

At around nine in the morning, the Marathas fired the first salvoes with their French-made artillery. The elevation was not correct and the rounds overshot their targets by a mile. The heavy guns had been chained together and dug-in and their fire could not be easily corrected. The Afghan artillery responded with their opening salvoes but their shots landed harmlessly ahead of the Maratha lines. The initial exchange of artillery fire was ineffective and just the tentative gambit of the titanic battle ahead.

At around nine thirty, the Marathas launched their attack with their Left flank under Ibrahim Khan Gardi. Amongst all the luminaries on the Maratha army, Gardi was perhaps the most professional and capable. He had been trained by the French General Busse and he himself was an expert in artillery. His troops were well equipped, well-trained and disciplined and he had managed to sustain them reasonably well even in the past difficult months. Although a Muslim, he was one of Bhau's favorites, a fact which caused considerable jealousy amongst the Maratha commanders. Ironically in this war – labeled as a Hindu-Muslim battle – this Muslim commander would prove to be Bhau's most steadfast ally.

Seeing that the cannon fire was ineffective – Ibrahim Gardi halted the fire and formed up his nine battalions for an attack on the Afghan Right flank. He attacked with seven battalions leaving two battalions deployed obliquely to meet any counter attack from the Afghan Cavalry. His seven battalions, with Gardi at the head, attacked in perfect order with bayonets fixed and their musket fire claimed a deadly toll on the Rohillas opposite them. The tightly disciplined fire-and-move formations of the Gardi musketeers brought them close to the Afghan lines. Their units moved in perfect unison, one advancing and firing as the other stopped to reload. Their coordinated advance brought down a withering hail of fire that almost broke the lines of the Afghan right flank. Then the Marathas made the first mistake of the battle.

The Maratha Cavalry under Vithal Shivdeo was to attack only when Gardi's foot infantry had driven a wedge through the Afghan

Right flank and then exploit this opening. But, impatient and restive, and perhaps a little jealous of Gardi's success, Vithal Shivdeo launched his cavalry prematurely. The Cavalry soon crossed the line of advancing Infantry and reached the Afghan lines. The result was chaos. The Gardi infantry could not fire their muskets because of the Maratha Cavalry ahead of them. The cavalry attack petered out in the face of heavy fire from the Rohillas. Most of the horses were simply too weak after weeks of near starvation and could not sustain the assault. The cavalry could not break through; the infantry could not follow up the attack and after three hours of bitter fighting Gardi's attack could not make any further progress. Yet by noon, in spite of heavy casualties, they were favorably placed. They were poised on the edge of the Afghan Right Flank and had killed around 8000 Afghans. The Afghan Right flank was considerably weakened and had barely succeeded in holding on.

THE EQUIPMENT

Marathas – The Marathas were short of finances and equipment even at the start of the campaign. Their situation worsened as the campaign progressed. Had a strong artillery contingent, but their guns were heavy, could not be easily deployed and maneuvered.

The men were usually equipped with swords, spears, bows and muskets. They wore little protective armour and Abdali derisively referred to them as "bare–backed".

Their horses were small ponies more used to mountain terrain and had limited strength and endurance.

Afghans – The men were well equipped with heavy armour which staved many injuries during close combat. The cavalry component was heavily protected and well armed, mounted on powerful Khurasami stallions.

The muskets fired heavier bullets with greater ranges and lethality than the lighter Maratha rounds.

Zamburaks – Camel mounted swivel guns were used to fire above the heads of their own troops into the Maratha ranks beyond. These lethal weapons were used in squadrons of 500 each to wheel around the battlefeild.

In the centre too the Marathas seemed to be having the upper hand, at least initially. Sadashiv Rao Bhau had launched a determined attack at the Afghan Centre held by Wazir Shah Vali Khan. The fine *Huzurat* troops, under the present command of Bhau tore though the Afghan centre, slaughtering over 3000 Afghans in the first two hours of battle. Bhau's personal direction led the attack through the crust of the Afghan lines and managed to reach three hundred meters of Shah Vali's position. As the centre began crumbling, Shah Vali sent an urgent message to Shuja-ud-Daula on his immediate left, requesting him for help, else he would surely perish. But Shuja-ud-Daula did not move, fearing that if he left his positions he would leave a gap which the Marathas could exploit. With the Afghan right flank almost broken by Ibrahim Gardi's attack and the Centre about to collapse – the Marathas seemed to be on the verge of a break through. At this critical juncture their lack of reserves began to tell. The Bhau had not a single unit of cavalry who could now tear through the crumbling Afghan lines and complete the break through. The Afghans rallied slowly but determinedly and held their positions. The Maratha attacks poised tantalizingly on the edge of victory and then the scales began to tilt.

Abdali had been following the events from his *Kazalbashi*, or command tent, from a vantage point around two kilometers behind the forward lines. Seeing the force of the Maratha attack and watching his Right Flank and Centre begin to give way, he passed instructions to his wives to mount their steeds and be prepared to leave if the situation worsened. He now gathered his reserve of 10,000 men from his slave squadrons and personal body guards. He also sent out his *nasagchis* (military provosts) to gather all able-bodied men available in the camp and round up all those who had fled the battle. The provost gathered up around three thousand fleeing soldiers, putting to death those who refused, and these were sent to reinforce the crumbling right wing. Another 6-7000 of his personal troops were sent to the beleaguered Shah Vali to bolster the centre. Abdali had reinforced both the Right Flank and the Centre with fresh troops without weakening his left flank. By 1 pm he was balanced once again and ready to counter attack.

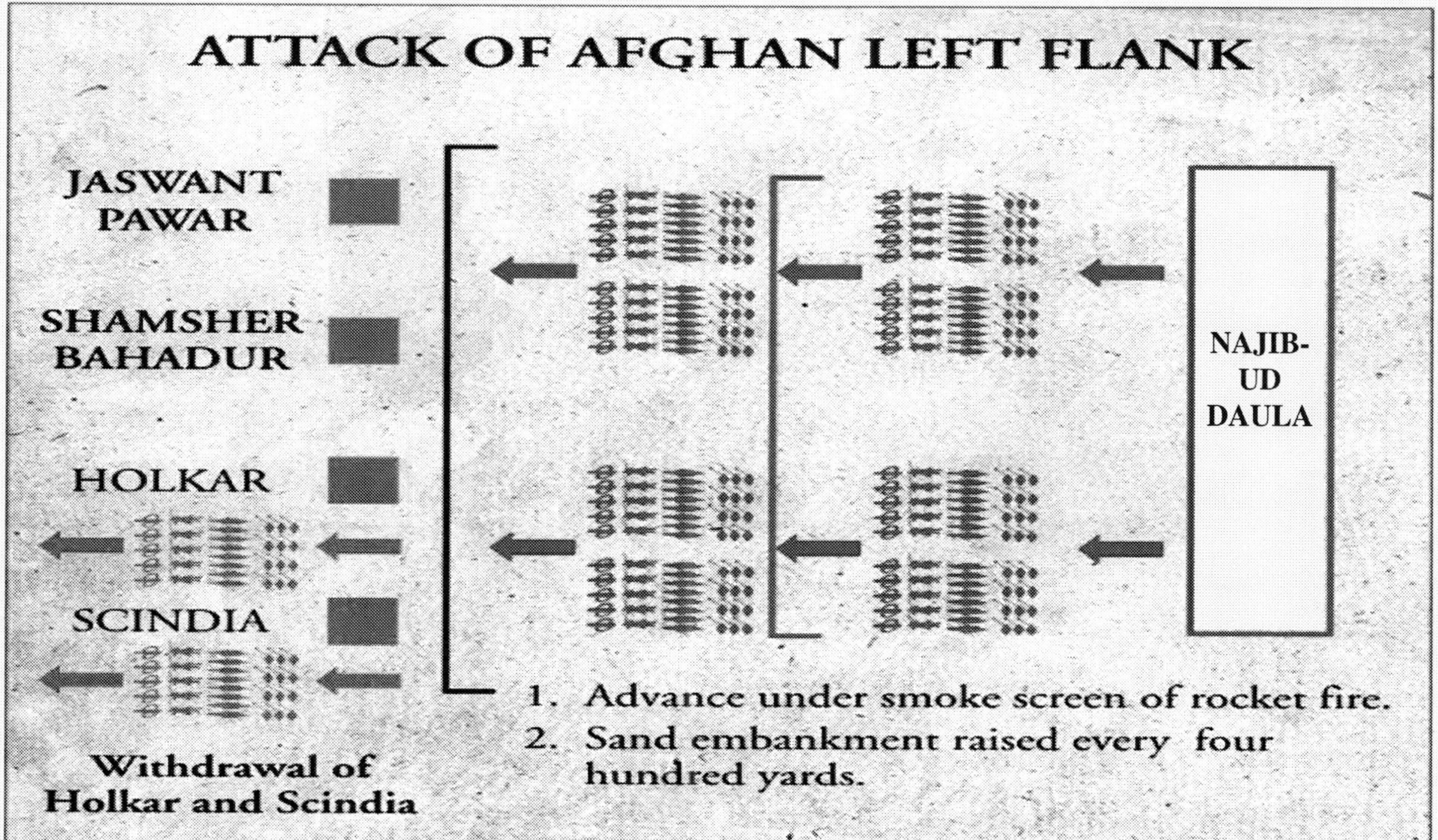
ATTACK OF AFGHAN LEFT FLANK
JASWANT PAWAR
SHAMSHER BAHADUR
HOLKAR
SCINDIA
NAJIB-UD DAULA
1. Advance under smoke screen of rocket fire.
2. Sand embankment raised every four hundred yards.
Withdrawal of Holkar and Scindia

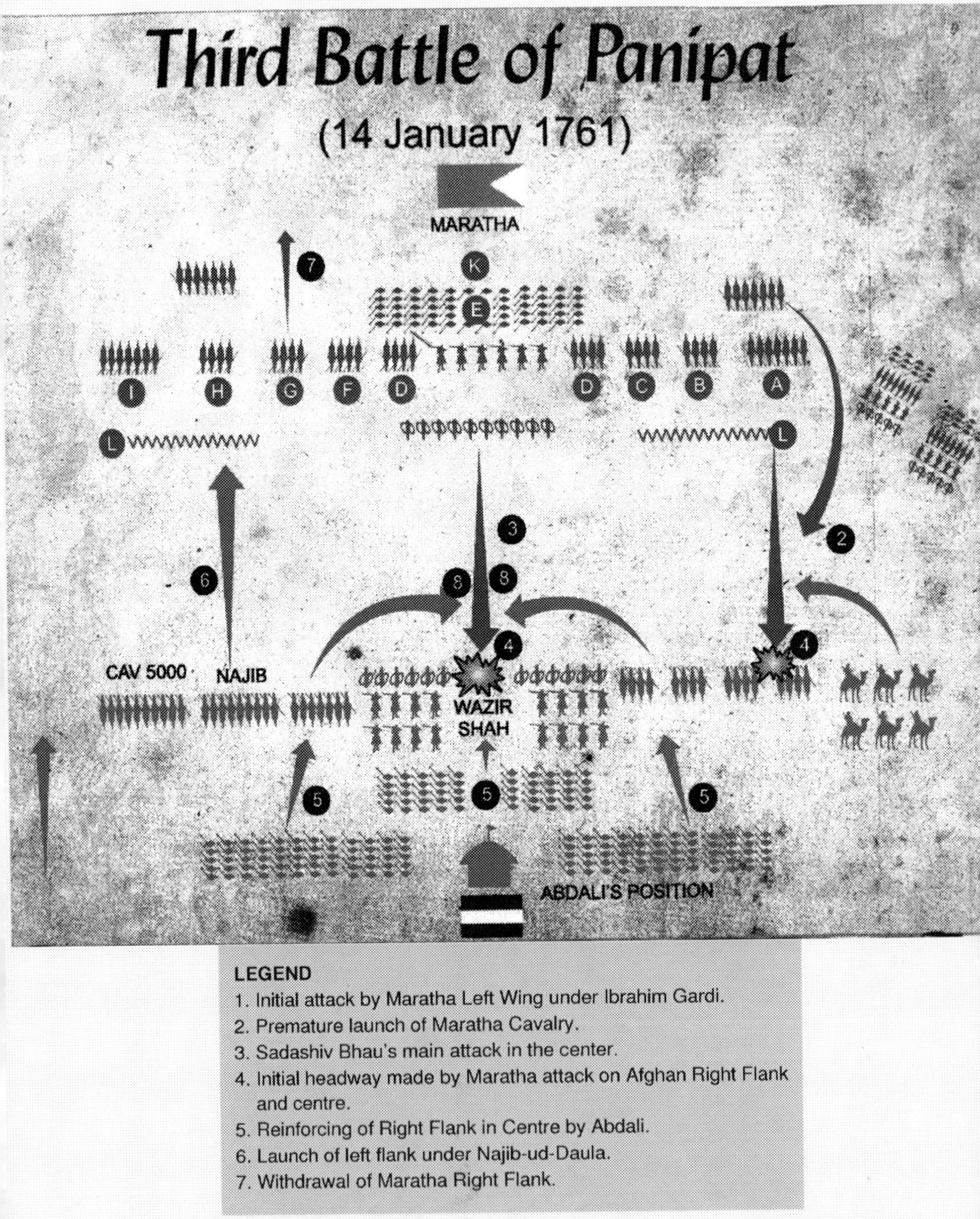

LEGEND

1. Initial attack by Maratha Left Wing under Ibrahim Gardi.
2. Premature launch of Maratha Cavalry.
3. Sadashiv Bhau's main attack in the center.
4. Initial headway made by Maratha attack on Afghan Right Flank and centre.
5. Reinforcing of Right Flank in Centre by Abdali.
6. Launch of left flank under Najib-ud-Daula.
7. Withdrawal of Maratha Right Flank.

Abdali's Counter Attack

Abdali now ordered his re-invigorated Centre to attack the Maratha Centre. Simultaneously he tasked his right flank to advance and recapture the ground they had lost to Ibrahim Gardi's attack. He also ordered Najib-ud-Daula to advance from the left flank against the Maratha Right flank and thus threaten Sadashiv Bhau's attack in the Centre.

The Maratha had been fighting bitterly since morning. Weakened as they were from the hardships and near-starvation of previous months, their strength was ebbing with each passing hour. No food or water had reached the battlefield and they sustained themselves with lumps of jaggery and handfuls of puffed rice. The Afghans had developed an effective replenishment system. The refreshments for the battle were carried by individual soldiers in the form of pieces of dried meats, fruits and bread. Their water carriers roamed the battlefield with leather pannier bags, providing much needed water to soldiers at the very front lines. At around 1 pm the reinforced Afghan Centre launched a furious attack, supported by the *Zamburaks*; camel mounted swivel guns which could fire above their own troops into the Maratha ranks beyond. Squadrons of 500 camel swivels wheeled around the Maratha lines in batches of around a hundred each, causing immense damage. Abdali also launched his reserve of 10,000 heavily armed cavalry in wide sweeping attacks on the flanks of the Maratha Centre which was gradually being compressed into a tight knot. In this mass the Afghan muskets and *Zambaruks* poured a withering hail of fire.

As the Maratha Centre fought valiantly against hopeless odds, the Afghan wings attacked as well. The Afghan Right wing was bolstered by reinforcements and now launched a massive attack on Ibrahim Gardi's forces on the left wing. By now most of the Maratha horses had collapsed out of exhaustion and the Cavalrymen fought dismounted as troopers. Ibrahim Gardi seven battalions were virtually wiped out. His brother was killed and he himself was wounded thrice and captured alive (He would later die a terrible death in captivity after being brutally tortured by the Afghans for choosing to fight on the side of the Marathas). Most of the Maratha Cavalry and the Gardi foot soldiers perished in the counter-attack and the remnants fell back and scattered across the countryside.

And what of the Maratha Right Flank. The Holkar-Scindia contingents took virtually no part in the battle. The just stood five kilometers away without advancing even as their own centre and right flank made impressive gains in the initial stages of the battle. Had they supported the attack perhaps Sadashiv Bhau may have been able to break through the Afghan lines. However the Holkar troops had suffered defeats in each of their previous skirmishes with the Afghans and their morale was low. Till the afternoon they passively waited in their position. At around 1 pm Najib-ud-Daula launched his attack from the Afghan Left Wing, advancing slowly and deliberately towards the Maratha Right Flank. His attack began with a salvo of 2000 rockets which caused an initial disorientation in the Maratha lines and terrified their horses. Under cover of its smoke screen his 15,000 infantry advanced slowly by fire and move, stopping every half a kilometer or so to raise an embankment of sand. The sand embankment provided cover to his men and also a raised firing platform for his rocket batteries. Najib-ud-Daula's attack drove a clear wedge between the Maratha Right Flank and the Centre and as the attack progressed, Holkar withdrew with his entire contingent of 5000 men. Scindia followed suit and suddenly the entire Right Flank disappeared leaving the area to Najib-ud-Daula. The Afghans now held the field of battle on the Right flank and with it they cut off the route of withdrawal of the Maratha centre which was still fighting valiantly under the Bhau.

Sadashiv Bhau had been holding on desperately against the reinvigorated Afghan attacks. In a last attempt to regain control of the situation he sent a message to Holkar to attack from the right flank and relieve pressure. Holkar did not respond. In fact by then, the Maratha Right Flank had already begun its withdrawal. The centre was now isolated and the Afghan launched attack after attack on the beleaguered Marathas. In spite of his situation, the Bhau launched three violent counter attacks which caused heavy casualties, but by then it was hopeless. The Afghans closed in, first firing their *Zamburaks* at long ranges then using their muskets as they neared. One such shot from a *Zamburak* struck the Peshwa's son, Vishwas Rao on the forehead and killed him instantly in the field of battle.

Vishwas Rao's death marked the beginning of the end. The Marathas lost heart and began to break. In the confusion, around 3000 Afghan prisoners who had been left behind in the Maratha camp, broke free and began looting and pillaging the camp. A rumor spread that the Afghans were behind them and the tired, demoralized Marathas lost cohesion. The battle degenerated into a brawl with adversaries battling first with muskets then with arrows and spears, closing in with swords and finally grappling with bare hands in a bitter fight to the finish. The heavily armored Afghan cavalry, mounted on their superb Khurasami horses swept in from

THE MOMENT

The initial Maratha attacks were making headway and the Afghan lines were crumbling when Abdali launched a counter attack with his personal reserves of 10000 heavy cavalry. This struck at the precise moment when the Marathas were exhausted and their limited reserves spent.

Abdali's perfectly timed counter attack halted the Maratha advance and allowed him to launch his own attack on the opposite flank. The scales tilted in his favour thereafter.

the flanks, firing muskets as they approached and then moving in for the kill with slashing sabers and spears. The cavalry attacks slowly compressed the Marathas into a tight knot where each Afghan bullet or cannon shot was bound to find its mark.

Vishwas Rao's death also broke the Bhau. He dismounted from his elephant and mounted a horse, plunging deep into the thick of battle. Three horses were shot beneath him, the last being but an emaciated country mare. In the carnage around him around 30-40000 Maratha soldiers fell on the blood soaked field – most of them mutilated and beheaded by the vengeful Afghans. Bhau was amongst the last to fall and his decapitated body was discovered at the scene of the bitterest fighting with around twenty dead Afghans around him. After the battle, Abdali in a rare gesture personally had his body and that of Viswas washed and then cremated at the spot where they fell.

The carnage followed till late at night and into the next day as well. Unfortunately it was a clear night and the moon though not full, was bright and clearly revealed the fleeing Maratha soldiers and civilians. The vengeful Afghans, who had lost around 35,000 of their own, pursued the defenseless Marathas into their camp and in the streets of Panipat. Another 10,000 civilians were killed in an orgy of revenge and around 20,000 women and children captured and taken as slaves. Barely 15,000 remnants of the Grand Maratha army succeeded in making their way across the Chambal and back into the safety of their own territory.

The destruction of the Maratha Army was one of the greatest tragedies of Indian history. Every household in Maharashtra lost at least one member, many families were wiped out completely. Balaji Rao Peshwa was crossing the Narmada River with reinforcements to bolster his army when he received news of the disaster in the couched words "Two pearls have been dissolved (the Bhau and the Peshwa's son) twenty seven gold mohurs have been lost (the chieftains) and of the silver and copper, the total quantity cannot be cast up." But then he himself was largely to blame for the debacle. He neglected to equip his army right from the beginning itself; he did not supply them or make arrangements for finances even after he heard of their precarious conditions. Finally when he eventually moved northwards with reinforcements, he delayed his departure by almost three months, being busy with his own second wedding. If only he had departed earlier he would have reached around October and his advancing army would have caught the Afghans in a pincer. He turned back from the Narmada, abandoning for ever his dreams of Northern India, but he never recovered from the shock. Six months later, he was dead in Pune and his death cast a further shroud of gloom on the already grief-struck Maratha Empire.

The Impact of the Battle

Abdali described the battle and its outcome in a letter "The flame of fighting blazed up and raged on all sides. The enemy distinguished themselves and fought well beyond the capacity of their races. The fighting passed from the exchange of cannon and rocket fire, to the discharge of muskets, from where it proceeded to combat with swords, daggers and knives. The grasped each other by the throat. Suddenly the breeze of victory began to flow as willed by the Divine Lord and the Deccanis suffered utter defeat. Forty to fifty thousand troopers and infantry men fell as grass before our pitiless swords......".

The scale of carnage at Panipat was unprecedented and the huge loss of life itself imprinted itself indelibly in the Indian, especially the Maharashtrian psyche. In Marathi there is a verb which is commonly used even today, "*Panipat Zaala*" which means that a great disaster has occurred.

There were many reasons for the Marathi defeat but the main is the failure of logistics. The army was just not geared to fight a sustained campaign in North India, especially in the winter. They did not know the land, its people and did not have adequate information of their enemy. The travelled without finances – and they travelled heavy. Without finances and friends, they exposed their long lines of communication to Abdali, who then played a waiting game for almost two months and allowed the Maratha army to starve itself to exhaustion.

Even when they fought they forgot their traditional strengths. Had Bhau simply left behind his huge entourage of civilians and camp followers he could have fought unhindered and his stocks would then have been adequate. Without civilians they could have fought a guerilla war unencumbered and harass Abdali long enough to force him to go back to his own country.

The Maratha failure to secure alliances was due to their high-handedness, arrogance and their habit of plundering the countryside. This antagonized the locals and left them without an ally even in this so-called Hindu-Muslim war. There were also too many differences within themselves. The Maratha Chiefs fought incessantly amongst themselves and once Ibrahim Gardi and Holkar almost came to blows in the presence of their troops – something which was bound to fray morale. The Marathas chiefs followed their own tactics and were not easily amiable to discipline as seen by the premature attack of their cavalry and the unauthorized withdrawal of the Right flank. On the contrary Abdali not only bound a cohesive alliance of divergent forces but held them together with rigid discipline. When his own Sunni soldiers misbehaved with Shuja-ud-Daula's Shia troopers, he had their noses pierced with arrows, strung a rope through it and led them to Shuja to forgive or execute as he deemed fit. The iron discipline helped hold his crumbling forces in the wake of the initial Maratha attacks.

THE TACTICS

The Marathas should have struck to their traditional strengths and engaged Abdali in a guerilla war instead of taking him on in a pitched battle. This would have worn him out and forced him to return to Afghanistan.

By fighting a pitched battle on the ground of Abdali's choosing, they were administratively unbalanced and played to Abdali's strength.

The Marathas followed the traditional tactics of launching frontal attacks supported by heavy artillery fire. However their artillery did not prove very effective, because the range could not be easily adjusted. There was little coordination between their artillery, infantry and cavalry. They had no reserves to exploit their initial success.

More than tactics, administration decided the issue. The Maratha replenishment lines were cut off and they were weakened by near starvation before the battle.

Abdali out-generaled his opponent in both diplomacy and tactics. Firstly, he stitched together a formidable alliance and won over many potential allies from the Marathas. He maneuvered beautifully to cut the Marathas from their source of supplies thus putting them at a disadvantage even before the battle. When the battle was joined, he did not plunge headlong into the fray, as the Bhau had done, but positioned himself where he could watch and coordinate each movement on the battlefield. His creation and move of reserves to reinforce the Centre and Right Flank was the major factor in his victory. His timing for the counter attack, just when the Maratha attack had reached its culmination point was the act of a cool, calculating General who weighs each action and prepares for each contingency. He looked into every detail, be it the provision of water and food to his troops on the battlefield, the minutiae of deployment; the equipping of his army and the maintenance of its morale. And the results were telling.

What of the Maratha Right flank? Many historians have blamed the Maratha defeat for its failure to attack. Many even accuse Holkar and Scindia of treachery. But the failure of this flank was not due to treachery but to plain military incompetence and cowardice. The Holkar-Scindia contingent had been defeated in repeated skirmishes prior to the battle and their morale was already low. In the face of the Afghan attack they simply turned and fled. Even had they attacked, it would not have significantly changed the outcome of the battle. At most, it would have delayed the inevitable by perhaps a day or so.

The huge defeat pushed the Maratha power back into the Deccan and put a halt to its expansion. But, the Marathas were fortunate that after the death of Baji Rao, Peshwa Madhav Rao I, one of the most capable Peshwas took over the helm. Within ten years he rebuilt his army, re-established Maratha supremacy in the Deccan and pushed its influence back into North India. But by then, it was a little too late. The Maratha defeat at Panipat had provided a vacuum of power at a crucial juncture in India's history, which was to be filled by another outsider. Almost at the same time when the Maratha and Afghan armies were engaged in their titanic clash, an Englishmen named Robert Clive was on his way to England to brief the Prime Minister on the feasibility of establishing an Imperial Empire in India. The British Empire, which had sown its seeds at Plassey now received a fertile ground in which to implant its roots. In the wake of the Maratha defeat at Panipat, India now stood ripe to be exploited by yet another foreign invader, a distant European power that would rule India for almost two hundred years.

8

The Establishing of Imperial Rule – The Battles of Plassey & Buxar

"Hail Mir Jafar, Emperor of Bengal, Orissa and Bihar" – Clive greeting the traitor, Mir Jafar after the battle.

❖ ❖ ❖

Background

It is difficult to gauge the importance of a battle merely by the number of combatants or the casualties incurred. By this yardstick, the Battle of Plassey – or Palasi as is the correct Indian word – would have been lost in the footnotes of history. In this battle the casualty count was virtually negligible and the actual battle lasted less than a day. Yet, in terms of impact, this was one of the most decisive battles in Indian history as it heralded the era of Imperial India. Till then British presence in India was just as traders of the British East India Company. After Plassey, they became more than just traders, they established an empire.

In the early 18th Century, the British East India Company had established a strong presence in India with three main bases at Fort Saint George at Madras, Fort William in Calcutta and Bombay Castle in Western India. As they grew stronger and the political condition in India deteriorated, they expanded the scope of their activities and began allying themselves with local rulers, promising security in return for trading concessions. They had to compete with the Dutch, the French and Portuguese and the rivalry of these nations in Europe soon reflected itself in the sub-continent. By a dint of skillful politics and military force they were gradually emerging as the most dominant European power in India and were strong enough to contest most local rulers. By the mid 18th Century the British had ousted the Dutch and the Portuguese in the Carnatic wars and had defeated the French and captured Arcot in 1855. With this victory, British influence was firmly established in peninsular India. Now they sought to consolidate their power in Bengal, then the richest province of India, which would pave the way towards control of all of North India.

India in that period was a maelstrom of perpetually squabbling states, devoid of any central authority. Aurangzeb died in 1707 and the Mughal Empire was on the decline. His successors were but figure-heads on the throne of Delhi with no control over their dominion and unable to counter the rise of different power centers all over the country. In the Deccan, the Marathas were emerging as the strongest force in India and had enlarged their empire virtually up to Delhi and Bengal. The Sikhs too were establishing themselves in Punjab but their power was curtailed by the repeated invasions of Nadir Shah and Ahmad Shah Abdali. In the East, the province of Bengal enjoyed relative stability under the reign of Nawab Ali Vardi Khan. However, his kingdom was repeatedly threatened by the constant raids of the Marathas who were knocking on the Southern boundaries of his empire. To counter their influence, he allowed the British

Siraj-ud-Daulah – The 20 year old Nawab of Bengal

to increase their presence in Calcutta and granted them trading concessions. The British capitalized on the opportunity and established themselves strongly around Fort William, building up its garrison and developing fortifications and defense works around the city. One of the major outcomes was the construction of the Maratha Ditch, a deep defensive trench which encircled the city as a protection against Maratha attacks.

With the death of Nawab Ali Vardi in 1752, his nineteen year old Siraj-ud-Daulah ascended the throne. The new Nawab of Bengal was young and inexperienced and relied heavily on his advisors – who themselves were engaged in the usual practices of court intrigue and treachery. Yet the young Siraj-ud-Daulah revealed a remarkable firmness and courage in establishing his authority. His major concern was the growing influence of the British in Calcutta, who had not only over-exploited their concessions but often transgressed them to establish a monopoly over all trade in Bengal. In those days the Seven Year war (1756 to 1763) between England and France was still raging in the continent – and the French and British representatives waged the same war in the Indian sub-continent often co-opting their local allies in the battle. As the proxy war intensified in India, both the British and the French began reinforcing their fortifications in Chandernagar, Calcutta and Qasimbazar. Siraj-ud-Daulah ordered them to halt the fortification that they were erecting in his own Empire without his permission – a demand to which the French complied with readily, but was repeatedly stalled by the British garrison. At that time, both the British and the French were the Nawab's subjects and under his protection and sovereignty. They could not construct fortifications or battle each other in his territory without his express sanction. British arrogance and disregard of local Indian rulers had been increasing as their strength in India grew. Their not-too-ethical trade practices had been slowly draining the Bengal treasury. The British repeatedly violated tariff and excise laws as they established a monopoly over trade in Bengal. But the unauthorized fortification was the last straw. With his supremacy being blatantly challenged,

Siraj-ud-Daulah set out from his capital of Murshidabad, in May 1756, at the head of 50,000 troops, to reassert his authority over the growing colonial presence.

By June, Siraj-ud-Daulah invested and captured the British fort and factory at Qasimbazar, the strongest and most important British trading station in Bengal. The small force soon capitulated and the commander of the fort, Lieutenant Ellis shot himself. With Qasimbazar secured, he marched on to Calcutta. The British garrison there had just around 515 men and their defenses were not prepared to withstand a strong onslaught. On 16 June, Siraj's forces entered Calcutta and Fort William. The British governor, Roger Drake, along with the notable luminaries fled the town on 19 June abandoning the small British population there to their fate. On 20th June the fort and its European inhabitants surrendered and Siraj formally took over the British settlement.

What followed became known as the Black Hole incident – an incident blown out of all proportion by British historians, which served as a trigger and an excuse for all their subsequent actions in Bengal. 146 British prisoners, including women and children were confined in a common dungeon of Fort William, known as the Black Hole. This dungeon was just 18 × 14 feet in size with two small windows, designed to hold only six prisoners. In the heat of the night, 123 prisoners died of asphyxiation and suffocation. This story gained widespread publicity not only in India but also across the

An Artist's rendition of the Black Hole

Robert Clive

shores to England and a clamor arose for retribution. Yet it cannot be stated with any certainty whether the Black Hole incident was true or a mere exaggeration. Siraj-ud-Daula's own role in this was negligible, but he was projected as the one responsible for the deed and the event provided the excuse for the British to re-assert their position in Bengal.

In August, the East India Council decided to dispatch an expeditionary force from Madras to Bengal to reclaim their lost possessions. Colonel Robert Clive, a relatively junior officer was appointed to lead the force of 900 European soldiers and 1500 sepoys. With him was a naval squadron of five ships under Admiral Watson. The mandate of the force to recover Calcutta and the lost British settlements, get all their earlier trading privileges restored and gain reparation for the losses suffered. In October, the force moved out of Madras with Clive marching by land while the fleet sailed into the Bay of Bengal towards Calcutta. By end December, the land and naval forces linked up at the mouth of the Hoogly River and then launched a combined attack on Calcutta with the naval ships providing fire cover to the assaulting land forces. By 2 January 1757, Calcutta was recaptured and Fort William was occupied once again. The British were back in their previous settlements and now they were strong enough to stave off even Siraj-ud-Daulah. The stage was set for another major confrontation.

If Siraj-ud-Daulah hoped that the British would be satisfied with regaining their previous settlements, he was wrong. On 9 January,

Fort William

Naval attack on Chandarnagar

a British force stormed the town of Hoogly, a French stronghold around forty kilometers north of Calcutta. Deciding to counter the growing British influence head-on, Siraj-ud-Daulah marched out of his capital, Murshidabad, and reached the vicinity of Calcutta by 03 February. With his superiority of numbers he hoped to launch a coordinated attack on the British positions around Fort William, but Clive pre-empted him. On the morning of 04 February, under cover of a dense fog, a force of around 2000 soldiers, amply supported by artillery attacked the Nawab's camp causing almost 600 casualties with little damage to themselves. The success of the attack unnerved Siraj and he agreed to sign the Treaty of Alinagar, in which he restored their factories to the British, allowed them to build fortification and restored all their former privileges. He then withdrew back to his capital at Murshidabad and the British consolidated themselves in Calcutta.

The uneasy truce lasted barely a month. Clive was not one to wait and with the Seven Year war still raging in Europe, he was fearful that the French would strike an alliance with Siraj-ud-Daulah to evict them once again from Calcutta. He decided to attack Chandarnagar, the strongest French settlement in Bengal and their main trading station even though the Nawab had expressly forbidden any military action in his territory. Clive used the same tactics of a combined land and sea assault with his land forces storming the outpost under a heavy naval cannonade from his five ships in the Hoogly River. The assault forced the French garrison to surrender on 23 March after just a day of fighting. Their defeat was made even easier by the fact that the Nawab's Governor in Hoogly, Nand Kumar had been heavily bribed and did not do anything to halt the fighting or assist the French. Nor did he report the attack to Siraj till it was too late. Siraj-ud-Daulah was furious as the attack on Chandarnagar, even though a French outpost still constituted an attack in his territory. British demands now grew as they now demanded the expulsion of all French personnel from Bengal, an unreasonable demand which was rightly refused by Siraj. As matters between Siraj-ud-Daulah and the British came to a head, Clive

Soldier of the 39th Regiment of Foot

decided to remove him from the throne and plant some one more amenable to their demands. Mir Jafar, the Commander in Chief, had been won over by the British with the promise of being made Nawab after the overthrow of Siraj. Most of his generals and senior members of his court were also induced by large bribes and promises of key positions if they joined the British. Within his own court, a conspiracy was building up and Siraj-ud-Daulah was losing the battle even before it was joined.

Clive managed to get the conspirators to sign a secret treaty, in which the British were to be allowed complete control over trade in Bengal after the overthrow of Siraj-ud-Daulah. The three main conspirators, Mir Jafar, Rai Durlabh, Yar Latuf Khan were promised key positions after the battle and in return agreed to provide Rupees One Crores for their war effort and Fifty Lakhs Rupees to the Europeans of Calcutta for their losses suffered. It was a virtually a sell-out of the state, but the subterfuge did not end there. Clive went to the extent of preparing a fake treaty with forged signatures, to overcome the objections of Omichand, another co-conspirator and ensure his co-operation. This fake treaty would later cost Clive his position and have him recalled to England in disgrace.

Sepoy of the Bengal Regiment.

Siraj-ud-Daulah was aware of the intrigue and treachery, but the 20-year-old Nawab was no match for the shrewd politicians of his court. After receiving repeated assurances from his Generals, especially Mir Jafar, that they would stand by him in his actions against the British, he marched out with an army of around 35,000 infantry and 18,000 cavalry along with 53 pieces of artillery. His force was supplemented with around 50 Frenchmen under St Frais who had got alongside a battery of six pieces of field artillery. Siraj's large and relatively well-equipped army would have been more than a match for the smaller British force but it was rive with internal dissension and most of his generals had already decided not to fight. Even before the battle, the army refused to move out of Murshidabad because they had not received their entire arrears of pay. The pay was released and the army marched out, but this open show of defiance on the very eve of battle revealed the fissures that existed within the army and its generals. These fissures would lead to its complete defeat at the hands of a force which was a fraction of its size.

The Battle Beneath the Palas Trees

As Siraj made his uncertain moves, Clive marched to counter him with a force of around 600 European infantry, 100 *topasses* (Eurasian Soldiers), 170 artillerymen and around 2100 native soldiers. He had with him six pieces of artillery and two small howitzers. The force was hopelessly outnumbered but was disciplined, well-led and effectively organized into compact units and formations. His entire battle plan to defeat a force more than ten times his size hinged around the fact that the bulk of Siraj's army, under the traitors Mir Jafar, Yar Lutuf Khan and Raj Durlabh would take no part in the battle. Yet as he moved out to confront Siraj, who was encamped on the banks of the Bhagirathi River near the village of Palasi, (the correct name which was later anglised to Plassey), he had received no confirmation from Mir Jafar and was uncertain as to whether he would keep his word.

The village of Palasi earned its name because of the large numbers of Palas trees that grew around it. These trees with their beautiful orange flowers were also called the 'Flame of the Forest', though at the time of battle, the trees were not flowering. The village was located on the East bank of the Bhagirathi River. A little North of the river, about 50 meters from its bank was the Laksha Bagh – or the Orchard of a Hundred Thousand Trees – a mango orchard around 500 meters long and 250 meters wide with hundreds of mango trees neatly planted in rows. The orchard was surrounded by a mud bank and a ditch. The entire area was plain, its landscape broken only by two small lakes, a small one around 500 meters away from the grove and a larger one a further 300 meters away. Both lakes were surrounded by mounds of earth which formed small hillocks that dominated the area around it. These little hillocks would play a vital role in the coming battle. About two kilometers away from the grove, Siraj-ud-Daulah had established his camp one night earlier. When Clive's forces reached Palasi at around midnight on the night of 22 June, they could hear the sounds of music wafting across from the camp. Siraj-ud-Daulah was in his camp surrounded by his troops, even then uncertain as to whether his own army would fight or turn against him. Even though Mir Jafar had assured him, Quran in hand, that he would stand by him, he had no way of knowing whether his Commander-in-Chief and senior generals

Soldiers of the Bengal Army

would actually support him in his battle. As events unfolded, his fears would be proved true.

THE MAN

Siraj-ud-Daulah – The 19 year old Nawab was young and inexperienced. He revealed great decisiveness and courage in initially containing British expansion, but was no match for the politics and intrigue of his own court.

Was weak and vacillating in battle and gave in despair even when he had the upper hand. Succumbed to the wrong advise given to him by the traitor Mir Jafar.

Robert Clive – Ruthless, unscrupulous and brilliant. He used every trick in the book and a few outside – to get his means, including forging a treaty.

Was cool and unperturbed even during the heat of battle when his forces were hopelessly outnumbered. Used his meager resources, specially his artillery optimally.

At around midnight, on 22 June, Clive reached Palasi and deployed the bulk of his forces inside the mango grove. He himself established his headquarters on a hunting lodge by the banks of the Bhagirathi River from where he could see the entire battle. Ahead of him were the vast, lush green plains and on the horizon the first black clouds of the monsoons were approaching. At daybreak, the vast army of Siraj-ud-Daulah marched out of its camp and occupied a crescent shaped line extending all around the British positions. To the North on the embankment of the large lake, the French contingents were deployed with their six guns. Behind them were around 5000 Cavalry and 7000 infantry under his only loyal General Mir Madan. The three traitors, Mir Jafar, Yar Lutuf Khan and Rai Durlabh had formed their divisions further to the south, in a crescent which extended all around the British positions. Just by virtue of this deployment, the British positions could have been swamped, if only Siraj's entire army had held together.

At around eight in the morning, the battle commenced in earnest. Clive had positioned himself on the roof of the hunting box, and was waiting for news from Mir Jafar to confirm his defection. But even at this late hour, no news arrived. He ordered his troops to move out of the mango grove and line up with the Europeans and Topasses in four divisions in the centre, flanked on both sides with the native infantry. Six of his guns were deployed in the gaps in between his positions but his two howitzers were concealed slightly ahead, under the cover of the brick kilns where they would get additional range. The French and Nawab's artillery brought down a furious cannonade on the British positions which killed 10 Europeans and 20 native infantry. The British artillery with just eight pieces could not retaliate effectively and after an hour, Clive ordered his men to withdraw back into the mango grove, where the trees and mud walls on the sides would provide same protection. Yet he wisely left his two howitzers and two additional field pieces hidden in a brick kilns ahead of the grove, and their fire prevented Siraj's infantry from attacking.

By around 11 AM, after three hours of battle, the situation was still inconclusive. Clive's men remained sheltered in the grove, the French artillery continued to occupy the embankment in the area of the lakes and the Nawab's forces, under his one loyal General, Mir Madan remained deployed behind it. The bulk of his army under Mir Jafar, Yar Lutuf and Durlabh Rai had made no move throughout the battle. Mir Jafar was not even in contact with Clive – and perhaps he was playing the classical traitor's game – waiting to see which side was winning and then act accordingly. Clive now ordered all his commanders to a conference to decide their future action. Most, Clive included, proposed a withdrawal since there was no intimation from Mir Jafar. But the younger officers, flush with their earlier easy victories, wanted to continue the battle. It was finally decided to hold their positions in the grove and then attack the Nawab's camp at midnight. It was a very courageous decision, because had Mir Jafar remained loyal to his Nawab and attacked the smaller British forces, they would have been encircled and annihilated. But then something happened that dramatically altered the situation. It began to rain.

The dark clouds coiling overhead burst around mid-day and the torrential downpour of an Indian monsoon drenched the troops and worse, soaked the gunpowder. The British were prepared and hastily placed their tarpaulins over their guns. The Nawab's gunners did not have the same foresight. Their ammunition was soaked and the guns which had caused such havoc in the morning were rendered useless. As the rain intensified, the cannon fire reduced and then stopped altogether.

After and hour or so the rains stopped and Mir Mardan Khan, the Nawab's only loyal general, launched his attack on the British positions. The British guns had halted fire to prevent exposing their guns to water and Mardan assumed that their guns too had been rendered ineffective by the rains. As he closed in, the British opened up a heavy fusillade of musket and cannon fire which broke the attack and inflicted heavy casualties. One of the casualties was Mir Mardan Khan who was struck by a musket shot and carried back mortally wounded to Siraj's tent.

THE MOMENT

It began to rain around midday. The torrential rain dampened the gunpowder and rendered the Nawab's guns ineffective. The British had the foresight to get tarpaulins and covered their gun powder. After the rains, they were able to continue firing and beat back the Nawab's much superior army.

It was here that the most critical moment of the battle was reached. Siraj's army (at least the loyal ones) was now commanded by the very competent General Mohan Lal, who was pressing the attack against the British. Under his guidance the attacks were making headway even though Mir Jafar and the other traitors had still not moved their divisions. Perhaps even now the situation could have been saved. But the death of Mir Mardan had thrown Siraj-ud-Daulah in a panic. In despair he sent for Mir Jafar. In a pathetic scene, he begged him for help, even removing his turban from his head and placing it at Mir Jafar's feet in an abject gesture of supplication. Mir Jafar pretended to help, but recommended that since the day was drawing to close, all the attacking troops should be ordered back and they would launch a coordinated attack in the morning. Another co-conspirator Rai Durlabh gave the same wrong advice to Siraj, who finally sent message to Mohan Lal telling him to cease fighting and withdraw. At the same time, Mir Jafar also sent message to Clive, telling him what he was doing and asked him to push forward his own attack.

Mohan Lal had been pressing the attack with great competence and initially refused to withdraw. But a personal message from the Nawab made him give up his attack in disgust and order his troops to retire. The entire attack ground to a halt and the advancing troops began withdrawing. At this juncture, Major Kirk Patrick, one of the veterans of Clive's army, sensed an opportunity and began advancing with two companies of 39th Regiment and two field guns behind the Nawab's retreating troops. Clive was resting when he received news of Kirk Patrick's move (which countermanded his

Clive meeting Mir Jafar after the battle

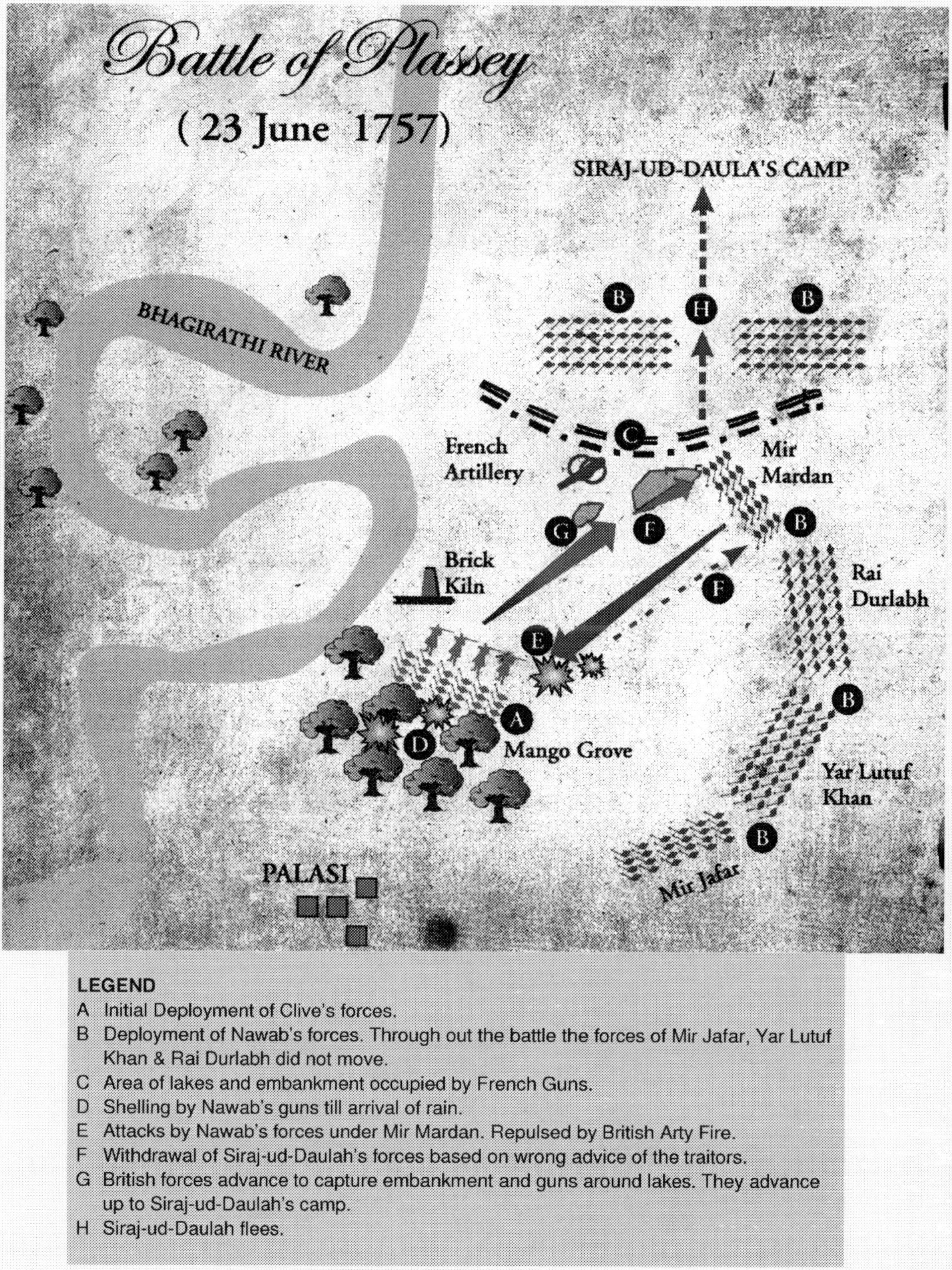

LEGEND

A Initial Deployment of Clive's forces.

B Deployment of Nawab's forces. Through out the battle the forces of Mir Jafar, Yar Lutuf Khan & Rai Durlabh did not move.

C Area of lakes and embankment occupied by French Guns.

D Shelling by Nawab's guns till arrival of rain.

E Attacks by Nawab's forces under Mir Mardan. Repulsed by British Arty Fire.

F Withdrawal of Siraj-ud-Daulah's forces based on wrong advice of the traitors.

G British forces advance to capture embankment and guns around lakes. They advance up to Siraj-ud-Daulah's camp.

H Siraj-ud-Daulah flees.

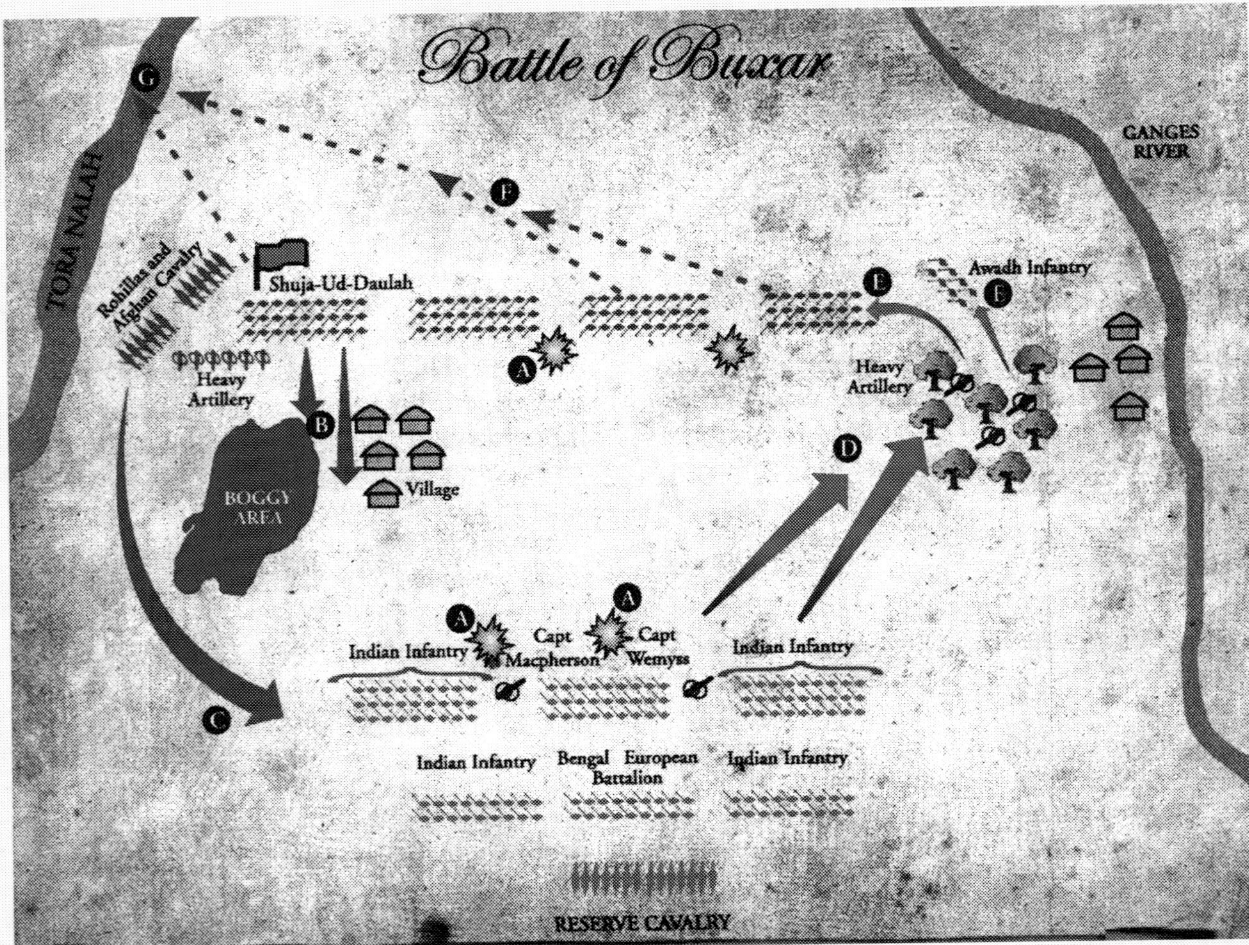

LEGEND

A Initial bombardment & counter bombardment.

B Advance by Shuja's forces - flounders in boggy ground.

C Cavalry attack from flanks. Repulsed by steadfast defense.

D British attack to capture grove and heavy artillery.

E With a firm base in the grove British infantry attack from the flanks.

F Shuja's army panics and withdraws.

G Shuja-Ud-Daulah himself withdraws across Tora Nalah destroying the bridge. His panic struck soldiers try to swim across, over 6,000 drown.

orders that no further action was to take place till midnight). He rushed after Kirkpatrick and severely reprimanded him for disobeying orders. But when briefed of the circumstance, he was quick to seize the opportunity. He ordered the rest of the army out from the grove and led an attack in the direction of the lakes which captured the French guns located on the embankment there. They now established their own guns in the high ground surrounding the lakes and began cannonading the Nawab's camp. Their infantry pressed forward an attack towards the Nawab's camp. In the Nawab's army, the troops were confused and faced with a barrage of conflicting orders. They were first told to advance and when they were succeeding, they were halted, then told to withdraw back into the camp. As the British forces counter-attacked they began retreating in confusion back into the direction of their own camp. By now all coordinated resistance had ceased.

With the British virtually on his camp, the Nawab mounted a fast camel and with around 2000 followers fled towards Murshidabad. The British followed up their attack, capturing the entrenchment surrounding the camp and then entered the very camp itself. Throughout these activities as their own comrades were being defeated and killed by the enemy, the three divisions of Mir Jafar, Yar Latuf Khan and Rai Durlabh made no move to help. The vast force of 45,000 soldiers remained inactive throughout the day. After having convinced Siraj to call off his own attack and flee, Mir Jafar moved his own division in the direction of the British Camp – to join them. This movement was construed as an attack and halted with musket and cannon fire. It was only when the situation became clearer and Mir Jafar's message was received by Clive, that the forces were disengaged.

By around five in the evening it was all over. Clive's advancing troops occupied the Nawab's camp and then chased the fleeing enemy for around ten kilometers before finally halting at Daudpur to claim the fruits of their victory. At the end of the day they had suffered just 22 dead and fifty wounded. The Nawab lost around

500 of his troops, including many of his key officers. Yet the casualty figures don't say it all. This battle was gauged not in the number of its casualties but on the impact it had on the subcontinent for the next 190 years.

Aftermath

Clive was quick to follow up his victory. The next day, Mir Jafar requested and was granted an audience with him at Daudpur, where Clive ceremoniously presented him with a plate of gold coins and proclaimed him as the Nawab of Bengal, Orissa and Bihar. He then sent him to the capital to prevent Siraj-ud-Daulah from establishing himself there. Siraj was forced to flee Murshidabad along with his consort, Lutf-un-nisa and some of his followers. He was chased, betrayed yet again before being captured and brutally put to death. His mangled remains were paraded through the capital in an ultimate rite of humiliation. At the time of his death he was twenty years old and had reigned for just fifteen short months.

Plassey established British supremacy both physically and psychologically. It demonstrated how a small body of well-led men could easily get the better of a larger, ill-disciplined rabble especially when its leaders could be easily brought off. In return for placing Mir Jafar on the throne, the British got over Rupees 100 lakhs in cash and jewels. Clive himself received over Rupees 200,000 and the co-conspirators Rai Durlabh and Yar Lutaf Khan also received their share. This sell-out bled the treasury and virtually bankrupted the richest Province of India. But the gains were more than just physical. With this battle the British completely destroyed French and Dutch influence and established themselves as the supreme power in Bengal. Fortunately for them, the Marathas – their only contending power – would be decisively defeated at Panipat in 1761 and this would remove the last hurdle to British rule in India. The victory gained at Plassey was further consolidated at Buxar and with it the sun began its rise for the British Empire.

The Battle of Buxar

With the establishment of a pliant Mir Jaffer on the throne of Bengal, the actual power shifted into the hands of the British East India Company, who now could do virtually what they pleased. The vast compensations given to the British bankrupted the state, but their demands did not cease. All state control disappeared as the East India Company took over the salt, betel-nut, tobacco, timber, silk, cotton and opium trades with impunity. Three year of systematic and unbridled exploitation followed where the company squeezed out each drop they could extract without paying even the trade tax or custom duty to the state. Eventually Mir Jaffer protested in 1760 and demanded the curtailment of the company's commercial activities and a re-imposition of trade tax and custom duties. The result was inevitable. Mir Jafer was deposed from the throne and his son-in-law Mir Qasim who was felt to be more amenable installed in his place.

Mir Qasim did not prove as pliable as the British hoped he would. In fact he proved to be quite a able administrator. Over the next three years he sorted out his finances and re-built his army, which he equipped with modern cannon and reinforced with European mercenaries. He also began curtailing the company's activities and gradually relations between him and the representatives of the East India Company shifted from antagonism to hostility and then to open war.

Things come to a head in June 1763 when the company's representative in Patna openly defied Mir Qasim by attacking the city and plundered its market. Mir Qasim retaliated and recaptured the town, inflicting a heavy toll on the British garrison and taking many prisoners.

Retaliation was swift. The British East India Company declared war on Mir Qasim, and sent an expeditionary force under Major Thomas Adams and John Carnac to recapture it. Patna was retaken in November 1760 and once again the company held sway over Bengal.

By then the Company's depredations had spread to most parts of the country and resentment had grown against British exploitation. Mir Qasim managed to persuade Shuja-ud-daulah, the Nawab of Awadh, and the Mughal Emperor Shah Alam II in a common cause against the British. It was at best an uneasy alliance with all three leaders being simultaneously approached by the British with the usual promises of great riches and power if they changed sides. But eventually the alliance held together and managed to put together a combined army of around 40,000 infantry and cavalry and 200 pieces of artillery. But the army, though large was disjointed. It was composed of diverse races such as Durranis, Mughals, Pathans, Hindus and Europeans and had little regimental discipline or common military training. Shuja-ud-Dualah was appointed as the Supreme commander by virtue of being the most powerful ruler, but his control over his allies, Shah Alam and Mir Qasim was nominal. The large army was more a heterogeneous mob often working at cross-purposes with each other.

The British army under Hector Munro had 18000 combatants, which included 1000 Europeans, 7000 Indians of the English army and 12,000 troops of Mir Jafar's army; the consummate traitor having changed sides once again in hope of future returns. But the army was well led, equipped and held together with the iron discipline which was the hall-mark of British armies. The British army reached Buxar on 2 October 1764 and saw Shuja-ud-Daula's army already deployed and waiting by the bank of the Ganges River. Shuja had chosen his site well. His left flank rested on the Ganges River and was protected by the village of Buxar and entrenchments which extended across the entire frontage. On his left flank were 5000 Awadh Infantry, who were not too well equipped or trained and whose fighting qualities were suspect. The bulk of his troops were deployed in the centre under Shah Alam with eight battalions lined abreast and field guns deployed between the gaps. The right flank was held with a large contingent of Rohilla infantry and around 5000 Afghan Cavalry. The fast flowing Tora Nala swept past his right flank and though this provided a measure of security to his right flank, it also cut off his lines of retreat. Mir Qasim himself was deployed in the rear as a reserve. Though he was the architect of the alliance he had been relegated to a relatively secondary position by the two more powerful rulers. On either flank were deployed heavy artillery guns under European mercenaries. Shuja-ud-dualah, although in command of the whole army was also located in the right wing and apparently he intended to utilize his right flank as the arm of decision. His plan was simple. He wanted to launch an assault with his best troops against the Europeans and keep his irregular forces to hold ground in case the British attacked. He planned to first use a heavy artillery bombardment to soften up the British lines before delivering an overwhelming assault with superior numbers.

Hector Munro had spent his time at Buxar conducting an extensive reconnaissance of the area along with his commanders. He intended to attack on the 24 October, but Shuja pre-empted him. On 23 October, Shuja moved his army out of his entrenched camp and into his battle array. As his scouts reported the news, Munro ordered his army in to their own battle array, something they had rehearsed and practiced many times before. Munro's deployment

THE TACTICS AND EQUIPMENT

In both battles the superior tactics utilized by the British decided the outcome. A high sense of discipline and regimentation ensured that their battalions did not panic even when faced superior odds. They held on resolutely in defense and attacked with almost parade ground precision.

They fine-tuned the tactics of fire and move and used artillery very effectively to provide covering fire at every stage of the battle. At Plassey, the ability of their guns to fire even after torrential rains turned the battle.

The Indian forces lacked similar cohesion and discipline. Most had come together from different armies and states and did not share common tactics or a joint doctrine. There was no central leadership and little coordination amongst the different components of the army.

was based on two compact lines held by a mix of Indian and European troops. In the front line were largely European troops commanded by Captain Wemyss on the right and four companies of under Captain MacPherson on the left. Flanking them were two battalions of Indian infantry on each side. In the gaps between the battalions were deployed the field artillery, basically six and twelve pounder guns. In the second line, deployed around two hundred meters behind were the Bengal European Battalion with two battalions of Indian infantry on either flank. The ground between the two opposing armies was open plain, with a large patch of boggy area on the left and a thick grove and a small village on the right. These three terrain features would be of great significance and play a major role in the battle.

At nine in the morning, the Indian guns began a furious cannonading of the British lines. The guns were of the latest screw type mechanism which meant that they could be elevated and traversed easily and fire was very effective. His troops advanced slowly from the centre under cover of the heavy gunfire from the batteries deployed on the flanks. Yet the attack floundered in the boggy ground ahead and was repulsed by heavy fire from the British guns. Shuja then ordered his cavalry to attack from the flank and though the attack was launched with speed and determination, it was repulsed by the British lines which held firm and continued firing even when the enemy cavalry was almost upon them. Three such attacks were launched but none could break the British deployment. Munro then gave the order for the British lines to advance. The two lines moved slowly and deliberately using fire and move tactics, moving around 100 to 150 yards under covering fire, and then going to ground to provide covering fire as the other line moved forward. The Nawab's gun's continued to take a heavy toll on the advancing infantry, but their iron discipline held and the attack did not waver. They assaulting troops reached the area of the Grove and Munro sent an Infantry Battalion to attack the heavy guns deployed there. The attack was a success and captured all twenty seven guns deployed there and the volume of fire now reduced considerably. With the grove captured, the Imperial troops followed up the success by capturing the village on the left flank of the Nawab's positions. Shuja-ud-dualah launched his reserves, but the counter-attack could not break the tight compact formations of the British units and sub-units. Munro now established a firm base in the area of the grove and turned the fire of the captured guns on Shuja's troops. As had happened so often in Indian armies of that period, the presence of an enemy close to their positions started a panic. Even though the Centre and the Right Wing were still intact and holding, the ill-trained troops of the Awadh levies on the left, broke and ran and that gave the signal for a general withdrawal. The withdrawal turned into a rout, as battalion after battalion left their positions with their leaders being unable to hold them. By around twelve, the entire front had collapsed as the disorderly forces fled towards the Tara Nala with the British in hot pursuit. Shuja-ud-dualah too was forced to flee, but in his anger and frustration he destroyed the bridge of boats across the Nala, which was the only escape route for his soldiers. Almost 6000 troops perished by drowning in the fast-flowing torrent, almost thrice as many as those who had fallen on the battlefield. By 3 PM or so it was all over. The British had won a decisive victory, but at a heavy cost. 1847 were killed and around two thousand wounded, though with typical English callousness, Munro described the casualties as being "mostly blacks".

Buxar once again demonstrated how discipline and superb leadership could wrest a larger disjointed opponent. It was very much a classic engagement of the kind that would occur regularly in battles across India for the next hundred years. The steadiness of the British battalions in defense and their ferocity in attacking with bayonet and sabers ensured that they would win the day. The lines of infantry remained stead fast in the face of repeated cavalry charges, firing carefully timed volleys, which invariably broke the attackers. When they attacked, the steady bayonet-tipped lines moved in disciplined formations of fire and move, absorbing casualties without breaking the momentum of the assault. In comparison, Siraj-ud-Daulah's forces broke easily when even a hint of resoluteness could have defeated their numerically inferior opponent. The lack of cohesion in the large army meant that there was no coordination or central leadership to control the situation which events began going awry.

Buxar was even more decisive than Plassey. It now advanced the frontiers of the British Empire up to Allahabad and the rich Province of Awadh came under their yoke. The British defeat of the combined armies Bengal and Awadh and the Mughal Emperor of Delhi was a psychological victory which imprinted itself on the Indian psyche. If Plassey laid the foundation, Buxar consolidated it. With these two battles, Imperial rule established itself firmly in India and the sun would continue its ascent on the British Empire for the next one hundred and ninety years.

Medals issued to commemorate Plassey

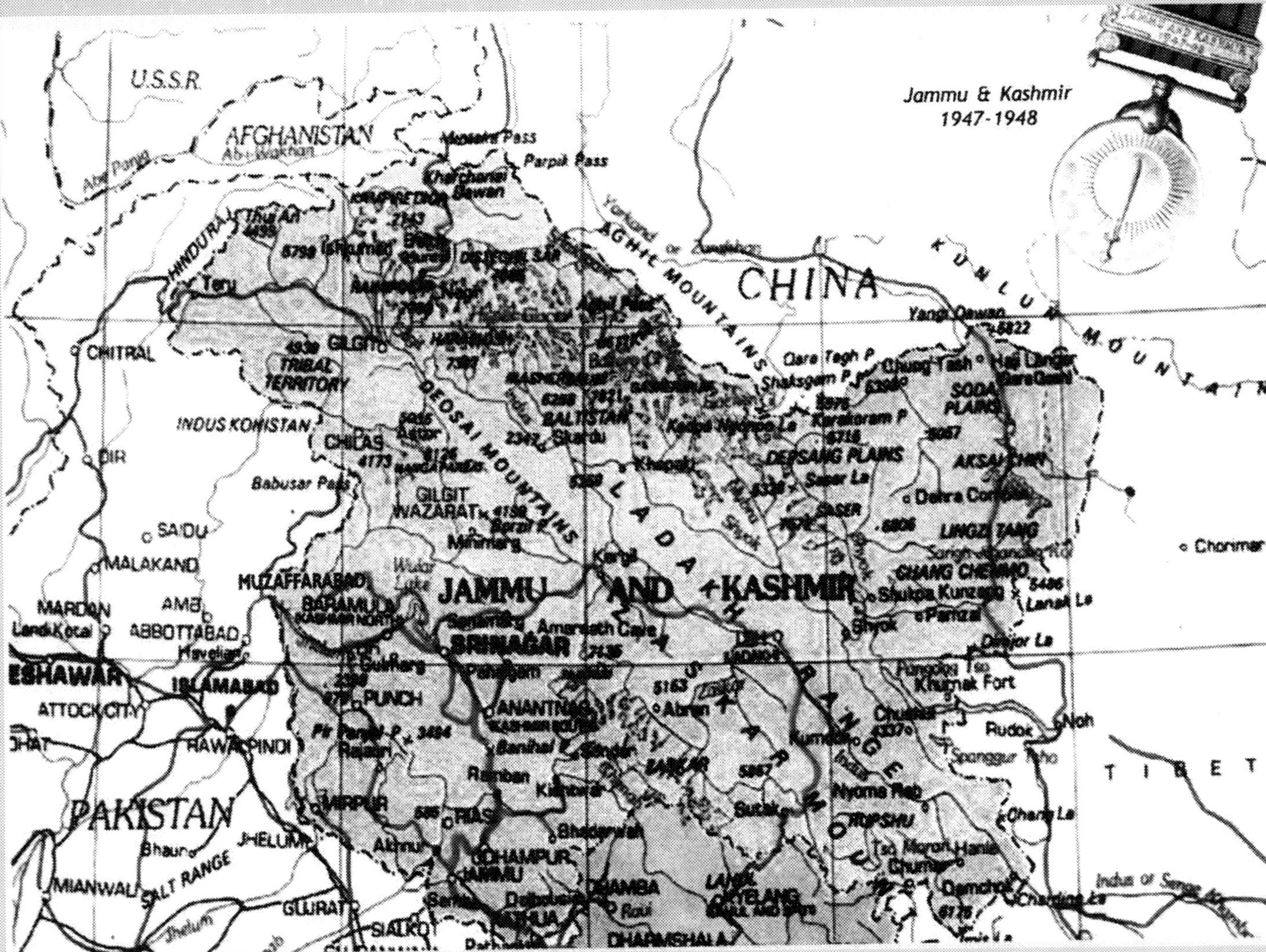
Jammu & Kashmir
1947-1948
U.S.S.R.
AFGHANISTAN
CHINA
KUNLUN MOUNTAINS
AGHIL MOUNTAINS
Parpik Pass
CHITRAL
TRIBAL TERRITORY
INDUS KOHISTAN
CHILAS
DIR
Babusar Pass
DEOSAI MOUNTAINS
GILGIT WAZARAT
SAIDU
MALAKAND
MUZAFFARABAD
JAMMU AND KASHMIR
LADAKH RANGE
MARDAN
ABBOTTABAD
SRINAGAR
PESHAWAR
ISLAMABAD
ATTOCK CITY
RAWALPINDI
PUNCH
ANANTNAG
Amarnath Cave
Kargil
Shyok
Khumak Fort
Rudok
Noh
TIBET
PAKISTAN
JHELUM
SALT RANGE
MIANWALI
GUJRAT
SIALKOT
MIRPUR
Ramban
Bhadarwah
DHARMSHALA
CHAMBA
DEPSANG PLAINS
SODA PLAINS
AKSAI CHIN
LINGZI TANG
CHANG CHENMO
Chorimar
Dehra Compas
Karakoram P
Qara Tagh P
Shaksgam P
Nyoma Rap
Chang La
Demchok
Indus or Singe

9

Independent India's First Battles – Jammu & Kashmir 1947-48

"If you do not see or hear Indian planes in the morning, shoot me in my sleep,"
Raja Hari Singh to his aide the night before the first Indian aircraft arrived at Srinagar

❖ ❖ ❖

Few nations have undergone as much trauma at birth as India did when she fulfilled her tryst with destiny at midnight on 15 August 1947. The creation of an independent India and Pakistan saw the partition of the nation and a human tragedy of unparallel scale. It is ironic that the only nation in the world which attained its independence purely through non-violent means should have witnessed such an orgy of violence amongst its own people after the hard-earned freedom was attained. Amidst the harsh pangs of birth, India and Pakistan emerged as two separate nations; carved out of the same soil and blood, but to be implacable enemies thereafter.

The arbitrary line drawn by Sir Cyril Radcliff, which formed the boundary between the two nations cut through states, districts, villages and in cases even streets and houses. The result was catastrophic. Hindus and Muslims who had lived together in amity for centuries now turned against each other. Twelve million people were uprooted in the largest displacement of humanity ever witnessed. Columns of refugees left all that they owned and moved with meagre belongings to the nation which their religion had ordained. Massacres, loot, rape and pillages took place as over two million people were killed in a frenzy of communal violence. While this wild fury was being perpetuated in Punjab and to a lesser extent in Bengal, a greater trouble was brewing in the scenic vale of Jammu and Kashmir.

At the time of independence, all states except for Junagadh, Hyderabad and Jammu and Kashmir had acceded to either India or Pakistan. Junagadh acceded to India on 09 November 1947 and Hyderabad was won over by police action. It was in Jammu and Kashmir that the first major confrontation between the two nations arose, a confrontation that remained unabated thereafter.

The Imbroglio of Kashmir

The beautiful state of Jammu and Kashmir, appropriately called "Paradise on Earth" encompasses an area of 148,000 square kilometres. It is strategically located at the northern tip of India and the North East of Pakistan. To its East and North lie Tibet and China. Almost all the major rivers, the Indus, the Jhelum, the Chenab, the Ravi, the Beas and Sutlej originate in the high Himalayas and then flow through its valleys into India and Pakistan. Strategically, it is vital to both nations.

Jammu & Kashmir is a pre-dominantly Muslim state with 77.1 percent of its four million strong population being Muslims. Hindus, Sikhs and Buddhists comprise the rest. The muslim majority state was ruled by a Hindu ruler, Shri Hari Singh, the Dogra Maharaja who had held the reins of the state for the past 22 years. Geographically it can be divided into three distinct regions – Jammu; Kashmir and the Northern Areas of Ladakh and Gilgit. The Pir Panjal range separates Jammu from Kashmir and the Great Himalayan range separates Kashmir from the Northern region. At the time of partition, the state was primarily connected to Pakistan with few lines of communication with India. Its main road ran from

Abbotabad in Pakistan to Muzaffarabad, Domel, Uri, Baramula and Srinagar. Srinagar was linked to Jammu and the rest of India via a 320 km long road though the Banihal Pass. Srinagar was also connected to Leh, the capital of Ladakh, with a 384 kilometre long road that passed over the critical Zojila pass. A longer, circuitous route connected Leh to Manali across a 400 kilometre stretch of difficult, mountainous terrain. At the time of partition the state had no rail connections with India and it had just two fair weather airfields; one at Srinagar and the other at Jammu.

As the other states acceded to either India or Pakistan, Hari Singh continued to vacillate. Both Nehru and Jinnah courted him but the Maharaja remained undecided and even toyed with the idea of an Independent state. As the Maharaja wavered, Pakistan decided to annex the state through force and launched "Operation Gulmarg" – an ingenious plan which came within an ace of succeeding and was thwarted only by the rapid, selfless action of the Indian army in its first battle after independence.

Operation Gulmarg

Pakistan's plan for the annexation of Jammu and Kashmir began as early as August 1947. "Operation Gulmarg", as it was code-named was the brain child of Major General Akbar Khan – the then Director of Weapons and Equipment. (Akbar Khan was to finish his career in prison on charges of plotting a coup against the government. His seditious tendencies apparently extended even to his own nation.) The plan was based on building up a force of tribesmen from the North West Frontier Province, arming them with weapons and equipment from the

Devastation caused by raiders

Pakistan Army and sending them into Kashmir to capture the state by force. The invaders were well organised into "lashkars" of around a thousand tribesmen each and led by officers of the Pakistan Army. Each lashkar had a Major as the Commanding Officer, assisted by a Captain and ten Junior Commissioned Officers from the regular army. The cadres were reinforced by demobilised soldiers and even the regular officers and men operated out of uniform. Around twenty such lashkars were created, each armed and organised on the lines of a Pakistan Infantry Battalion. They were well-equipped with civilian lorries, service rifles, mortars, machine guns, explosives, radio sets and supplies of rations, petrol and medical stores. The plan hinged on the belief that the pre-dominantly Muslim population would readily join and support the Pakistani invaders and an intense propaganda campaign was unleashed to wean them over prior to the actual invasion. An economic blockade was also enforced by halting all supplies and essential commodities from Pakistan. These were just the measures to soften the state before the actual invasion. It was felt that if the raiders succeeded in capturing enough territory, especially the capital of Srinagar, the entire state could be annexed and Hari Singh would be forced to accede to Pakistan.

The main thrust of the offensive was directed at the Kashmir valley. Six lashkars were to advance along the Muzaffarabad – Domel-Uri-Srinagar road for the capture of Srinagar. Two subsidiary thrusts of two lashkars each advanced astride the flanks of the main thrust. In the South – the Jammu Sector, a force of ten lashkars was to advance along Poonch-Rajauri and then move to

Baramula in the aftermath of the Pak Invaders

The crucial Baramula Bridge whose destruction by Brig Rajinder Singh delayed the invaders by two vital days

block the Jammu-Srinagar road and cut off Kashmir from the rest of India. In the Northern region the offensive was directed in the areas of Gilgit with the aim of moving on to Skardu, Kargil, Dras and then capturing Leh, the capital of Ladakh. It was an unconventional and audacious plan and came within an ace of success.

In early September the plan was set in motion as the lashkars concentrated in the areas around Abbotabad and launched armed raids along the entire border. Even as the incursions occurred virtually across the entire state, no information was received either by the state authorities or the Government of India. For almost a month intelligence agencies remained oblivious of the growing threat. Then on 22 October 1947, the main offensive burst through on the Abbotabad-Srinagar road and stormed into their first objective – Muzaffarabad.

Muzaffarabad was occupied by one Infantry battalion of the Jammu & Kashmir state forces consisting of Poonchi Muslims and Dogras. The Muslim troops had already been won over and as the lashkars approached, they killed the Commanding Officer and their Dogra comrades and joined the enemy. Muzaffarabad fell on 22 October and there the tribesmen unleashed their first wave of bestiality. The town was sacked, plundered and the women taken away to be brutally raped and sold into captivity. Domel, the next objective, fell the next day and the enemy advanced towards Uri and Baramula on the way to Srinagar.

On night 22 October the officiating Chief of Staff of Jammu & Kashmir State forces, Brigadier Rajender Singh received a desperate message that around 5000 armed men in 300 civilian trucks were advancing on the Uri-Baramula road heading for Srinagar. It was the first confirmed indicator of the threat. He collected some 200 men and rushed to Uri where he managed to blow up the girder bridge on the road which kept the frantic, blood thirsty invaders at bay. For two days he rallied his defences, but was killed on 24 October, fighting to the last. His gallant delaying action provided a vital two days which in the final analysis, perhaps saved the rest of the valley. Brigadier Rajender Singh was later awarded a posthumous Mahavir Chakra – the first gallantry award of Independent India.

Uri fell on 24 October and the invaders pushed forward towards Baramula, a prosperous town, just 56 kilometres from Srinagar. The same orgy of violence was repeated here as the town was plundered, the inhabitants killed and the women subjected to inhuman bestiality. By now the invaders, flush with victory and plunder did not discriminate between Muslims and Non-Muslims. The helpless citizens were easy prey and even the Christian missionaries were

The first Indian troops landing at Srinagar airfield

not spared. The nuns were repeatedly raped and then burnt alive in the Missionary hospital.

The ransacking of Baramula delayed the invaders by three to four days. Many of the raiders were so laden with loot that they decided to go back to their villages, deposit their ill-gotten gains and then come back for more. Had they gone on without stopping there was nothing between them and Srinagar and the town was defenceless and vulnerable. It would have fallen and with it so would the rest of the state.

The wonton desecration of his state finally galvanised Maharaja Hari Singh into action. On 24 October he appealed to India for help. While arms and ammunition were flown into Srinagar, it was decided not to send troops till the Maharaja formally acceded to India. On 25 October the Defence Minister, Mr Krishna Menon along with Lieutenant Colonel Sam Manekshaw, then a director with Military Operations flew into Srinagar to get a first hand assessment of the situation. On 26 October the Maharaja signed the Instrument of Accession which Menon brought back by hand to Delhi the same day. Kashmir was now legally a part of India and India was free to respond in any manner to defend its territory.

Operation Rescue

On 26 October, the Indian Army and Air Force galvanised for the first military operation of Independent India. At that time, most of the army was out on internal security duties and the closest infantry unit, 1 SIKH, which was operating in Gurgaon was hastily called to Palam airport by 0400 hours on 27 October. Like most other units, 1 SIKH was not up to full strength and to make up its deficiencies, Sikh personnel from 13

A picquet in Uri Sector

Armoured cars on patrol

Field Regiment, which was in Red Fort at the time, were placed under the battalion.

On 27 October at 0600 hours, the first Dakota, with the Commanding Officer, Lieutenant Colonel Dewan Ranjit Rai, on board took off. A total of 28 Dakotas carrying 464 soldiers were launched in a combined Army-Air Force operation. Even as the sorties took off, the exact situation was unclear. It was not even known if Srinagar airfield was safe or in the hands of the enemy. Rai had been instructed to establish wireless communication with the airfield and land only after receiving confirmation that the airfield was safe. Else he was to land at Jammu and then move to Srinagar by road. As the Dakotas reached the contact point, the confirming crackle of the wireless message reached Rai and at 8.30 am the first Dakotas touched down at Srinagar's tarmac airstrip. The Indian army had arrived.

Even then, the operation was a tight rope walk that could have gone either way. The initial strength of just an infantry battalion was not enough to counter the hordes of invaders converging onto Srinagar. On landing, Rai was briefed of the presence of the raiders at Baramula and decided to confront them there, instead of waiting for them to reach Srinagar.

Indian troops on the offensive

Param Vir Chakra

Maj Somnath Sharma PVC (Posthumous)

Leaving one company behind for the security of the airfield, he moved with three companies to Baramula, where he organised a hasty defensive position east of the town. Yet, he was unaware of the strength of the invaders or the heavy weaponry that they were equipped with. On 29 October, the heavily armed raiders launched repeated attacks on his defences and soon outflanked his position. Rai ordered the battalion to move back from Baramula and occupy an intermediate position at Pattan, halfway between Srinagar and Baramula. As Rai was conducting a skilful withdrawal, a burst of enemy fire killed him on the spot. The actions of 1 SIKH and its gallant Commanding Officer have gone down in history. Even today, 27 October, the day the unit landed in Srinagar, is celebrated as Infantry Day – the day when the Indian Army saved the valley.

The delaying action of 1 SIKH stayed the invaders away from Srinagar and gave time for additional troops to build up. 161 Infantry Brigade which was deployed near Delhi was airlifted into Srinagar. Its arrival was inauspicious. Within two days its commander was wounded and had to be evacuated. He was replaced by Brigadier (later Lieutenant General) LP Sen, a dynamic leader whose determination soon transmitted itself to his command.

Indian troops recapturing an enemy position

As 161 Brigade gradually built up, so did the enormity of the threat. The enemy now began advancing towards Srinagar airfield from the direction of Badgam, a small

A mountain battery in action

village just a few kilometres from the airfield. Badgam was occupied by a Company of 4 KUMAON under Major Somnath Sharma and his position was viciously attacked by a horde of almost 700 of the enemy. Hopelessly outnumbered, the company held on against insurmountable odds, before it was finally overrun on 03 November. Major Sharma's last radio transmission was "The enemy is 50 yards from us. I will not withdraw one inch but fight to the last man and the last round". The actions of the company delayed the enemy and saved the airfield. Somnath Sharma's selfless gallantry earned him a Param Vir Chakra, the first recipient of India's highest gallantry award.

In face of the growing threat to Srinagar, 161 Brigade re-deployed around the town in a tight, compact formation. The Brigade was a hotchpotch of units comprising of 1 SIKH, 1 KUMAON, 1 PUNJAB, two companies of 4 KUMAON and a company of 1 MAHAR. One squadron of armoured cars from 7 CAVALRY had also joined the formation, boosting up its fire power considerably. With forces being gradually air-lifted into Srinagar, the strength of the Brigade built up and it was soon strong enough to withstand an enemy attack. Yet it was a close-run thing. Had the invaders reached Srinagar even a day or two earlier, the outcome of the entire campaign would have been different.

On 7 November, aerial reconnaissance revealed around 3000 enemy raiders in an open area around Shalatang, 30 kilometres west of Srinagar concentrating for an attack on the town. Sen decided to

Enemy invaders surrendering to the attacking Indians

go onto the offensive and using a battalion to engage the enemy from the front, moved two other battalions to attack from the flanks along with a troop of armoured cars. When all elements were in place, they opened fire simultaneously. The enemy was out in the open and in a wide freshly ploughed field without cover, their vehicles parked on a side. With fire pouring in from three sides, they collapsed. Now the roles were reversed. It was a classical conventional battle which the Indian army excelled in and after five hours of intense battle, the enemy was virtually decimated and the balance took to their heels. Over seven hundred of the enemy were killed and most of their transport destroyed. With this major victory, the enemy was now incapable of taking any further action in this sector and the threat to Srinagar receded. Flush with victory, the Brigade recaptured Pattan, Baramula and Uri. In the momentum of their advance, the army planned to recapture all the lost areas up to Domel and then Muzaffarabad, but then a grave situation developed further south in the Jammu sector.

Actions in Jammu Province

In conjunction with the actions at Srinagar, a force of ten Lashkars advanced further south in Poonch and Rajouri sector with the aim of moving up to Jammu. By the first week of October, they had swarmed into the region rapidly overcoming the meagre state forces and captured Mirpur, Bhimber and Mendhar by 03 November. These helpless towns, especially Mirpur, were subjected to the same brutal slaughter, loot and rape that were witnessed in the other towns and the stream of refuges carried terrible tales of the atrocities. The refugees fled into Poonch and political pressure mounted to reinforce the town and save the population from the

General Thimmayya with his Field Commanders

carnage of the towns captured earlier. On 14 November the army was ordered to despatch troops to save Poonch.

Actions now shifted from the Srinagar sector towards Poonch. 161 Infantry Brigade which had made such spectacular gains in the past week was ordered to halt its offensive actions and move from Srinagar Sector towards Poonch approaching the town from the North. From the South, 50 Independent Para Brigade advanced from Jammu and a link up of the two formations was planned south of Poonch. On both sides, the advance was difficult. Bridges were blown up, ambushes took place at each bend and the formations were encumbered with the task of looking after refugees at each town that they relieved. As the leading elements of 161 Brigade approached Poonch, elements of the State militia holding the town, mistook them for a Pakistani column and blew a vital bridge on the outskirts of the town. Further advance or a link up was now impossible and so 1 KUMAON under Lieutenant Colonel Pritam Singh was inducted on foot into the town. Pritam Singh rapidly reorganised the defences of the town using his own battalion, elements of the state forces and even raised a local self-defence militia. A small airstrip was constructed which allowed it to be maintained by air. Completely isolated, the garrison held on for over one year in the face of repeated enemy attacks before it was eventually relieved in the Indian army's summer offensive. The defence of Poonch was one of the most heroic sagas of the war.

Even though Poonch was reinforced the situation in the entire Jammu Sector remained grave. The enemy pushed forward with over 10,000 tribesmen and troops from the regular army and captured Jhangar on 25th December. They then moved ahead to contact Naushera. If Naushera was lost the enemy would be within striking range of Jammu. It was ironic that though Pakistan hailed this war as a 'Jehad', a Hindu-Muslim war, it was an Indian Muslim, Brigadier Mohammed Usman – the commander of 50 Independent Parachute Brigade, who was the energy and driving force of the actions in this sector. Brigadier Usman was born in Allahabad and had been under considerable pressure to join the Pakistani army after partition, but chose to stay in the land of his birth. He, like hundreds of Indian Muslims, lived, fought and fell in the best

A convoy meanders along the Leh-Zojila raod

A patrol moves along a typically difficult track in Kashmir.

traditions of the Indian army and the actions of men like him proved the lie of Pakistan's 'Two-Nation' theory.

By February 1948, around 12,000 to 15,000 riders concentrated around Naushera and on 05 February, launched an all-out offensive, hoping to overrun its defences by sheer weight of number. 50 Para Brigade had been built up to five battalions and Usman deployed it effectively on the high ground surrounding the town. In some of the fiercest fighting of the campaign the defences held firm, fighting back wave after wave of frenzied assaults with artillery, mortars, small arms fire and often with bayonets and bare hands. As the assaulting forces closed in, artillery guns levelled their barrels and fired at them through open sights. For three nights the enemy continued their attacks only to be repulsed each time. When the fighting finally subsided, not a single defensive position had been penetrated and over 2000 of the enemy lying dead or dying on the features around them. Naushera was a crucial victory which broke the enemy in the Jammu sect. This success coming as it did in the wake of the reverses of the past two months boosted Indian morale. From now on the situation changed and the Indian army went on the offensive.

The Indian Army's Offensives

With two vital victories at Shalatang and Naushera under its belt, and the arrival of fresh troops into J&K, the Indian army moved to re-capture the areas occupied by the raiders. Major changes took place which impacted the conduct of operations. The first was the appointment of General Cariappa as the first Indian Commander-in-Chief of the army. His identification with the country and its troops gave impetus to the operation and provided a fresh dynamism. The other was the reorganisation of the Jammu and Kashmir Division, then the only Indian division operating in Kashmir, into two divisions – the Srinagar Division (later 19 Infantry division) under Major General Thimayya, DSO, and the Jammu Division (later 26 Infantry division) under Major General Atma Singh. This divided the responsibilities of the widely dispersed area and gave a separate, well defined sector to each formation.

In the midst of a harsh, bitter winter, the Indian army gradually recaptured its lost areas against stiff enemy opposition. The major objective was the re-capture of Jhangar, whose loss had hurt hard. Brigadier Usman had vowed not to sleep on a cot till Jhangar was re-captured and in the months following the loss he kept his promise. By early March, the formation closed in around Jhangar and on 17 March launched a two pronged attack in a raging snow storm. Jhangar fell the next day and that night a makeshift camp cot and a couple of blankets were brought forward from the Advance Dressing Station for Brigadier Usman to sleep on a cot for the first time in months and fulfil the promise that he had made

A mountain Battery moves into position along the rugged tracks

Locals belles watch the landing of the first Dakota at the newly constructed Leh airfield

to himself. Unfortunately, just three months later, this brave hero was to be killed by an enemy shell in the vicinity of his greatest triumph.

Flash with the victory at Jhangar, the Indian army rapidly closed in and re-captured Rajauri on 11 April 1948. It was a bitter-sweet victory. As the triumphant troops entered the town, they discovered huge pits full of the bodies of men, women and children massacred by the enemy in a final orgy of senseless violence before their retreat. These scenes of unimaginable horror and wanton destruction would be witnessed in many of the town and villages that the army recaptured.

By now summer was in the air and with it came the plans for a summer offensive. Two additional brigades had moved into the area and planning was afoot for the recapture of the lost areas. The Srinagar division (19 Infantry Division) under Gen Thimayya was given the task of recapturing areas up to Muzzafarabad. By June the formation had secured its intermediate objectives but by now the enemy had moved almost two brigades of regular Pakistan army troops in the Domel-Muzzafarabad sector and the forces were virtually evenly matched. Ferocious fighting took place in these heights and the army made slow progress winning back lost territories feature by feature, village by village and town by town. Then on 10 July 1948, on the appeal of United Nations, the Indian Government ordered a cessation of the offensive and the advance to Muzzafarabad came to a halt. The Pakistani Army had no such compunctions. Taking advantage of the pause they recaptured Kishanganga and Pandu and along this line operations gradually wound up. This line would then become the Line of Control – a jagged, uneven line which would erupt sporadically for years thereafter and form a tense demarcating boundary between the two nations.

Operations in Ladakh

To the North and East of Kashmir lies the starkly beautiful region of Ladakh. This high, remote region is connected to Kashmir by a scenic road from Srinagar to Leh which passes through the 3500m high Zojila Pass – one of the highest passes in the world which aptly means "The Pass of Blizzards." The only other road link to Ladakh is over the circuitous caravan route which meanders across a series of mountain ranges from Manali to Leh. The region provided a backdoor entry into Kashmir but its vast immense spaces and poor lines of communication made it virtually impossible to defend. At the time of partition, the area was lightly held by members of the Jammu and Kashmir State Forces who were strung in penny-packets across this vast region. In this strategically vital area, Pakistan launched a major offensive in conjunction with its operations in the Kashmir valley.

A Jawan stand guard at Zojila Pass as the first convoys rumble through it

The raiders poured into the region in November 1947.

Gilgit and Baltistan were lost even before the Indian Army could even react. Ladakh was thrown into panic as the refugees streamed in from the Northern Areas, carrying tales of atrocities and debauchery committed by the marauders. In the wake of the enemy advance most of the State forces fell back to Skardu, a small town which guarded the approach to Leh. The town was held by a small garrison of around a thousand men under Lieutenant Colonel Sher Jung Thapa. Skardu was contacted by the enemy in early January, but each of its attacks was determinedly beaten back. Besieged on all sides and heavily out numbered; the garrison held on for over eight months before finally capitulating on 14 August 1948.

While Skardu was grimly holding out, the enemy by-passed the town, moved towards Kargil and Drass and soon overran the small detachments there. By the first week of May, both the towns were in enemy hands and now he was in a position to threaten both Leh and Srinagar. Even worse, he succeeded in capturing the crucial Zojila Pass and thus cut off the land link from Srinagar to Leh. With the capture of Zojila, Leh could only be connected by air or the long, tortuous route from Manali. The fall of Leh, and with it all of Ladakh seemed imminent.

As the threat to Leh intensified in the early months of 1948, it was decided to reinforce the small garrison there. In the height of

Aerial view of the forbidding Zojila Pass.

winter, a small detachment of three officers and 70 volunteers from 2 DOGRA moved out from Srinagar and after braving blizzards, snow-storms and avalanches reached Leh on 8 March 1948 after a month long trek. This brave company under Major Prithi Chand carried along additional rifles and weapons to raise a local militia for the defence of Leh. Under Prithi Chand's dynamism, Leh's defences were reorganized with the state forces personnel already there and a local defence force was raised from volunteers. He also constructed a make-shift airstrip with the help of local labour and on 24 May 1948, a single Dakota, flying over uncharted territory without maps, oxygen or landing aids landed on the highest airstrip in the world. This aircraft, piloted by Air Commodore Meher Singh, had on board a distinguished passenger, General Thimayya himself, who had come to personally assess the situation. With the airfield operational, two more companies were flown in. An additional company marched across the hazardous 400 kilometre Manali route to strengthen the garrison. Gradually the defences of Leh were considerably reinforced and the town was now ready to withstand any enemy attack.

The use of tanks at Zojila Pass was a masterstroke that led to its capture

As the Indian army was moving feverishly to save Leh, the enemy was making his own moves. By mid-May the raiders reached the outskirts of Leh and here inexplicably paused their operations. At that time Leh was weakly held and had they pressed forward, it would have fallen. The delay of two odd weeks gave the vital time required to make the airstrip functional and reinforce Leh by air. It also provided time for additional troops to march in from the Manali route and build up the defences of the town.

Though Leh was reinforced, the town was still effectively isolated by the capture of Zojila Pass. The loss of the pass had also cut off the entire Ladakh region. The priority now lay in the recapture of the pass to open the land route to Leh. Zojila was a tough nut to crack. The pass was held by a battalion with three main positions; Mukand Ridge and Chabutra Ridge – on the right and left shoulders and a depth position on Machine Gun Ridge. The defences in these forbidding heights were virtually inassaultable and Indian troops were exposed to the withering fire of Machine Guns dug into well-sited positions in the natural caves of the mountain side. These positions were virtually immune to air or artillery fire and could only be captured by a ground assault across difficult and treacherous terrain which was dominated by enemy fire.

THE MOMENT

The crucial moment of the campaign was undoubtedly the morning of 27 October 1948, when the first aircraft carrying troops landed at Srinagar airfield and were then able to stave back the invaders from Srinagar.

It was a touch and go. A delay of even a few hours may have resulted in the fall of the airfield and with it there would be no way to move troops into the valley to counter the raiders.

Two attempt to capture the pass by infantry attacks failed. The enemy was too well dug-in and effectively sited. Air and artillery attacks had no effects. As September drew to a close and winter was setting in, time was running out. If the pass held for just a month or two more, it would be impossible to capture it in winter and then Leh would have automatically fallen. The entire Indian operations in this sector depended on the capture of Zojila.

Thimayya realised that the only way to eliminate the enemy from their positions would be by using the direct fire of tanks. But then no tanks had ever reached these heights and no tanks had ever operated as such altitudes before. Yet it was decided to take the chance and a squadron of Stuart tanks of 7 LIGHT CAVALRY was moved from Akhnur to Zojila. The turrets of the tanks were removed to reduce their weight which would enable them to cross the numerous small bridges en route. Bridges were reinforced, tracks were hurriedly widened, crossings were made and the tanks trundled up the long, difficult climb towards Zojila. It is a credit to the drivers that not a single tank gave way to mechanical failure or was struck on the slushy narrow tracks, even though the move was made purely by night to ensure secrecy. By 15 October the squadron was in position, the turrets refitted and the stage was set for the historic assault on Zojila.

Operation "Bison", the code name for the attack, was scheduled on 20 October, but when all was ready it began to snow. Zojila lived up to its name. The Pass of Blizzards was hit by raging snow storms and twice the operation was postponed because of the weather. Finally D-Day was set for 01 November and with winter approaching, it was literally now or never.

On 01 November, in spite of another raging snow storm, General Thimayya gave the order to attack. Beneath a leaden sky, with snow flakes swirling all around them, the tanks rumbled across the start line at 10:15 A.M. As the tanks roared through, with Thimayya in the leading tank, the infantry attacked from the flanks and on the shoulders of the pass. The poor visibility and atrocious weather actually aided surprise as the enemy did not expect an attack in these conditions. With the infantry moving along the flanks, the tanks sprayed the pass with machine gun and high explosive fire. The sight of the tanks unnerved them and in a panic the enemy fled, leaving behind his dead and wounded and vast stocks of equipment. Tanks and infantry swept through the pass, the tanks firing into the bunkers and caves, the infantry clearing the shoulders. By the next evening the depth position was captured as well and on 02 November the tri-colour was raised once again on the wind-swept pass.

THE TACTICS

The Pakistani tactics of sending in irregular forces reinforced with regular officers and troops was novel and unconventional and almost succeeded. They managed to assemble the raider in absolute secrecy and news of the their activities was concealed till the last moment. Thus total surprise was attained.

Indian tactics were largely conventional. In the difficult terrain they had fight a unconventional adversary and then re-capture lost areas virtually village by village, town by town and crest line by crest line. Its counter offensive to recapture all Kashmir was halted by the advent of the cease fire.

The use to tanks at Zojila was a tactical masterstroke . Moving them to the forbidding heights in absolute secrecy and then using them to assault the well entrenched Pakistani positions was the major factor that helped recapture the vital pass.

Zojila was the most important battle of the campaign. Had the attack not succeeded, it would never have been captured at all and then Leh and all of Ladakh would have fallen. The threat to Srinagar would have intensified from its Northern flank and the very geography of the nation would have been altered. This victory marked the turning point of operations in the sector. Pushing forward in sub-zero temperatures in some of the worst terrain imaginable, the rejuvenated Indian troops surged forward and on 16 November – Guru Nanak's birthday – 1 PATIALA celebrated the auspicious day by capturing Drass. On 23 November the leading troops entered Kargil. On the same day a column sent from Leh linked up with the advancing troops at Kargil. The long isolation of Leh was over. Leh and Ladakh were saved.

Just a month later, on night 31 December, the cease fire came into being under the auspicious of the United Nation. The Indian Army had faced a daunting challenge thrown up within less than a month of Independence. The Army fought for over a year in some of the most difficult terrain in the world, often against impossible odds and yet came out trumps. At the end of hostilities, almost a third of the state was still held by Pakistan. Had the army been permitted to continue its offensive in the wake of the victories at Shalatang, Naoshera and Zojila, the lost areas too would have been recaptured. As it is, the unfinished task would result in three other flare-ups, in 1965, 1971 and in the 1999 Kargil war. The uneasy state of no-war-no-peace endured across the Line of Control for the past four decades and has bedevilled relations ever since. The actions of the Indian Army saved the state and held together the Union in its present form. It was its first challenge, but the fledging army of independent India would face more such challenges, encounter set backs and victories and soldier on in war and peace in service of the Nation. The operations of 1947-48 helped forge the sword of Independent India. It would be further tempered by the wars that lay ahead.

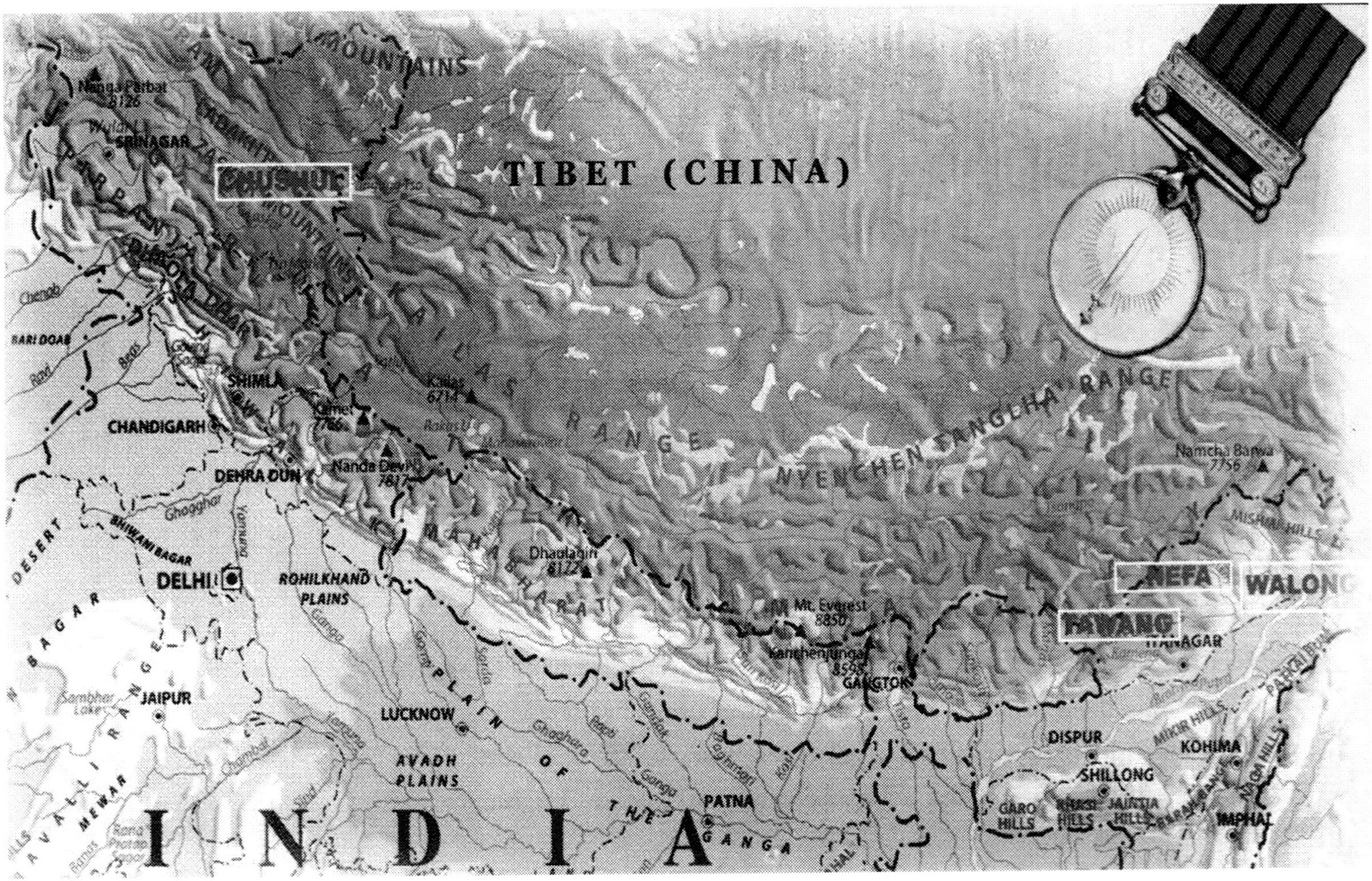
TIBET (CHINA)
CHUSHUL
NEFA
WALONG
TAWANG
Nanga Parbat
8126
SRINAGAR
SHIMLA
CHANDIGARH
DEHRA DUN
DELHI
JAIPUR
LUCKNOW
PATNA
GANGTOK
ITANAGAR
DISPUR
SHILLONG
KOHIMA
IMPHAL
Kailas
6714
Kamet
7756
Nanda Devi
7817
Dhaulagiri
8172
Mt. Everest
8850
Kanchenjunga
8598
Namcha Barwa
7756
ROHILKHAND
PLAINS
AVADH
PLAINS
GARO
HILLS
KHASI
HILLS
JAINTIA
HILLS
MIKIR HILLS
BARI DOAB
BHIWANI BAGAR
DESERT
MEWAR
NYENCHEN TANGLHA RANGE
I N D I A

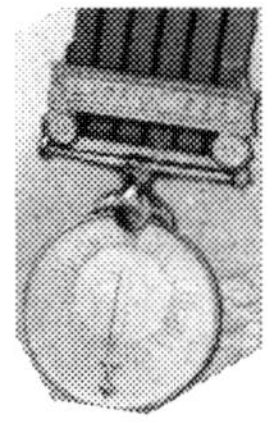

10

Debacle in the High Himalayas – Sino-Indian Conflict – 1962

"In 1962, the Indian Army was short of equipment, weapons, ammunition, rations, clothing, everything—, everything except guts"

❖ ❖ ❖

Background

For millennia, the Himalayas have stood guard over the Northern frontiers of the Indian Sub-Continent, its mighty mountains standing like sentinels on the approaches to India. These high, craggy ranges, often uncharted and unmapped, allowed a peaceful co-existence between the nations that lay astride them, namely India, Tibet and China further to the north. Then in 1950, China invaded Tibet and rapidly annexed that helpless country. India and China now became neighbours with an undemarcated border running through the Himalayan ranges between them. This uneasy situation would be a festering sore between the two emerging Asian powers and culminate in the 1962 Sino-Indian border war; a short, brutal war which gave independent India its first and only, military defeat.

The root-cause of the border dispute goes back to 1913, when

Air dropping of stores on a remote post. Many posts occupied as part of the "Forward Policy" were isolated and could only be maintained by air

the dividing line between India and Tibet was decided under the auspices of Sir Henry McMohan, the Foreign Secretary of the British Government of India. In this agreement, the border between India and Tibet would run along the watershed – the highest line of mountain ranges. The map showing this draft agreement was signed by Indian and Tibetan representatives and though the Chinese representative initialled the document, China did not accept or reject it. Due to the inhospitable nature of the terrain the boundary was never marked and most of the areas were so inaccessible that barring the odd expedition, no one ever visited them. The alignment of the McMohan Line, as shown on the map, was also subject to different interpretations. Thus when India gained independence in 1947, she inherited land boundaries with Tibet which were not demarcated on ground and not accepted by China. With the Chinese annexation of Tibet the unmarked border now became the disputed border between India and China.

The border between India and China runs from Ladakh in the West right up to the Indo-Burmese border in the east. The disputed area in the West is Aksai Chin – "The Desert of White Stones" a vast, arid area the size of Switzerland, which India claimed as part of Kashmir and the Chinese as part of Western Tibet. Due to the inhospitable nature of the terrain, the area was totally uninhabited and as was famously brought out in Parliament," not a blade of grass grew". The Central Sector runs along the Indus River up to Nepal and was clearly demarcated and thus not subject to dispute. Further east, along a 1360 kilometre stretch East of Bhutan all the way to Burma is the Eastern Sector, notionally demarcated by the McMohan Line and claimed by China as part of Southern Tibet and by India a part of its territory. To facilitate administration of the region (the present day area of Arunachal Pradesh), India had established the North Eastern Frontier Agency (NEFA) with its Headquarters in Tezpur. It was in the undemarcated Eastern and Western Sectors that the seeds of conflict lay.

When China took over Tibet, the Tibetans, though peace-loving and passive, did not prove to be easy subjects. In spite of brutal suppression, the Tibetans organised an armed revolt against Chinese occupation and a long guerrilla war began. To facilitate move of troops and equipment into Tibet and strengthen its hold on the region, it began the construction of the Sinkiang – Tibet road in 1956 passing through the disputed area of Aksai Chin. It is shocking that India got to know of the construction of a road passing through its own territory only in September 1957, when the Chinese press jubilantly announced its completion. Worse, these reports were followed up by maps that showed Aksai Chin and even parts of the Eastern Sector South of the McMohan Line as Chinese territory. It was a shocking intelligence failure and India was to pay a heavy price for this lapse.

India awoke to the threat too late. Those were the days of "Hindi-Chini Bhai Bhai" and Nehru and the Chinese Premier, Chou En-Lai shared a special relationship. The occupation of Indian Territory provoked a flurry of diplomatic protests, with proposals and counter-proposals initiated by both sides, each of them inconclusive. Yet in spite of the major border dispute lurking in the

Indian troops in summer clothing faced as much a threat from the elements as from the enemy.

background, the tenor of Indo-China relations remained cordial. Then another incident took place which further acerbated tensions. In 1959, after the brutal Chinese suppression of the Khampa rebellion in Tibet, the Dalai Lama fled to India where he was readily accepted and given sanctuary. The Chinese viewed India's support to the Dalai as indicators of its designs on Tibet (even though by then, India had virtually accepted Chinese sovereignty over Tibet). A personal exchange of letters between Nehru and Chou-en-Lai proved inconclusive. Even a week-long visit by Chou-en-Lai, in April 1960 did nothing to resolve the vexed border issue. At that stage China showed indicators that it was willing to accept the Indian position in the Eastern Sector, in return for acceptance of their claims in Aksai Chin. This compromise formula was turned down by the Indian leadership who insisted on a complete Chinese withdrawal before any talks on the issue could commence. Chou-en Lai was greeted with cheers of "Hindi-Chini Bhai Bhai". The same cry would be taken up by Chinese troops as they closed in to attack Indian positions just a year later.

As diplomatic parleys and overtures continued the Chinese were building up for a future confrontation. The situation was soon coming to a pass, but the Indian leadership seemed oblivious to the growing threat. The army's warning of increased Chinese activity was brushed aside and it was told to focus itself on the threat from Pakistan. Perhaps due to a sense of delusion or misplaced confidence, the Chinese threat was ignored. When the growing storm finally burst, its impact overwhelmed all of India.

The Brewing Storm

In August 1959 the first major border incident took place. The Chinese attacked an Assam Rifles post at Longju, along the McMohan Line in the disputed area of the Eastern Sector, killing three and forcing the remainder to withdraw. In the Western Sector an even more ominous incident occurred. On 20 October, the Chinese ambushed a routine Indian patrol, near Kongka Pass around 64 kilometres inside Indian Territory, killing nine and capturing ten. In both cases the Chinese claimed that the Indians were inside their territory. The Chinese stance was now hardening palpably. A reconnaissance patrol sent to Aksai Chin to confirm the existence of the Chinese road were captured, detained for 40 days, and sent back with a stern warning not to expect such "reasonable treatment" in future. Diplomatically too, the Chinese were asserting their claims not only over Aksai Chin in the West, but across the entire McMohan Line in the East with some maps showing the entire area up to the foothills of NEFA as part of

Indian 'Jawans' in hastily prepared fox holes. Most defenses lacked even the basic amenities

Chinese territory. Along with diplomatic and political manoeuvring, the Chinese were steadily building up its military forces and infrastructure to enable them to launch a rapid offensive at an opportune time. Its 54th Army based in the Tibetan plateau was made responsible for the offensive.

After the Longju and Konka incidents the entire operational control of NEFA and Ladakh was handed over to the army. A new Corps – 33 Corps, was raised to look after the Eastern Sector. But it was had just one division – 4 division based at Tezpur, and its operational area encompassed the entire North Eastern region including Sikkim, NEFA, the Indo-Burma border and the Indo-East Pakistan border. Even this meagre increase in troops was not backed by any improvement in infrastructure. No roads existed on the Indian side. There was only one jeepable track from Tezpur to Bomdila. Beyond Bomdila no tracks existed and it required a gruelling seven-day climb using porters and mules just to reach the operational area. It had been assessed by the army that it would require three divisions to successfully hold the area, but on ground only two brigades were available. The Chinese on the other hand had brought up three divisions of acclimatised, battle hardened troops and extended their road communications right up to the border. Their own defences were gradually built up on their side of the McMohan Line, often in plain sight of the Indian positions, while deeper inside their offensive forces were being marshalled in absolute secrecy.

In spite of this yawing gap, the Indian government completely misread both our own capabilities and the Chinese intentions. Nehru and the Defence Minister, Mr Krishna Menon had been incorrectly advised by the Intelligence Bureau and were convinced that China would not attack. To further stake its claim on the area, the Government adopted the disastrous "Forward Policy" in 1960, a policy that entailed depicting Indian presence right up to the line of the claimed borders. This involved sending troops to occupy high, remote posts and picquets bang on the border – or rather the perception of the border. All though 1961-62 Indian posts were established well-forward, even though most of the posts were tactically indefensible and many were so remote that they could only be maintained by air. Some of the posts were even established beyond the line of Chinese posts, in effect cutting them off. A dangerous game of "I Dare" began as posts were established like pawns on a chessboard, each move signifying a claim and evoking a counter-move from the other side. Even though the activities were provocative and likely to evoke a strong response, the government persisted even against the advice of the army, which was keen on developing its own defensive capabilities before establishing the forward posts. The Indian army's rapid liberation of Goa in 1961 had infused a false sense of confidence and the top leadership were not willing to see that the Chinese were a different preposition all together. They were convinced that they would not attack – their violent reactions at Longju and Kongka were conveniently forgotten and our own glaring inadequacies were blithely overlooked. When the Chinese attack came, it was in a way, almost inevitable, but still took the nation by surprise.

The establishing of forward posts led to sporadic instances of firing and patrol engagements causing casualties on both sides, although no major clash of arms took place. On 10 July 1962, the first major Chinese reaction manifested itself. Chinese troops encircled a platoon size post in the Galwan Valley in Ladakh and came within 15 metres of the post. It was a tense stand-off but neither side fired and after a day or two the Chinese withdrew, although they still continued surrounding the post. This should have set alarm bells ringing, but instead the incident reinforced the perception that the Chinese would not attack. Rather than infuse fresh caution, 33 Corps was ordered to establish twenty four new posts along the McMohan Line – much against the protests of the Corps Commander, Lieutenant General Umrao Singh, who wanted to first develop the defensive capabilities before undertaking this provocative move. As part of this deployment, in June 1962, an Assam Rifles post was established at an isolated place called Che Dong which became the flash point of the war.

Che Dong was nothing more than a cluster of shepherds' huts lying a short distance from the tri-junction of the boundaries of India, Tibet and Bhutan. It had no tactical or functional significance and in fact, 33 Corps had selected a location a little in the rear as the site for the post. The post commander found the proposed site to be inhospitable and moved forward to Che Dong instead. Unfortunately the new site selected was inside Chinese territory – a crucial fact overlooked by the lack of maps or a demarcated boundary. Che Dong also faced the Chinese Thag La ridge, a tactically important feature to which they were understandably sensitive. Their reaction was violent. In early September, they encircled the post and occupied the ridge line behind it – Dhola ridge and effectively entered Indian Territory. Encircled by belligerent Chinese, the post commander reported that he was surrounded by over 600 Chinese troops; an inflated figure which he later admitted was done just to get early help. The situation now worsened and 7 Infantry Brigade under Brigadier John Dalvi was ordered to move forward to Dhola area. Two battalions of the brigade, 9 PUNJAB and 2 RAJPUT were ordered to move up and occupy defences along the Namka Chu River – an area that lay in a deep valley dominated by heights on either side. The ill-equipped and poorly clothed troops were moved up without adequate acclimatisation to occupy indefensible positions along the river. The Corps Commander, General Umrao Singh, protested against this hasty, ill-considered move and it was decided to ease him out. A new Corps Headquarters was raised – 4 Corps – with Lieutenant General BM Kaul, the then Chief of General Staff at Army Headquarters – as the more amenable head of operations in NEFA. General Kaul was an officer from Army Service Corps with no combat experience, but had risen to one of the highest positions of the army largely due to his relation with Nehru and the political patronage that he enjoyed. Brash and vain-glorious, his lack of tactical or strategic vision and ignorance of ground realities made him the wrong choice for such a sensitive appointment. The creation of a new Headquarters to orchestrate the battle at a time when hostilities

Indian troops fight back a Chinese attack under overwhelming odds

were imminent was again a hasty, ill-considered move made for political expediency and personal gains rather than military logic. Kaul's appointment and his ineffective conduct of the battle was to have disastrous results for the army.

While the Indian Army and political leadership knee-jerked, the Chinese had planned months, if not years in advance. They had built up three divisions of well-trained acclimatised troops; their dumps were stocked and established well forward, their supply lines were in place and their intelligence network and guides were already in Indian Territory to pass back detailed information to their attacking columns. One high-ranking Chinese agent was working as a roadside tea shop owner on the Bomdi La road, with two pretty local belles as an added attraction, to radio back information of Indian troop movements on the road. Their offensive plans were in place and they were just waiting for the opportune time to make their move. The Che Dong post incident gave them the excuse to move forward into Indian territory on the Dhola Ridge. As the tense stand-off continued, on 12 October 1962, the Prime Minister, Pandit Jawahar Lal Nehru passed instructions to the army to "free our territory"; a statement misreported by the press as "Armed forces ordered to throw out the Chinese aggressor from NEFA." With that the dam burst. On 20 October 1962, Chinese troops debouched from their well-concealed concentration areas and poured out into the Indian positions in both Ladakh and NEFA. The Indian army was now to face its sternest test by fire.

The Chinese Offensive

With the main bone of contention laying in NEFA it was but natural that the main weight of the offensive would fall there. The main offensive was directed in the Kameng sector with a secondary offensive launched in the Walong Sector on the Indo-Burma boundary. In conjunction, a massive offensive was also launched in Ladakh, the area of the disputed Western Sector. It was in Kameng that the bitterest battles were fought.

Kameng is the western most district of NEFA which borders Bhutan. Here, the major town was Tawang, a town of great religious significance which holds Asia's second largest Buddhist monastery. Tawang lies just forty kilometres from the boundary. On the boundary stands Bum La, a crucial pass which guards the direct approach to Tawang which was held by a platoon of 1 SIKH. South of Tawang, the area dropped, falling down to the Tawang River (Tawang Chu) and then rose again along the next ridge line towards Se La which stands at an altitude of 4180 meters above sea level. From Se La the ground drops to the Dirang Valley, rises again to the next ridgeline at Bomdi La and then falls into the Tenga Valley and the foothills of Assam.

In this crucial sector, one solitary road existed from Bomdi La up to Tawang which was capable of taking only limited jeep traffic. Beyond Tawang, all moves were on foot or mule tracks. 7 Infantry Brigade, under Brigadier John Dalvi was responsible for operations in this sector, a hopelessly inadequate force for the 150 kilometre long area. 7 Brigade had been ordered to move forward to occupy positions along the Namka Chu River in the wake of the Che Dong

Stores being delivered by air on a dusty airstrip in the Walong Sector

incident and at the commencement of operations on 20 October, the brigade had two battalions 9 PUNJAB and 2 RAJPUT strung along the river in indefensible, low-lying positions which could be easily overrun. The third battalion, 1/9 Gorkha Rifles were in depth. A fourth battalion 4 GRENADIERS had arrived recently, ill–equipped with no experience of the terrain or high altitude warfare and were deployed along the flanks of the valley. The deployment placed Brigade out on a limb, where it could be isolated and destroyed in detail.

From 8 October onwards, the Chinese had been building up for the attack. But even as they prepared, they continued to talk to Indian soldiers in their isolated posts in broken Hindi, offer them tea and cigarettes and at times even hand over air-dropped supplies which had fallen on their side. In spite of their friendly overtures, their offensive preparations were getting more and more apparent. On 19 October, Dalvi made one last frantic call to withdraw from the Namka Chu to more defensible positions in the rear, a militarily sound suggestion which was curtly turned down. At 5.00 A.M. on 20 October, the deathly silence of the Namka Chu valley was broken by the roar of Chinese guns as their artillery unleashed an intensive, hour long bombardment on Indian positions. Two Chinese Divisions of the 54th Army, fully acclimatised, well-equipped and clothed, and supported by intensive artillery fire poured in towards the positions of 9 PUNJAB and 2 RAJPUT in the valley below. Wrongly deployed, exposed to enemy fire and without artillery support, the Punjabis and Rajputs fought valiantly. But it was a lost battle even before it had begun. The odds were simply too much and their positions were soon overrun. The intensity of the battle can be gauged by the casualties suffered by 2 RAJPUT, the unit that took the brunt of the initial attack. Out of the 513 ranks who held their positions at daybreak; 282 were killed, 161 wounded or captured and only 60 managed to escape by withdrawing in small groups through difficult gullies, streams and tracks into adjoining Bhutan. The Gurkhas and Grenadiers on the flanks were cut off and similarly mauled. By 12.30 it was all over. The gallant Brigade, which had achieved renown by its performance in Africa during World War II virtually ceased to exist as an entity. Brigadier Dalvi and his party tried to escape but lost in the forbidding mountains without food or water, they could not get far and were captured by the Chinese on 22 October.

With 7 Brigade systematically cut off and destroyed, the Chinese launched a fresh Division against Tawang on 23 October. The solitary platoon of 1 SIKH holding the border post at Bum La withstood three attacks before being overrun. The rest of the battalion (the same unit, whose prompt arrival at Srinagar Airfield in October 1947 saved the valley) were in delaying positions North of Tawang – spread out and without artillery support. One by one, its companies were overrun or bypassed. In just a few hours, the Chinese converged onto Tawang in a three-pronged advance, using one Regiment along the main axis and two others infiltrating from difficult tracks along the flanks. By 4 P.M., it was clear that Tawang could not be held and the garrison was ordered to pull out and fall back to Bomdi La. That same night the orders were changed and it was decided to hold Se La instead, a formidable 4180 meter high feature which lay between Tawang and Bomdi La. 62 Brigade was ordered to hold Se La with 1 SIKH, which had already been badly mauled, and 4 SIKH LI which had just come in from Punjab. A third battalion 4 GARHWAL RIFLES was guarding the vital bridge at Jang on the Tawang Chu River. Se La was a formidable position and if held resolutely would have halted a further Chinese advance. Also by now, the Chinese had already outrun their supplies and were forced to make a pause at Tawang – a pause which allowed the Indian defenders to consolidate their positions.

On 23 October, Chinese troops occupied Tawang and with meticulous forethought began preparations for the next phase of the operations. Stocks were built up, the troops replenished and re-kitted and the road system extended from their side up to Bum La and then on to Tawang where it would link up with the Indian road beyond. The road construction was completed in just fourteen days – an astounding feat, especially at these altitudes. The rapid construction of the road surprised the Indians planners who had expected a much larger pause in operations.

The Indians too were trying to come to grips with the situation. The Corps Commander 4 Corps, Lieutenant General BM Kaul, who was largely responsible for the state of affairs, took ill and was evacuated to Delhi. Yet rather than leave the battle to his successor, he tried to control the battle from Delhi. Five days later he returned to take over the Corps once again. Meanwhile fresh troops were inducted into the sector. But not many troops could be pulled out because of fears that Pakistan would use the situation to its advantage and reignite the Western Theatre. The battalions that were inducted marched directly from the plains, carrying little with them except their pouch ammunition. The troop build up was jerky and ill-planned and the most crucial element, logistics, was neglected all together.

By mid-November, 62 Brigade established itself at Se La with five battalions in a compact defended layout. A second brigade, 65 Brigade, was located behind in Dirang, holding it with two battalions. The third brigade of 4 Division, 48 Brigade was arrayed behind at Bomdi La, holding the vital pass with three battalions. Yet even these ten battalions were well short of the strength of seventeen

Indian troops operating in high altitudes. The antiquated .303 single shot rifles are held in their hands

battalions required to hold the sector against the Chinese threat which was estimated at three Divisions. The battalions were new to the area and not familiar with the operational role or the nuances of fighting in high altitude area. Most units were spread out in company sized localities, often digging down in the ice-packed earth with bayonets, mess-tins and bare hands. There were no mines or barbed wire for defences. There were no defences as such; after all it takes weeks of coordinated labour to prepare a defensive position in these altitudes. The men were still in their summer uniforms, holding antiquated bolt-action .303 rifles in their hands with perhaps twenty additional rounds in their pouches. No emergency supplies were provided and instead of the chocolate based energy snack that they received during World War II, they carried only jaggery and *shakarparas* (a coarse kind of biscuit) in their haversacks. A replenishment system simply did not exist and most isolated posts subsisted on whatever little they had. No kerosene or petrol could reach these heights. The army just did not have twenty litre jerrycans since some wise bureaucrat had replaced all jerrycans with two hundred litre barrels to reduce expenditure. These barrels could not be hauled up to these altitudes by man or mule. When dropped by air, they often landed in deep valleys where they could not be retrieved and carried up to the posts. A few consignments of the new 7.62 mm semi-automatic rifles and 81 millimetre mortars had recently been received, but their ammunition had not arrived and these vital weapons remained packed in their crates. All this was not known to the nation or the leadership safely ensconced in Delhi. After the initial setbacks, the nation had rallied solidly behind its army, the media was playing its build up and it was felt that the spirit of the army and its tough soldiers would once again prevail. The optimism was reflected in the name given to the plan for the defence of Se La – "Operation Olympus", a grandiose name which could not hide the glaring inadequacies of the preparation. It would be not long before the misplaced optimism soon dissipated.

The Second Phase

By mid-November with their new road constructed up to Tawang, the Chinese launched the next phase of their operation directed at Se La. 62 Brigade was in position by then, but its troops were still not acclimatised and woefully short of the most basic equipment for a defensive battles. On the night of 17 November, the Chinese out-flanked the defences of Se La from the East, using a difficult track called the Bailey Trail to move over 1500 troops in absolute secrecy. Another equally strong detachment outflanked the defences from the west. Se La itself was attacked frontally by two crack Divisions, 54 Division and 11 Division. Even in the face of such numerical superiority, the position could have still held, but with the fear of being outflanked and cut-off, GOC 4 Division ordered the brigade to withdraw and fall back to Bomdi La. Initially the Brigade Commander, Brigadier Hoshiar Singh refused. After all his defences were stocked for over ten days of battle and he could hold Se La as fortress if he could be supplied by air. But on night 17/18 November, the Chinese breached the defences from the North attacking when the forward battalions were in the process of readjusting their positions. By 18 November, half of Se La's formidable defences were in Chinese hands and Hoshiar Singh ordered the rest of the Brigade to withdraw to Dirang. The withdrawal turned into a rout. Unknown to the defenders, the Chinese had established a road block on the road and as the withdrawing columns approached scattered them with effective fire. The columns broke up into small parties and tried to escape through the hills and find their way back into their own lines. In the absence of any cohesive leadership, it was virtually every man for himself. Most were killed or taken prisoner and Brigadier Hoshiar Singh himself was ambushed and killed. The Battle for Se La was an unmitigated disaster. 34 Officers, 43 JCO's and 1610 other ranks were killed, captured or missing in action and the brigade disintegrated in just two days of battle.

With Se La abandoned, the next position at Dirang, then held by 65 Brigade with two battalions also became untenable. The battle followed the same pattern and with the same results. The Chinese bypassed the defences, infiltrating in large numbers along the *nullahs* and streams to outflank the defences. The presence of enemy troops behind them again unnerved the defenders and 65 Brigade was ordered to withdraw towards Bomdila and join 48 Brigade which was already deployed there. The withdrawal was a replay of the Se La battle. The withdrawing battalions stumbled on to the road blocks established by the Chinese and were repeatedly ambushed. One battalion 19 MARATHA LIGHT INFANTRY managed to withdraw in relatively good order – the second 4 RAJPUT ran into a major ambush in the vicinity of Bomdila and lost over 200 men including their Commanding Officer.

As the disjointed battles were being fought at Se La and Dirang, the senior leadership seemed unable to come to terms with the fast unfolding turn of events. Decision making was slow, since all decisions were invariably referred to General Kaul. The battle of Se La saw the confusion which characterised the decision-making. First Se La was to be held at all costs. Then an ambiguous signal was sent from Kaul stating, "Hold on to the present position to the best of

Indian troops patrol around the picturesque Pangong Lake

your abilities. When any position becomes untenable, I delegate the authority to withdraw to any alternate position you can hold" This signal was sent on 18 November at a time when the brigade was already cut-off and no withdrawal was possible. Such lack of clear-cut orders and repeated changes in plans sent out mixed signals to the troops who soldiered on in their summer uniforms, their antiquated .303 rifles clutched grimly in their hands. When ordered to fight, they held on, when ordered to withdraw, they left. When no orders were received they merely held on to their ill-prepared defences, fighting on with nothing except sheer guts and tenacity.

With the fall of Se La, the battle converged on to Bomdi La which was then held by 48 Brigade. It was hoped that the withdrawing elements from Se La and Dirang would fall back and reinforce the defences, but very few reached Bomdi La. Those that did arrive were scattered and exhausted and in no condition for further battle. The defences of Bomdi La were denuded by sending out two companies to attack the Chinese road block on the Dirang-Bomdi La road. As the companies left their defences, the Chinese attacked using a circuitous route and occupied the positions that had been vacated by the two companies. The weakened battalions repulsed three attacks, but by 1500 hours on 18 November, the Chinese managed to drive a wedge in the defences At 1630 hours, the Commander gave the order to withdraw towards Rupa, 14 kilometres to the South. Unfortunately, the withdrawal order did not reach one of the Battalions, 1 MADRAS which was out of communication with their Headquarters and completely isolated. The battalion tried to withdraw by night, only to run into ambush and suffer heavy casualties – including that of their Commanding Officer.

Even as 48 Brigade was withdrawing, a fresh brigade, 67 Brigade, was moving to Bomdi La. By the time its leading elements reached Bomdi La, it had already been vacated. Further confusion followed. 48 Brigade was ordered to move back and re-occupy Bomdi La. When it turned back it was told to move on to Rupa. In the chaos and confusion, the Chinese attacked – their timing was invariably unerring – and pushed the two Brigades back in disarray towards Rupa on 19 November. On midnight 20 November, the Chinese announced a unilateral cease fire effective from midnight of 21/22 November and gradually the sporadic fire that reverberated in the hills reduced and then stopped all together. The broken battalions tried to reform and count their losses and the Headquarters tried to come to terms with the magnitude of the

AMX-13 Tanks in action near Chushul

defeat. The curtain slowly rang down in the last act of this tragedy of arms.

The Ladakh Sector

While the litany of unmitigated disasters was continuing in the east, Indian operations in the Ladakh sector showed a greater sense of purpose. The hostilities had commenced in the Ladakh sector with the initial confrontations at the Galwan and Kongka posts. Here too, the Indian government had persisted with its ill-conceived "Forward Policy," occupying post after isolated post in a long line extending from Daulat Beg Oldi in the North to Demchok at the Southern end of the sector. Opposite them, the Aksai Chin road had been completed and the Chinese now had the capability to build up and transport its troops rapidly to any part of the four hundred kilometres long sector. The Indian army had asked for one division with four brigades to counter the Chinese threat, but only one brigade - 114 Brigade with two battalions was available. The third battalion, 13 KUMAON arrived only on 2 October, a scant two weeks before actual hostilities erupted. As in the eastern Sector, the forces were hopelessly outnumbered, but here the state of preparedness was better, the leadership more decisive and the positions better sited and coordinated.

Maj Shaitan Singh, PVC

In conjunction with the offensive in the Eastern Sector, the Chinese attacked in the early hours of 20 October, launching simultaneous assaults on the series of isolated Indian posts across the entire frontage. Surprise was complete. No indicators were received of an impending attack in the sector; in fact the forward posts were in the process of thinning-out with the onset of winter. By 22

October most of the posts had fallen and the Chinese were poised for the next stage of their operations; the capture of Chushul and its vital airfield.

The beautiful Chushul valley guarding the approach to Chushul lies at an altitude of 4300 meters. To its north is the Pangong Tso (Lake) – a wide, crystal blue, salt water lake which is pristine in its natural beauty. Lofty mountain ranges soaring over 5000 meters high stand as natural barriers, with just one gap; the Spangur Gap providing an open avenue of approach. This gap leads straight to Chushul and was the obvious approach for the offensive. The Chinese had improved their tracks all the way to the Spangur Gap and could even bring tanks to the area. 114 Brigade under Brigadier TN Raina (later General Raina, COAS) entrusted with the defence of Chushul had three battalions and was later reinforced by an additional battalion, a troop of AMX-20 tanks, an artillery battery, heavy mortars and a Machine Gun Company. Raina had organised his defences well. The positions were well sited, the troops dug-in and protected by wire and minefields. The brigade held six second line scales of ammunition and morale was high – in spite of the initial reverses. The effect of this preparation, the basic degree of preparedness for any defender was revealed in the much improved performance of the Indian army in this sector.

The Indian defences extended across a 40 Kilometre long frontage, largely poised against the Spangur gap. One battalion held a position north of the gap, the newly arrived 13 KUMAON was in the South with one of its companies holding an isolated post at Rezang La. This position overlooked a narrow track that could by-pass the Spangur Gap and led directly towards Chushul. Chinese activity and their preparation opposite the Spangur Gap was clearly visible to the Indians – and with reason. This was an elaborate ruse because when the attack came it was not launched at Spangur. It came at Rezang La.

On 18 November, on a bitterly cold, foggy Sunday, the Chinese launched a silent attack on C Company of 13 KUMAON at Rezang La. The company under Major Shaitan Singh was ten Kilometres away from the rest of the battalion and had no artillery support. Yet the company held on in the face of repeated assaults forcing the enemy to bring up 75 millimeter cannons on wheel barrows to destroy the position by direct fire. In the face of intense fire the defences slowly gave way and the company fell, fighting virtually to the last man and to the last bullet. Out of the 128 who attended the "stand-to" in the morning, only 14 survived. Shaitan Singh himself was amongst the last to fall. Mortally wounded by a burst to the abdomen, he refused to be carried to safety and continued firing from his position to allow his comrades to withdraw. His gallant stand was immortalized in the film "Haqeegat' which reflected the horrors and the rigors of the 1962 War with great accuracy and helped bring home to Indian audiences the courage of the individual Indian soldiers and the abysmal conditions in which they fought and fell.

The Chinese also launched a simultaneous attack on the Northern flank of the Gap, held by 1/8 Gorkha Rifles. For thirty hours, this battalion fought back wave after wave of Chinese attacks even using their artillery guns in direct firing roles when they came too close. Finally at 15.30 hours on 19 November, the feature fell. With its capture, the Chinese were in a position to roll down from the dominating heights on the flanks and encircle the Indian troops – a tactic they had utilised so successfully in the Eastern Sector.

THE MOMENT

There was no specific moment that defined the battle. The year long build up of the "Forward Policy" set the tone for the confrontation. It was a period which the Chinese used to make their offensive preparations, but in which little was done to improve Indian defensive capabilities in spite of the fact that posts were being established well forward. That period was critical in deciding the eventual outcome of the battles that followed.

Raina realised the gravity of the situation and the futility of holding on. He ordered his brigade to commence thinning out and slowly and methodically the troops moved back to establish a new defensive line in the area of Chushul village. Virtually the entire brigade with its complete equipment and stores were in their new positions by 20 November. The Chinese were unable to follow up and Chushul with its vital airfield remained in Indian hands. That night the Chinese announced a unilateral fire and as the operations drew to a close, 114 Brigade remained unbent and undefeated.

THE TACTICS AND EQUIPMENT

The Chinese followed a sound strategy of gradually building up both their offensive and logistic capability before launching their offensive. They concealed their preparations virtually till the last moment and when they did attack, they used excellent deception measures. They repeatedly used difficult terrain to outflank the Indian defences and then attacked from the rear or the flanks.

Chinese troops were acclimatized and well equipped for operations in high altitude. What stands out was their speed in constructing roads and infrastructure in difficult, inaccessible terrain which helped them develop their logistics.

Indian tactics were invariably reactive. The occupation of forward posts exposed troops in isolated company and platoon size posts, which could be cut off and destroyed in detail. There was little coordination and an absence of clear-cut orders. The battles for Tawang, Sela and Bomdila were characterized by conflicting orders and there was no coordination between different formations.

Yet more than tactics it was a gross failure of logistics. Troops were ill-equipped to operate at these heights. They lacked winter clothing, had antiquated 303 rifles, usually held only pouch ammunition and had few supporting weapons. The lack of roads and basic infrastructure made it impossible to sustain the troops. There was only one jeepable road and troops had to march seven days just to reach their forward positions. Air supply repeatedly failed in the difficult terrain.

The coordinated actions of 114 Brigade and its relative freedom to operate without external interference showed just how a defensive battle could have been fought, even in the Eastern Sector. Yes – there were too many handicaps in the functioning of the army. The Forward Policy deployment spread out troops in remote, indefensible posts which dissipated the combat potential and left them open to destructions in detail. Confused, rapidly changing orders further disoriented the troops. Overall the operations ended in a crushing, unmitigated defeat. When the firing finally stopped on the night of 21 November, the army had lost 1423 killed, 3018 wounded and 1655 missing, most presumed dead in the scattered encounters that characterised the fighting. 3587 were taken prisoner, including Brigadier Dalvi, the Commander of 7 Infantry Brigade. If we look at the fact that only around 24,000 of all ranks were engaged in both sectors (NEFA & Ladakh) it works out to a casualty rate of almost 40 percent – a very, very high figure by any standard. In the wake of the cease-fire, the Chinese withdrew back to their original positions (except in Ladakh where they retained the territory that was captured) and with time the Indians reoccupied their lost areas. Yet the withdrawal was not an act of goodwill. It was a planned tactical move, since the Chinese had outrun their communications and it would have been impossible to hold the captured territory against the Indian counter-offensive, especially with winter approaching.

The Indian army came out bloodied, chastened and perhaps the wiser. The defeat brought about a radical change in its strategic thinking and once again the focus shifted to developing a modern, professional army. New equipment came in, formations and units were raised, training began in earnest and a spirit of professionalism, free of political interference began to permeate the army. It was a rude wake-up call, but a timely one and the army responded to it in style. Just three years down the line it faced another major challenge – this time on the Western borders and the army showed that the lessons of 1962 had been well imbibed. The mantra in the army, post-1962 was, "There is a blot on our faces which water can never wash. Only one thing can clear it – blood." Over the years, with its redeeming actions in 1965 and 1971, the blot has been erased, perhaps permanently. But hopefully the lessons of 1962 will remain, not only for the generation which witnessed it, but for the ones that followed and are entrusted with ensuring that it never repeats itself.

The Long Vigil of Rifleman Jawant Singh

Brave soldiers don't die. They just go into a long sleep. For the many Indian soldiers who fell in these hills, their sleep has been long and venerated. Across the stretch from Bum La to Bomdi La, small memorials dot the sides of the road in homage to those who made their last stand there.

Amongst the many small memorials, one stands just ahead of Se La, at Jaswantgarh, named after Rifleman Jaswant Singh who fell along with his comrades after fighting off four Chinese assaults. A small temple has been created at the spot and he is venerated there as a baba. His shrine is offered the soldiers tea every morning. All passers by make a small prayer before crossing the site. If a sentry dozes off at night, an unseen hand slaps him awake. Rifleman Jaswant Singh also goes on leave once a year. His photo is carried on the shrine, and taken to his village in Punjab. After two months his photo returns to his place of duty at the shrine.

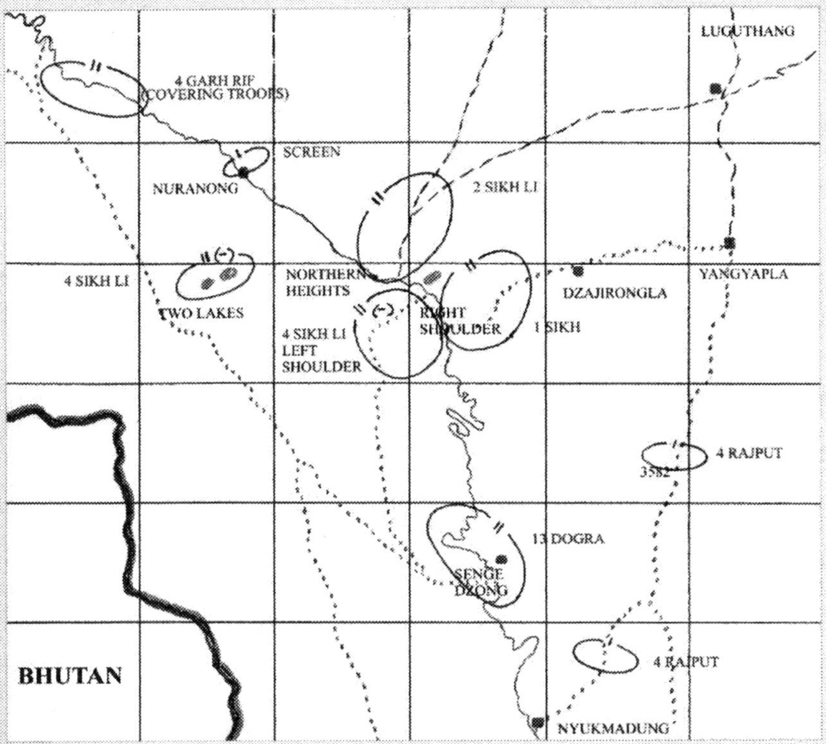

Plan for defense of Sa La

A present day view of Se La in winter

CONDUCT OF OPERATIONS : 1965 INDO-PAK WAR

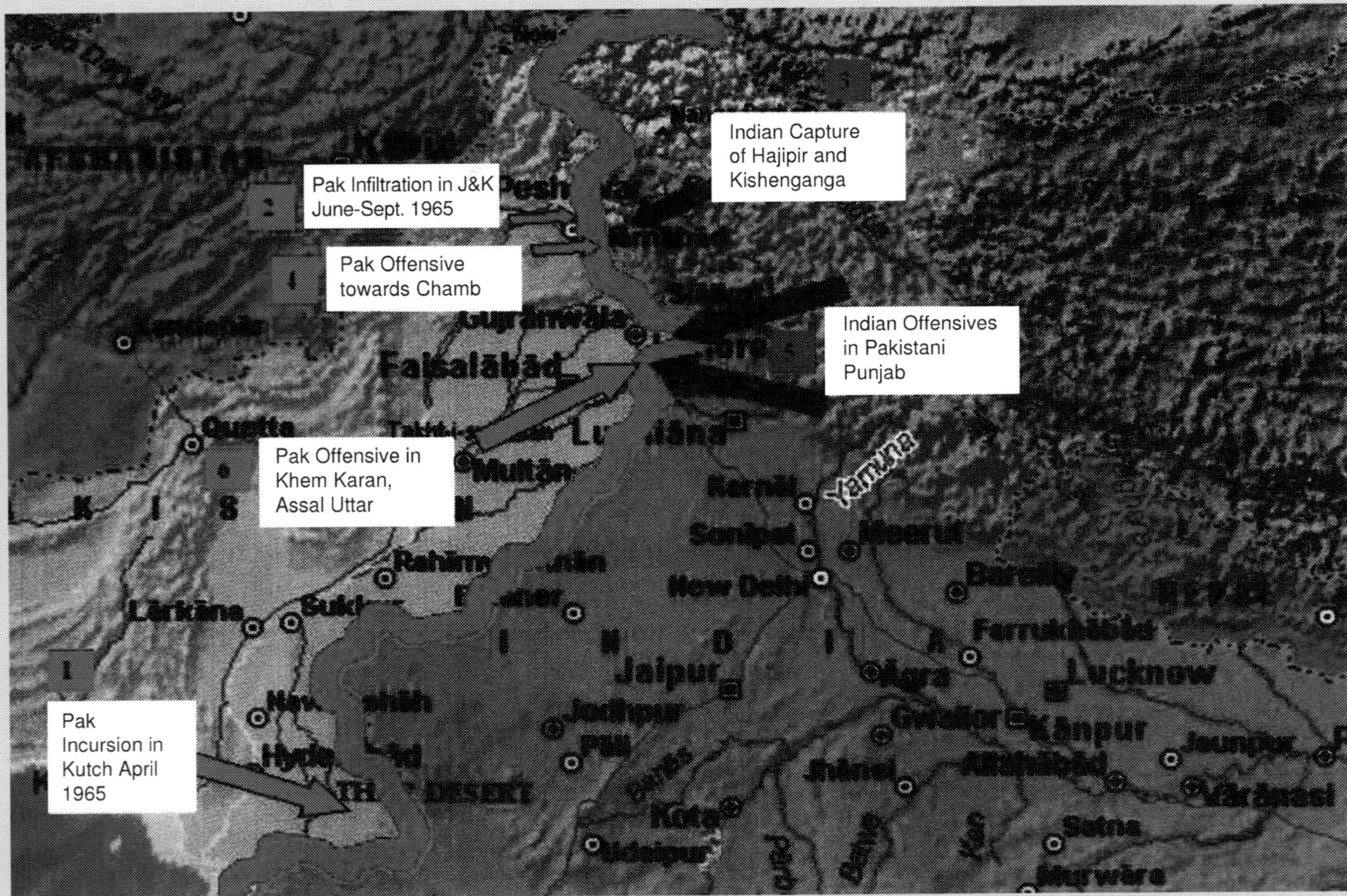

11

Redemption and More – The 1965 Indo-Pak War

"*Pakistan ahead – No Passport required – BASH ON REGARDLESS*" – Sign on the Punjab Border

❖ ❖ ❖

The years following the humbling experience of 1962 were years of difficult transition for the army. The humiliation of the war had pierced the psyche of the nation and wounded every man in uniform. Yet, it brought in its wake much needed lessons. The army slowly rebuilt itself, fresh formations were raised, new equipment came in and the lost ethos of professionalism slowly permeated within the ranks once again. But then it takes years, if not decades for an army to re-consolidate, especially after such a haunting defeat. The Indian army was not to be given that grace period. Barely three years after the 1962 debacle another equally grave crisis appeared, this time on its western borders. It was once again put through a test of fire, a test in which it eventually came out trumps and gained some measure of redemption in their own eyes and that of the nation.

The Indian army's defeat in 1962 was too good an opportunity for Pakistan to let pass. She was still smarting after the failure of its 1947-48 campaign and in her eyes Kashmir was an unfinished item on the agenda. Politically too, India had weakened considerably after the death of Nehru in 1964 – the great man never really recovered from the trauma of 1962. His successor, Lal Bahadur Shashtri, was a small, frail looking man who lacked Nehru's stature, but his diminutive frame concealed an iron core within. If India's military and political strength was at ebb, Pakistan's own stars seemed on the ascendant. She had joined the SEATO and CENTO pacts in the mid-fifties and in its wake came a flow of the latest US equipment; M-47 and 48 Patton tanks, F-6 Sabre jets, Sidewinder missiles, naval vessels and artillery. It had also made common cause with China and ceded 6500 square kilometers of area in the Hunza region of Kashmir – an illegal act since the area was legitimately part of Indian territory. Assured of Chinese support and flush with new equipment, the Pakistani army was convinced that it could get the better of a recuperating Indian Army and win over Kashmir by military force.

Politically, the army was the undisputed power in Pakistan. General (Later Field Marshal) Ayub Khan had staged a military coup in 1958 and the nation was under its first spell of military rule (a trend which would follow repeatedly in the coming decades). Ayub was from that generation of Pakistani officers who remembered how tantalizingly close they were to capturing Srinagar in 1947-48. With the reins of power in their hands, the army embarked on a similar plan to usurp Kashmir by force – this time by direct military intervention.

The plan was to be conducted in three distinct phases. In the first phase, they would engage the Indian army far away from the actual theatre of Jammu and Kashmir to divert troops. This would also give them an opportunity to test their new weapons and gauge the Indian response The next phase would be akin to the plan of 1947-48. A guerilla invasion was to be launched in the state to incite the population and provoke a revolt. In the third and final phase the army would launch an offensive in the garb of helping the people of Kashmir, to decide the issue militarily once and for all. Strategically it was a sound plan. But it under-estimated the capabilities of both the Indian military and its politicians. When the Indian response came, it was far stronger and more vehement than they expected. The plan unraveled and they were once again pushed on to the back foot.

Opening Forays in Kutch

The Pakistani Army chose the Rann of Kutch, a bleak salt–caked stretch of desert on the north western tip of Gujarat, for the opening forays of its campaign. Pakistan claimed around 9025 square kilometers of its area and in 1956 had tried to establish a post there. The Indian side was inadequately patrolled by police and paramilitary forces, a meager strength which could not effectively keep guard over such a vast area. In January 1965, Pakistan's Indus Rangers occupied Kanjarkot, a disused mud-fort two and a half kilometers inside Indian territory. India responded by establishing Central Reserve Police Force posts around it – an act which Pakistan claimed violated their own territory. On 9 April, came the first serious clash of arms as one of the newly established posts was attacked by troops of the regular Pakistan army complete with artillery support. The situation was now coming to passé and India responded by moving 31 Infantry Brigade and 50 Independent Para Brigade into the area. A new formation Kilo Sector was also established to look after the area. On 22 April, Pakistan attacked in force using their newly arrived M-48 tanks and M-113 Armored Personal Carriers which pushed the Indian defenders back from their newly established posts. The stage was now dangerously close

Indian troops in the Rajasthan Sector

to all-out war and fresh formations were moved from the Eastern Theatre against Pakistan. Prime Minister Shashtri publicly announced in the Lok Sabha "If Pakistan persists in its aggressive activities, our army will decide its own strategy and employment of its manpower and equipment in the manner it deems best". It was a clear indicator that India would expand the theatre of war and take it to another level. As tensions rose, so did the pressure from the world community to halt hostilities. Finally on 01 July, Commonwealth leaders brokered a cease fire and both sides returned to their original positions. Yet it was but a pause and the stage was being set for larger battles ahead.

Operation Gibraltar

Flush with the manner in which they achieved easy victories during the initial days of the Kutch operation, Pakistan was convinced that the time was ripe to start the main operation in Kashmir. Over the next three months or so, it began building up a force of 'mujahids' and razakars, basically irregular forces officered by Army Officers, who would infiltrate into the state, stir the local population and incite a revolt. The force was to capture the airfield and radio stations and destroy roads and bridges to isolate Kashmir valley from the rest of India. Military installations and bases were also to be attacked to tie down the army. In the aftermath, the regular army would attack. It was a plan that had been practiced in 1947 and fine-tuned to a great extent. However they forgot the major lessons of the campaign and this attempt would end even more disastrously.

In the months following the Kutch expedition, Pakistani infiltration had been steadily on the rise in Kashmir. Ten guerilla columns, named after famous Muslim conquerors, Babur, Ghaznavi, Ghori, Salauddin and so on infiltrated across the cease fire line from Kargil to Jammu. Their intrusions were actively supported by Pakistani artillery and in the initial days the infiltrators did cause great havoc and confusion. They closed in towards Jammu and

Prime Minister Shri Lal Bahadur Shashtri addresses troops in the Western Sector. His decisiveness was instrumental in the Indian Army's rapid response

Srinagar and in the Kargil Sector their actions threatened the critical Srinagar – Leh road. Yet while the infiltrators left a trail of raids, ambushes, destroyed culverts and bridges in their wake, they failed in their basic aim of inciting the local population. Most of the locals were not swayed by Pakistani propaganda, many still remembered the atrocities of 1947-48. In most cases the population was not only unresponsive but actively supported and helped the Indian army.

Yet the increased infiltration was a threat that could not be ignored and the Indian army decided to throttle the very routes of infiltration. In Kargil, Pakistani picquets overlooking the Leh-Srinagar road were captured. Further South, in Tithwal, Indian troops advanced all the way to Kishanganaga effectively blocking all ingress from the area. An even more ambitious plan was chalked out to capture the crucial Haji Pir Pass. This pass lay in the Haji Pir bulge created by the 1948 cease fire agreement which helped provide a direct approach to Srinagar. Most of the infiltration took place through this area and it was used to support and maintain the infiltrators. Its capture was vital if the infiltration was to be stopped, but Haji Pir would be a tough nut to crack. It was held in strength

The Indian tricolour atop Haji Pir after its capture by 1 PARA. Its capture was a feat of courage and endurance

by elements of the regular army and razakars, well supported by artillery. 68 Brigade with four battalions was tasked to capture the crucial pass. Its plan was to launch a two pronged attack to initially capture two vital features, Sank and Bedori which guarded the approach to the pass. Once these were captured, a fresh battalion would attack and capture Haji Pir Pass. The route was difficult, the enemy was well-prepared and the objective was one of the most strongly defended areas in the sector.

By 23 August, the brigade built up and also constructed a 1 Ton track and laid a 21 meter Bailey bridge to support its operation. All actions were done by night in atrocious weather conditions. Twice the attack was postponed because of the weather but on night 25 August, the attack on Sank and Bedori went in. After three bitter attacks, 1 PARA captured Sank, but on the other side Bedori still held on. As long as Bedori was held by the enemy, the rest of the brigade could not move ahead for the capture of Haji Pir and the operations seemed to have ground to a halt. At this juncture, 1 PARA volunteered to go ahead to capture Haji Pir even though by now the Pakistanis were alerted and fully prepared for an attack. It was a tight, calculated gamble, but the prize was well worth the risk. In torrential rain with a light mist enveloping the valley, one company under Major Ranjit Singh Dayal (later Lieutenant General Dayal, MVC) made a grueling approach march to the base of the pass and then made a circuitous climb along the difficult Western shoulder on to the flank of the defenses. With one platoon engaging the enemy, the balance of the company rolled down and charged the surprised defenders who fled in confusion. By mid-day the pass was captured. Bedori fell thereafter and the soon the outlying positions were captured as well. Haji Pir bulge was back in Indian hands.

The Indian successes at Haji Pir, Kishanganga and Ladakh surprised the Pakistani planners who saw their grandiose plans fast unraveling. They had not attained any of their aims in Kashmir and had lost critical areas on their side of the Line of Control in the bargain. On 01 September, General Ayub Khan made a radio broadcast to his people that it was Pakistan's bounden duty to help the "Kashmiri Freedom Fighters" and now decided to launch the third and final phase of their plan; an armed attack across the International Boundary directed towards Chhamb and Akhnur. This would cut off the valley and help decide the issue through sheer force of arms. It was a gamble and like many of their plans, hinged on too many intangibles for success. Ayub Khan, the consummate bridge player appropriately code-named it "Operation Grand Slam". This operation too was destined to be trumped.

The Trumped GRAND SLAM

The actions in Kutch and the infiltration of armed raiders in Kashmir were the opening gambit of Pakistan's grand design. The

Anti-aircraft gun in action at Chhamb

ace of spades was to come in final phase of the operation, the armed attack on Kashmir. At 0330 hours on 01 September 1965, Pakistan unleashed its final trump card as their artillery opened up across the ceasefire line opposite Chhamb and Akhnur. 12 Infantry Division along with two armored regiments from 6 Armored Division pushed through the Indian positions at Chhamb and headed for the vital Akhnur Bridge over the Chenab River which was the sole link from Jammu to the Kashmir valley. The sector that the Pakistanis chose for their attack was then held by 191 Infantry Brigade with four infantry battalions and a squadron of light tanks (AMX 13 from 20 LANCERS). In fact just two days prior to the offensive, a newly raised formation, 10 Division had been moved to Akhnur to look after the sector, but it had no staff or communications and the entire command and control system was in a flux. In this sector, the infiltrators had been active and there were signs of the impending offensive in the air. But when the assault came, it took the Indians by surprise. Pakistani tanks and infantry launched multi pronged thrusts which pushed the Indians back to the Munawar Tawi River. Inexplicably the Pakistanis chose this crucial juncture for a change in command and the General Officer Commanding 12 Division was replaced by General Yahya Khan, perhaps for political compulsions. This change in command provided a vital twenty four hour delay to their operations which allowed the Indians to consolidate in their new defensive positions around Akhnur.

By noon on 03 September, Pakistani troops recommenced their advance, crossed the Munawar Tawi River and headed towards Akhnur. By now additional troops had been moved up and a new defensive position was established at Akhnur with an intermediate position around ten kilometers ahead. For three days the Pakistanis launched repeated attacks to break through and though they succeeded in penetrating the intermediate positions their offensive was slowly reaching its culmination point and was effectively spent.

As these actions in Chhamb were underway, India was implementing its own plans for a counter-offensive. It had repeatedly warned Pakistan that an attack on Kashmir would be taken as an attack against India and retaliation would not be confined to Kashmir but at the place and time of its own choosing. Pakistan obviously chose to discount this as a mere threat. On 06 September, India launched her own counter stroke – the offensive in Punjab directed at Lahore. The Indian offensive forced Pakistan to hurriedly pull out a brigade and an armored regiment from its offensive to counter their advance in Punjab. Their offensive in Akhnur petered out as the action shifted southwards towards the Punjab sector.

THE MOMENT

The decisive moment of the war was the crossing of the Ichhogil Canal by Indian forces on 06 September. Pakistan had not anticipated a strong Indian offensive in Punjab. This actions posed a direct threat to Lahore and forced it to recoil from Kashmir.

The Indian Counter Offensive

The Indian Army had been given a carte blanche by Prime Minister Shashtri to attack at the time and place of their choosing in response to the Pakistani offensive. With this freedom of action, the army was not restricted to Kashmir and free to open up another front. General JN Chaudhuri, the Chief of Army Staff, had drawn out the offensive plans almost three months in advance and the plans had been war gamed in July to test their efficacy. The plan called for a two pronged offensive into Pakistani Punjab. 11 Corps,

Gen Choudhury, COAS on the Ichhogil Canal along with other senior officers.

then based in Punjab was to launch a thrust directed towards Lahore. The second thrust was to be executed by the newly raised 1 Corps, further north in Pakistan's Shakargarh Bulge towards Sialkot. The two thrusts would strike the very heartland of Pakistan and carry the war into its territory forcing it to halt actions in Kashmir.

On 6 September Indian forces crossed the International border. 11 Corps launched its offensive with three divisions towards Lahore, the largest town in Pakistani Punjab. The operations of all three divisions were based on securing a crossing on the Bambanwali – Ravi-Bedian Link Canal, popularly known as the Ichhogil Canal, a formidable irrigation canal ahead of Lahore. The canal had defense fortifications and many of the villages ahead of it had been developed as strong points which had to be cleared before any crossing could be attempted. As per 11 Corps plans 15 Division, the northern most division was to advance along the Grand Trunk road which passed from Delhi-Amritsar-Lahore and beyond and secure a crossing on the Ichhogil Canal. In the centre, 7 Infantry Division was to advance along the Khalra–Barki road to approach Lahore from the South East. To the extreme south, 4 Mountain Division moved along the Khem Karan–Kasur axis. The initial tasks of all three divisions were to secure the Eastern bank of the Ichhogil canal and then establish bridgeheads across it at selected places to threaten Lahore. To achieve surprise, all three divisions moved

The enemy destroyed many of the bridges on the Ichhogil canal to delay the Indian crossing

directly from their peace- time locations to their assembly areas near the border just a few hours before the attack. This naturally made coordination and the fine-tuning of the attack difficult and in many cases units and supporting elements could not marry up in time. Communications were not tied up and often failed at critical stages of the impending battle. The divisions held only two brigades each, which drastically limited their offensive potential. Yet, the armored component had been greatly reinforced by 2 Independent Armored Brigade, which was placed under command 11 Corps. Its Centurions and Shermans were to play a vital role in the coming battle.

The initial advance of all three divisions was rapid and most of the initial objectives were captured. The offensive achieved complete

Prime Minister Shri Lal Bahadur Shashtri congratulates Lt Col Hayde, CO 3 JAT on the Dograi crossing

surprise, but the Pakistanis were fast to react. After the cease fire in Kutch, Pakistan had not moved its field formations back to their peacetime locations and they remained in forward concentration areas close to the border. Within hours of the offensive, they regrouped and hit back. Their Air Force was particularly effective and appeared over the skies as early as 0700 hours on 06 September, repeatedly strafing the advancing columns. Their defensive formations launched vigorous counter attacks to reclaim lost territories. Their response to 15 Infantry Division moving along the Grand Trunk road axis was particularly violent. The Division had made a good initial progress and had succeeded in establishing a crossing on the Icchogil Canal by 3 JAT near Dograi and another one around nine kilometers up north at Bhaini Dhilwan. The crossing of the canal by 3 JAT provided a bridgehead which directly threatened Lahore and in fact Indian troops reached right up to Batanagar, a suburb of Lahore. But this singular success was not exploited and instead the valiant battalion was ordered to pull back and abandon its hard earned positions. The subsequent advance of 15 Division floundered in the face of repeated counter attacks. By 8 September, the enemy had reinforced this sector with additional armor and infantry and no further advance was possible. 15 Division

4 SIKH launches its assault for the capture of Barki

Pak troops surrender to the advancing Indians

pulled back, anticipating a threat to Amritsar and by around 10 September actions in this sector slowly died down.

7 Infantry Division moving to its South along the Khalra – Lahore axis made greater progress. This Division was to cross the Ichhogil Canal and threaten Lahore from the South Easterly direction. Its two brigades 65 and 48, were tasked to secure the canal crossing sites with 65 Brigade capturing Bedian and 48 Brigade capturing Barki. The border outposts were captured in a rapid pre-dawn operation and at first light on 06 September; the two brigades crossed the International Border. 48 brigade moved rapidly along the main Khalra-Lahore road, clearing the initial opposition en route, till it reached the Hudiara Drain, a wide, formidable obstacle around three kilometers short of the Icchogil canal. Here the enemy was well entrenched and as the leading troops approached, opened up with a torrent of machine gun fire. Further move was impossible in the face of the withering fire. As the leading troops went to ground and engaged the enemy, one battalion was sent on a wide outflanking move to cross the Drain from the North and then attack the enemy from the rear. It took the better part of the day to clear the position but by nightfall Hudiara Drain was in their hands. The enemy demolished the bridge before withdrawing but by midday on 07 September a Bailey bridge was in place and the advance resumed towards Barki.

By 9 September, 48 brigade had consolidated itself around the outskirts of Barki and captured the outlying defenses. On the night of 10/11 September, 4 SIKH along with a Squadron of Central India Horse launched a determined attack on the town, capturing it bunker by bunker, pillbox by pillbox. Barki was a major success as from here Lahore cantonment and the city airport were within field artillery range. With Barki secured, the brigade advanced towards the Ichhogil canal and contacted it by midnight. Yet the enemy managed to destroy the bridge across the canal and prevent a crossing. By now, 7 Infantry Division was in a position to cross the canal and threaten Lahore from the South East. Yet its success could not be exploited as a critical situation developed further south with 4 Mountain Division.

4 Mountain Division, the Southern most division of 11 Corps had been tasked to advance South of Bedian, cross the Ichhogil Canal in its sector and then secure areas right up to the Sutluj River to deny the enemy a launch pad for an offensive. It was an ambitious task and the division was not equipped for its role. It had been badly mauled in the 1962 war and had only recently been reformed and reorganized. It was designed primarily for mountain warfare. The men were not trained for fighting in plains and the formation was weak in anti-tank weapons. Unknown to it, its advance would bring

Jubilant Indians atop a destroyed Pakistani Tank

it in the path of Pakistan's 1 Armored Division and 11 Infantry Division, lying concealed in the area of Kasur, poised to launch an offensive in to Indian territory. The clash of 4 Division with the two formidable formations would see it advance, withdraw and then repulse an enemy offensive in one of the most fiercely contested actions of the war.

4 Division left their lines in Shimla Hills at 0200 hours on 5 September and moving without a pause reached their assembly areas around 10 P.M. Yet by 5.30 the next morning, its leading elements crossed the International Border and by 11 am had captured its initial objective, a crossing on the Rohi Nala on the Khem-Karan – Kasur road. It was then to secure the eastern bank of the Ichhogil canal, and capture Ballanwala, a large village guarding the approach to the canal. The village was strongly held by the enemy with armor and infantry but the enemy skillfully concealed his deployment with tight fire discipline. The first Indian attack reached almost 50 meters of its objective before the enemy opened up and repulsed it with heavy fire. The divisional artillery could not support the attack due to a failure of the radio sets and the attack gradually petered out. Another attack by night proved equally abortive and it soon became apparent that enemy opposition in the area was much stronger than was initially presumed. The exact nature of his strength only came to light when the enemy counter attacked on night 7/8 September, using elements of 1 Armored Division and 11 Infantry Division which lurked in the area in preparation for their own counter offensive into Indian territory. At around 0200 hours their attack came in, driving back the Indian troops with heavy casualties and considerable confusion. Many of the battalions withdrew in the face of the onslaught. Seeing that it was impossible to hold on, the Division Commander, Major General Gurbaksh Singh decided to withdraw back to the Indian side of the border and occupy a defensive position in the vicinity of Asal Uttar, a large village on the road leading to Amritsar. The withdrawal was well coordinated and covered by the fire of the entire divisional artillery which continually pounded the positions in the path of the Pakistani advance. Almost 40,000 rounds were fired that night- the

road and rail bridges on the canals were specially targeted and one of the rounds damaged the crucial bridge on the Ichhogil Canal. This chance round halted the further move of armor till it was repaired and the crucial twenty four hour delay gave the Indians time to move back and consolidate in their new defensive positions around Asal Uttar. When the Pakistani advance resumed most of the troops were in their positions. As the roar of tank engines broke the night around the sleepy village of Asal Uttar, this little hamlet with its meandering water distributaries and high sugar-cane fields was to witness the most titanic clash of arms seen on Indian soil.

The Graveyard of Pattons

Pakistan's plan for its offensive in Punjab was, as always, ambitious in scope and scale. It was launched with 1 Armored Division under Major General Nasir Ahmed Khan and 11 Infantry Division under Major General Abdul Hamid; a strong force, well equipped with five regiments of brand-new Patton tanks and one of M-24 Chaffee. As per the initial plan, they were to move into Indian Punjab and capture Khem Karan in the initial phase. Then one of the prongs was to move southwards to capture the rail-road bridge on the Sutlej River at Harike and cut off Punjab from the south. A stronger prong was to advance northwards to capture first capture Jandiala Guru, a small town 19 Kilometers east of Amritsar and then capture the bridge on the Beas River – thus cutting off virtually all of Punjab. The entire action was to be completed within three days. If it was successful it would have isolated 11 Corps and most of Punjab. The offensive was preceded by a drop of a Company of paratroopers near the forward Indian airbases of Pathankot, Adhampur and Halwara to cause sabotage and destruction behind enemy lines. This force was dropped as scheduled on the moonlit night of 07 September, but they landed too far from the target areas, got dispersed and after the initial confusion they created were soon rendered ineffective. Most of the force was rounded up and captured, in many cases by angry villagers who chased them from their fields.

The Pakistani offensive would have been greatly affected by the Indian attack. The advance of 4 Mountain Division led it straight towards Kasur, the area chosen for the Pakistani concentration areas. To give them credit, they not only managed to halt the advance of 4 Mountain Division directed at its launch pads, but also managed to push the formation back to its start point and consolidated in time to launch their own counter offensive. On the other side, 4 Division, though initially surprised by the presence of a large offensive force in its path, managed to withdraw in good order and establish a well laid out defensive position in the area of Asal Uttar which blunted the enemy offensive. In these see-saw actions of offensive-counter offensive one of the most critical factors was the delay of 24 hours caused by the damage to the bridge on the Ichhogil canal. While Indian accounts state that it was caused by artillery fire, the Pakistanis maintain that it was result of a tank which crossed it incorrectly and damaged the bridge. Whatever be the cause, after one third of their armor had got across, the balance had to wait for almost a day till a new bridge was erected. This allowed the Indian to consolidate in their new positions and also breach their distributaries and flood the areas in the path of the enemy advance.

On 08 September, the leading elements of Pakistan's 1 Armored Division crossed the International Border at day break. Their armor moved on a broad front along the main Khem-Karan – Amritsar road. Khem Karan fell in the first onslaught and its capture provided a major propaganda victory. Pakistani papers carried glowing accounts and photographs of their troops at Khem Karan railway station, but this was to remain the limit of their achievements. By now 2 Independent Armored Brigade with two Sherman and one Centurion Regiment (3 CAVALRY) had moved in to the sector and the infusion of fresh armor, especially the modern Centurions, proved vital to contest the enemy's armor superiority. The Indian tanks, often out-gunned and out-armored by the heavy Pattons were skillfully concealed in the tall sugarcane fields and opened up only when the enemy was at close range. Superior gunnery and the use of skillful tank tactics helped negate the advantage of range that the more sophisticated Pattons possessed.

For the next three days, from 8-11 September, the enemy tried to break through the main defenses of 4 Division without success. In the face of furious armor and infantry assaults, the units of 4 Division held their positions, often fighting back armored assaults with their anti-tank weapons. In a grim contest at Bhikhiwind, Havidar Major Abdul Hamid of 4 Grenadiers engaged four Patton tanks with a recoilless anti-tank gun, destroying three before being killed by a round from the fourth tank. Hamid's valor, won him a posthumous Param Vir Chakra. His memorial stands on the Bhikhiwind-Amrisar road at the spot where he fell, like many other small memorials that commemorate individual acts of courage.

While the enemy armor was being held, Indian armor deployed in a sickle shaped formation around their axis of advance. The area had been heavily flooded and the fields were boggy and impassable. Attempts to outflank the Indian positions failed and at around 1530 hours the enemy made one last desperate attempt to breakthrough with two Patton regiments. As enemy tanks advanced, they came into the range of Indian Centurions of 3 CAVALRY concealed in the tall sugarcane fields. Heavy tank fire reinforced with the murderous fire of the divisional artillery trapped the enemy in a deadly killing ground, whose boggy fields provided no scope for maneuver. The GOC of 1 Armored Division moved forward to push the armor onwards, but his party was spotted and engaged with heavy artillery fire. The fire wounded the divisional commander, killed the artillery brigade commander and decimated most of the group. The remnants surrendered along with a prize cache of documents which revealed the complete details of the ambitious plan.

CHM Abdul Hamid, PVC
4 GRENADIERS

By around 11 September, the offensive had spent itself. No further attempts were made to breakthrough towards Amritsar. The ferocity of their initial assaults died down, with many tank crews simply abandoning their brand new tanks when engaged. Across the area, the damaged and smoldering remnants of burning enemy tanks littered the fields; many more simply stood undamaged and abandoned. A later count revealed that 97 Pakistani tank were destroyed or captured, including 72 of their prized Pattons. 32 abandoned Pattons were captured in mint-condition, some showing just 200-300 kilometers on their odometers. The tanks are visible even today, standing on crossroads and monuments to commemorate this epic clash of arms.

With the offensive having ground to a halt, Khem Karan remained the only objective attained by the enemy. The recapture of Khem Karan now became a matter of prestige. Additional troops were called into the sector, including 2 MAHAR and 4 SIKH. 4 SIKH was the Army Commander's own unit and he was keen that it be given the honor of recapturing Khem Karan. The valiant unit had battled long and hard at Barki and was actually quite exhausted and had suffered casualties to men and equipment. The date of the attack was scheduled on 12 September (also the day when 4 SIKH celebrated their Battle Honor Day of Saragarhi). After a long

Indian officers inspect damaged Pakistani Pattons

approach march, the Regiment blundered into an enemy tank harbor around midnight and most were killed or taken prisoner. Two attacks were launched on Khem Karan between 12 and 14 September but the enemy held on and repulsed all attacks with well coordinated fire. A final divisional attack was launched on night 21 September, which again proved inconclusive. The enemy held on and at the time of the cease fire on 23 September, Khem Karan remained the only achievement of his ambitious offensive.

The Offensive in Sialkot Sect

In conjunction with the 11 Corps offensive, the newly raised 1 Corps launched a simultaneous offensive from Jammu towards Sialkot. 1 Corps had been raised only a few months earlier in April 1965, and had been unable to fine-tune its coordination within its units and formations, aspects which takes months to develop. It had 1 Armored Division, 6 Mountain Division, 14 Infantry Division and 26 Infantry Division on its Order of Battle, a large enough force but with many shortcomings. For one, its armored division held only one armored brigade and one motorized Brigade and had inadequate artillery and air defense resources. The infantry too suffered from similar drawbacks. 6 Mountain Division was not trained or equipped for fighting in the plains and 14 Infantry Division like the Corps Headquarters had only been raised in April. The units and formations had not trained together and the finer drills and coordination which make all the difference in battle were just not tied up.

1 Corps debouched from its concentration areas in the areas of Jammu and Samba at first light on 06 September, at the same time that 11 Corps was crossing the International Border towards Lahore. It planned to advance towards Phillora – Chawinda and Pagowal, and then move further westward to cut the Sialkot–Lahore road. The two infantry divisions, 6 and 26 Divisions were to secure the flanks of the advance by initially capturing Maharajke, Charwa and Bajragarhi. 1 Armored Division was then to advance and capture Phillora and Pagowal by last light 08 September. After that they

were to capture Chawinda, a major road-rail junction whose fall would help isolate the sector.

The initial advance commenced as per schedule and by night 07 September, 6 and 26 Divisions succeeded in capturing their objectives. 1 Armored Division also moved as per plan in a two pronged advance with 1 Armored Brigade on the right and 43 Lorried Brigade on the left. The advance was lightly contested, but the move was too cautious and slow. In fact both brigades followed the out-dated concept of moving into harbor at night, a practice which reduced the advance into a crawl. Nonetheless by 10 September, 1 Armored Brigade was at the outskirts of Phillora and had captured the outlying localities. Phillora was well defended with two regiments of enemy armor prowling the vicinity and they fought a skilful covering battle to delay the approaching Indians. On 11 September, the opposing armored units clashed in what has been described as the biggest tank battle in the sub- continent. Two units, 17 POONA HORSE and 4 HORSE (HODSUNS) outmaneuvered the enemy and advanced towards Phillora from a difficult, unexpected direction drawing out the enemy armour. As Indian and Pakistani tanks engaged in a grim battle, the infantry moved forward under

Indian troops at Phillora – the town was captured after bitter fighting

a barrage of artillery fire and launched a determined assault on the town. In spite of heavy casualties they succeeded in wresting Phillora by 3.30 P.M. on 10 September. Phillora was repeatedly counter attacked and subjected to intense air and artillery fire, but the Indian troops held on. In the confused fighting, with positions and localities changing hands, a Pakistani helicopter was seen hovering south of the town and was shot down by tank fire as it attempted to land. It was later revealed that the GOC of Pakistan's 15 Division was killed in the engagement. Pagowal fell thereafter and in spite of repeated enemy counter attacks the Indians held on to their hard won prize. The action now shifted for the capture of Chawinda, five kilometers south of Phillora.

The delay in the capture of Phillora gave the Pakistanis time to reinforce Chawinda and additional infantry and two armored regiments had been inducted in to the area. On 14 September the first Indian attack went in, which succeeded in capturing Jassoran and Butur Dograndi on the outskirts of the town. The locations were counter attacks and lost, recaptured again, counter attacked once more as localities changed hands with bewildering frequency. The enemy's propensity to launch immediate and determined counter attacks on any lost locality was clearly visible and acts of great valor took place on both sides. In the face of fierce enemy opposition the attack on Chawinda was repeatedly postponed, as 1 Corps struggled to fight back the intensive counter attacks on its captured localities. With each delay in the operation Chawinda became stronger and was now virtually a fortress. A night attack was launched around midnight 18 September but it petered out in the face of intensive enemy fire. Eventually the attack on Chawinda was called off and the Indians consolidated the area they had captured. Till the last day of the war, Pakistani counter attacks and continual air and artillery fire came down on the captured positions, which held on grimly. When

Lt Col AB Tarapore, PVC
17 HORSE

Senior Officers inspect a damaged Pakistani Patton Tank

the cease fire came into effect, 1 Corps still held 490 square kilometers of prime territory. It had destroyed over 130 enemy tanks, and killed over 700 and captured 138 prisoners. Their own casualties were high. 29 tanks destroyed and 41 damaged. Personnel casualties were even higher with almost 600 killed and over 1600 wounded or missing. What was significant was the high number of officer casualties. 38 officers were killed in these actions, including two Commanding Officers. And while roll of honor is long and the acts of gallantry almost too numerous to recount, one name requires mention – Lieutenant Colonel A B Tarapore, the Commanding Officer of 17 HORSE, who though wounded, led his regiment in repeated assaults. Under his leadership, his regiment claimed 60 enemy tanks for the loss of 9 of their own. He was killed leading one final assault and his courage and leadership was recognized with the posthumous award of a Param Vir Chakra- the first earned by the Indian Armored Corps.

On 20 September the UN Security Council passed a resolution for a ceasefire from 12.30 P.M. on 22 September. The cease fire actually came into being on 23 September 1965, but the guns

The Graveyard of Pattons at Asal Uttar

continued their sporadic clatter. Over 566 violations by Pakistan were reported even after the ceasefire. Losses were high on both sides. 2902 Indian soldiers fell in the field of battle, with 359 missing believed killed. Of this a very high proportion were officers, 177 officers, including 10 commanding officers were killed, revealing a very high caliber of leadership which perhaps made all the difference. 8444 were wounded and over 200 tanks were destroyed

THE MAN

One of the most decisive figures of the war was Prime Minister Lal Bahadur Shashtri. His diminutive frame concealed an iron nerve.

His rapid decision to permit the Indian Army to open another front in Punjab in response to the Pakistan's offensive in Kashmir and the Indian army's action thereafter changed the complexion of the war and forced the Pakistani Armed Forces on the back foot.

General Ayub Khan had the dubious distinction of staging the first military coup in Pakistan. He was over confident of his army and seriously under estimated the Indian army (still recovering after the 1962 Indo-Chinese War) and the political leadership (weakened after the death of Nehru). He had evolved a tactically sound plan but did not cater for the strong Indian response.

in the war. Pakistan's human losses would have been around the same, but its equipment losses were heavier, especially the tank losses that it incurred in the battles of Asal Uttar and Phillora. In terms of territory, the Indian army secured 1528 kilometers of prime land in Pakistan – largely in Punjab while Pakistan claimed 544 square kilometers in the Khem Karan and Chhamb sectors. It was a hard fought, bitter contest and to some extent, was inconclusive as neither side could fully achieve their operational goals. In the Tashkent Agreement signed after the war between Prime Minister Shashtri and President Ayub Khan, both sides agreed to return to their original positions. This act conceded all the captured territories back to Pakistan – including the crucial Haji Pir Pass. When the guns finally fell silent, perhaps there was little to show for the three week long battle that had cost so much in both men and equipment.

Yet the achievements of the war were measured not in terms of territory captured or the casualties incurred. Its effect was more –

much more. Yes, there was lack of cohesion and coordination in the initial stages, there were problems of artillery, air support was often found wanting and our intelligence was faulty, often guess work. But overall, the army acquitted itself well. It blunted the enemy designs in Kashmir and captured vital territory, especially in Haji Pir and Kishenganga that turned the tables. The tenaciously fought defensive battle in the fields of Asal Uttar and Khem Karan, virtually wiped out Pakistan's armored division and put paid to their entire offensive capability. In the Sialkot sector, even though the eventual objectives were not realized, impressive gains were made by the 1 Corps offensive. But the impact was more than that. The impact came in the new pride and fresh confidence that the army now developed. The stigma of the 1962 war was being slowly erased and the blot on their faces was in the process of being completely washed away – with blood and tears. Its fresh confidence and rejuvenated outlook would be further revealed six years down the line when the army embarked on the even more decisive, geography altering actions of the 1971 war.

THE TACTICS AND EQUIPMENT

Pakistan resorted to the fairly sound tactics of first provoking actions in Kutch to test their new equipment and gauge the Indian response. This was followed by armed incursions in Kashmir followed by a conventional military attack directed at Chhamb and Akhnur.

The Indian tactics hinged on throttling infiltration (by capture of Haji Pir and Kishenganga) and then holding the Pakistani offensive in Kashmir. When pressure mounted they wisely shifted the action towards Punjab.

Both sides were evenly matched though Pakistan held a definite edge in equipment. Their tanks and aircraft especially F-6 Sabres and M-48 Patton tanks were superior to their counterparts although their handling of sophisticated equipment was poor. Superior armour tactics helped decide the issue in Punjab.

12

The Birth of a Nation – 1971 Indo-Pak War

"It took only twelve days for the Indian Army to smash its way to Dacca, an achievement reminiscent of the German offensive across France in 1940. The strategy was the same-'Speed, Ferocity, Flexibility' "
– *The Sunday Times*, London.

❖ ❖ ❖

It is rare, if ever that an army is called to fight three major wars in the span of less than a decade. Yet in the tumulus era of 1962-71, the Indian Army was called to fight in three different arenas, in vastly different types of terrain and in completely different situations. In 1962 an unprepared army took on a much superior adversary in the freezing heights of NEFA and Ladakh and suffered a shattering defeat. In 1965 the same recovering army fought the over confident Pakistanis to a standstill and then took the war into their territory. The 1971 war was different. This time the army was extremely well-prepared and given clear-cut directions under a magnificently dynamic leadership which gave it an opportunity to fight on its own terms and at the time and place of its choosing. The amazing results demonstrated just what the army could achieve in the right conditions and gave India its most decisive victory since independence.

To understand the backdrop of the 1971 Indo-Pak war, we must first understand the circumstances that led to the war. It all began with the turbulent political climate of Pakistan and the upheaval taking place in East Pakistan. In 1969, General Yahya Khan had taken over as President of Pakistan after yet another spell of military rule. He had announced the National Assembly Elections in 1970, but the results took the nation by surprise. The East Pakistani Party, the Awami League under Sheikh Mujibur Rehman won an outright majority, securing almost twice the number the number of seats as its nearest rival, the Pakistan People's Party of Zulfiqar Ali Bhutto. This implied that a East Pakistani Party would now come to power and Mujibur Rehman would be President of both wings of Pakistan.

Pakistan's birth, mid-wifed by the ruthless strokes of Sir Cyril Radcliff's pen, had led to the creation of two wings – East and West Pakistan – separated by over 1600 kilometers. Both wings had entirely different cultures, different languages and little in common, except religion. West Pakistani often referred to their Eastern counterparts as "small, dark-skinned rice-eaters" and they were considered inferior to the Punjabi stock that comprised the main gentry of Pakistan. The resentment between the two wings was simmering beneath the surface for many years now. The jute, rice and textile exports of the East was pumped into the Pakistani economy, but very little was invested back in return. Rather, East Pakistan was systematically exploited and ignored. Perhaps the final denouement came with the killer cyclone that struck East Pakistan in March 1970, which brought in its wake unprecedented devastation and claimed over one and a half million lives. This

Shiekh Mujibur Rehman addressing a rally at Dacca

national calamity was virtually ignored by West Pakistan and this brought to the fore the underlying differences between the two geographical wings of the entity called Pakistan. Now in 1970, the years of exploitation seemed to be coming to an end as Sheikh Mujibur was all set to take over as President of Pakistan in the wake of his resounding electoral victory.

Yet in the West, they had little intentions of letting power slip out of the hands. On 21 February, Yahya Khan, instigated by Zulfiqar Ali Bhutto, imposed martial law and dissolved the cabinet, preventing Mujibur Rehman from forming the government. It was a travesty of democracy and a deliberate move to deny political power to an East Pakistani party. Mobs hit the street of East Pakistan and political protests erupted. As violence intensified, the Pakistani army was called to maintain peace and order, and additional troops were airlifted from the West. Gen Tikka Khan – "The Butcher of Baluchistan" was appointed as Governor and Martial Law Administrator of East Pakistan, with the mandate to suppress the revolt at any cost. His tactics were predictably blunt and ruthless. The army was let loose and a brutal orgy of violence followed. Bengali intellectuals and students were rounded up and killed, women were raped, houses razed and Mujibur himself arrested. By mid April, Tikka Khan managed to attain some measure of stability and bring the situation under control. "Thank God!! Pakistan has been saved," exclaimed Bhutto when he heard the news. He was wrong. Pakistan was not saved; on the contrary it was merely the beginning of the end.

The violent army action had three important fall-outs. Firstly, it was felt that the Bengali officers and men were not loyal and many of them were disarmed, jailed and shot. This turned the East Pakistan Rifles and members of the Para military forces against them and they revolted to form the freedom force that later became the Mukti Bahini. The second was that it let loose a flood of terrified, starving refugees into adjoining India – a flood that reached almost 10 million by April. The massive influx of humanity caused logistical

Pakistani Army atrocities in East Pakistan

nightmares and a demographic upheaval of dangerous proportions in Bengal. The influx of refugees affected India directly and gave her a major stake in the speedy resolution of the problem. Lastly and most importantly – the atrocities of the army transformed the political protests of the Bengalis into a movement for Independence. Mujib himself declared the independence of Bangla Desh just before his arrest and the call spread. The movement for independence would gather rapid momentum in the coming months.

India's Response

In end April, the Indian Cabinet met to discuss the East Pakistan issue; a crucial meeting attended by General Manekshaw, the dynamic Chief of the Indian Army and perhaps the greatest hero it has produced post-independence. Here he was bluntly told "Go into East Pakistan" even though it would lead to war. At that juncture, the army was not ready. Its equipment required extensive refitting and refurbishing; its formations had to be reorganized for the new operation and at this time of the year the Himalayan passes were open and the Chinese threat would make it impossible to move troops from that sector. It took a man of great moral courage to stand up to the iron determination of Prime Minister Mrs Indira Gandhi and Sam was the man for the moment. He refused to be rushed into the war and bluntly stated "I guarantee you hundred percent defeat if we go in now".

The blunt statement had its impact and Manekshaw had his way. The operation was postponed till winter when the Himalayan passes would be snowed in and the Chinese threat would recede. By then the troops would be ready and the Mukti Bahini would be built up sufficiently to play a more vital role in the operations. In December too, the notoriously marshy land of East Pakistan would be hard and permit easier movement – during the monsoons the army would have been road bound and easily blocked. The timing of the operation was perfect and made all the difference to victory or defeat.

From April to November both sides built up for the war which now seemed inevitable. In the East, border clashes became more frequent, often accompanied by mortar and artillery exchanges.

Gen Manekhaw with Field Commanders. His inspiring leadership was instrumental in India's decisive victory

A Field Gun is pushed into position.

Pakistani troops attacked Indian positions in the areas around Boyra within which Mukti Bahini positions had been established – a major incident that involved the use of artillery and tanks on both sides. Thirteen Pakistani Chafee tanks were destroyed in this action. In the air, three F-86 Sabres, which had intruded into Indian airspace, were shot down. As a result of this Indian troops were now given permission to cross the border in self-defense and attack in case of aggression by Pakistani posts against Indian Territory. In the West too, border incidents were on the rise with artillery duels and exchanges of fire taking place regularly across the International Border and Line of Control. The Pakistani press followed up the jingoistic propaganda often accompanied by statements by General Yahya Khan saying "In ten days I will not be here (in Islamabad), I will be off fighting a war". The Pakistani strategy was to provoke a series of clashes and then launch an attack in the West (where they were stronger) and thus reduce the threat to the East. It was confident that if her troops made gains in the Western sector and the troops held on in the East, it would give them time to enable China and USA to come to its aid. Then with captured territory under its belt, it would be able to negotiate from a position of advantage. On the other hand, the Indian strategy hinged around fighting a holding action in the West, while launching a rapid all-out offensive in the East, which would allow them to proclaim Bangla Desh. It was a delicate game of nerves as both sides built up to launch their own offensives while containing the other. Pakistan hoped to attack by October, when the Chinese passes would still be open – but it waited too long to build up its own offensive and defensive capability. When it finally struck on 3 December 1971 – it was a little too late. By then the Indians had not only developed their offensive capabilities in the East, but were well poised to blunt any offensive in the West. Better still, the Himalayan passes were closed and two much needed divisions opposite the Chinese could now be utilized.

THE MAN

Two great personalities stand out in this war. Mrs Indira Gandhi and General Sam Maneckshaw. They provided a political and military leadership of the highest standards and attained a synergy rarely seen. Both were strong, dominant personalities and their actions complemented each other to help attain India's greatest victory since Independence.

General A K Niazi, the Pakistani Commander in the Eastern Theatre made the mistake of dispersing his troops in fortresses based on towns on the approaches to Dacca. He did not plan for the contingency of being by passed. Adequate thought was not given to the defence of Dacca. His actions were not coordinated with the activities on the Western front. He was not even informed of Pakistan's pre-emptive strike on 3 December that initiated the war.

On 3 December 1971 at 5.45 P.M. Pakistan launched a series of pre-emptive air strikes at Indian airfields of Srinagar, Avantipur, Pathankot, Utharlai, Jodhpur and Ambala, an action akin to the Israeli strikes on Arab airfields that crippled the Egyptian Air Force in 1967. The actions were similar, but the results were vastly different. Not enough sorties were launched, too many targets were selected and as a result none could be effectively engaged. Also by this stage they had lost the element of surprise. The Indian aircraft were well-dispersed and parked in protected hangers. Damage was minimal and not a single aircraft was lost on ground.

Gen AK Niazi – Commander-in-Chief Pakistan Eastern Command

Indian response was rapid. That same night, the Indian Air Force swung into action and launched a series of strikes on air bases, railway yards and radar installations within Pakistan. In the wake of the air strikes, Pakistan launched her land offensive in the Chhamb and Poonch sectors at 8.30 P.M. on 3 December. That same night, General JS Aurora, General Officer Commanding Eastern Command, received the go-ahead for the offensive into East Pakistan. The third Indo-Pak war had begun.

Operations in the Eastern Sector

By daybreak, 4 December, the campaign in the Eastern Theatre was underway. It had been meticulously prepared and coordinated, but the scale of its success surprised even its planners. A country larger than Greece was overrun and captured; 93,000 prisoners were taken and a new nation was created – all within 12 decisive days.

It was not that the Pakistani army was weak or ill-equipped. Their forces in the East under General AK Niazi comprised of around four and a half divisions, 25,000 Para Military Forces, five squadrons of Chaffee tanks and adequate artillery and engineer support. A squadron of around twenty F-86 fighters was deployed at Dacca airfield. The Navy did not have any major vessels based in East Pakistan but had a large number of gunboats and merchant vessels. Opposing them, the Indian army held seven divisions, including two recently pulled out from the Indo-China Border. It had three armored regiments, two independent reconnaissance squadrons and a mechanized infantry battalion – overall a 7:4 superiority in land forces, not enough for a offensive operation of this nature. What tilted the scales were the air and naval assets, the help extended by the Mukti Bahini and the support of the local population which proved invaluable in this new, unfamiliar terrain.

On 4 December the Indian Air Force launched a series of sorties against the airfields near Dacca, an effective strike which destroyed most of the aircraft on the ground. The remnants were effectively grounded as the runways were damaged and rendered unfit for subsequent use. By 6 December, the IAF had attained complete control of the skies over East Pakistan. The army was free to move without fear of enemy air attacks.

The navy pitched in by establishing a complete naval blockade of East Pakistan. Eastern Naval Command had a strong flotilla in the Bay of Bengal, including the aircraft carrier "Vikrant", the

The Indian Navy played a stellar role in the blockade of East Pakistan

frigates "Brahmaputra" and "Beas"; two Petya class Missile boats, one submarine and some light vessels. The Indian dominance of the seas was established on the first day itself, when the Pakistani submarine "PNS Ghazi" was sunk off the coast of Vishakapatnam. It was never really clear whether the submarine was sunk by depth charges, blundered into a mine or was destroyed by an accident, but the major loss subsequently confined the Pakistani navy to a purely defensive role. By 5 December a complete naval blockade of East Pakistan was tightly established. Three major Pakistani naval ships; 'Jessore", "Comilla" and "Sylhet" were sunk and 17 merchant vessels captured or destroyed in the ensuing naval operations in the Bay of Bengal. The close knit coordination between the Army, Navy and Air Force was a major factor in the success of this operation.

On land, the geography of East Pakistan did not suit the attacker. The ground was marshy and wet and almost one fourth of the area was covered by lakes, rivers and streams. Three major rivers flowed through the country; the Ganga (called Padma locally), the Brahmaputra (or the Jamuna) and the Meghna. The rivers flowed from North to South and formed a network of deltas and tributaries, which increased to the South of the country. Across the rivers, only two major bridges existed; the Hardinge Bridge across the Ganga and the Ashuganj Bridge across the Meghna. The low-lying countryside with its network of streams, rivers and tributaries made it an attacker's nightmare. It would require tons of bridging equipment to cross the many obstacles en route. Eventually the Indian army laid over 10,000 feet of bridging material on its advance to Dacca.

Even though geography favored the defender, defending such a vast area was never going to be easy. General Niazi had to hold ground as far forward as possible, to prevent India from capturing a vast tract of territory and declaring an independent Bangladesh. While it would not be possible to hold each inch of land, he decided to hold important towns and communication centers as 'fortresses'. These fortresses were well stocked with supplies and ammunition, with instructions to hold on and not withdraw till they had suffered over 75 percent casualties. The towns of Jessore, Jhenida, Bogra, Rangpur, Jamalpur, Mymensingh, Sylhet, Bhairab Bazar, Comilla and Chittagong were developed as fortresses with other smaller towns developed as strong points to provide depth. However with the paucity of troops to hold the vast area, there were no reserves. No thought was given to the defense of Dacca. Dacca lay at the apex of the Meghna and the Brahmaputra (Jamuna) rivers, but the rivers were unguarded and there were virtually no troops in Dacca for its defense. He expected his fortresses to hold on long enough for China and USA to force a halt to the war and his fortress concept was actually the best option he had in these circumstances. Yet the many weaknesses of this strategy would unravel in the face of the rapid Indian advance which bypassed most of the major fortresses and headed straight towards Dacca itself.

The Indians on the other had realized that the key to the liberation of Bangladesh was to advance fast enough to capture enough territory to announce the liberation of Bangladesh. In the initial stages, no plans were made for the capture of Dacca. The advance was only planned up to the line of the rivers along four major sectors as under:

- **South Western Sector**. 2 Corps consisting of 4 Mountain Division, 9 Mountain Division, 50 Para Brigade (less a battalion) to advance between the Bay of Bengal and the Ganga (Padma) river.
- **North Western Sector**. 33 Corps with 30 Mountain Division and 71 Mountain Brigade to advance from the Siliguri Corridor between the Ganga (Padma) River and the Jamuna River and capture area upto Bogra and Rangpur.
- **Central Sector**. 101 Communication Zone comprising of 95 Mountain Brigade and FV Sector were to advance South of Meghalaya between the Jammu River in the West and the Meghna in the East and capture Jamalpur and Mymensingh and then Tangail.

- **Eastern Sector**. 4 Corps with 8, 57 and 23 Mountain Division to advance from Assam, capture area from Sylhet in the North to Chittagong in the South up to the line of the Meghna River.

Operations in the South Western Sector

2 Corps, under Lieutenant General MV Raina, planned to advance up to the Padma River in two divisional thrusts. Pakistani strongholds were to be contained and only the ones obstructing the advance were to be captured. Concurrently fast moving columns were tasked to bypass the enemy fortresses and race for the river line and prevent the enemy from withdrawing across the rivers towards Dacca. Opposite 2 Corps was Pakistan's 9 Infantry Division with two brigades; 57 Brigade in the North based on the stronghold of Jhenida and 107 Brigade in the South holding the Jessore sector. Raina planned to advance with 4 Infantry Division in the Northern Sector, which was to first secure Magura and then move on to

Indian soldiers survey a destroyed bridge over one of the numerous small rivers in East Pakistan

Jhenida. It was then to be ready to advance up to the line of the Jamuna River and capture the ferry near Goalpura Ghat. In the south, 9 Infantry Division was to capture Jessore – the most important fortress in the theatre, and then be ready to assist 4 Division in the crossing of the Jamuna.

Both divisions moved fast using local resources in the form of cycles, rickshaws, bullock-carts and rafts to negotiate the marshy land. By 6 December, 9 Infantry Division contacted Jhenida, approaching it with a rapid speed march and cutting it off from the rear. The surprised enemy was surrounded and surrendered by 1430 hours on 6 December itself. The fall of Jhenida also triggered a rout at Jessore. Jessore was contacted on 7 December, only to find it abandoned. It had been held by a Pakistani Brigade Group well supported by armor and artillery and the Indian Army had braced itself for a long siege with heavy casualties. Yet the enemy simply ran away, and this prize fell into Indian hands within just twenty four hours. As the enemy withdrew across the Jamuna River they destroyed the vital Hardinge Bridge thus denying the sole crossing place on the wide river. Most of Pakistan's 9 Infantry Division was also trapped east of the River with the destruction of the Hardinge Bridge. But, with their escape route cut off, other fortresses in the sector, especially Khulna and Kushtia held on grimly. Both the Indian divisions got embroiled in battles to capture the enemy strongpoints which held on till the end of the war. When the announcement of the cease fire on 16 December, the GOC, Major General Ansari along with the rest of his division laid down their arms and surrendered to the victorious Indians.

Operations in the North Western Sector

To the North of 2 Corps, 33 Corps advanced from the North Western Sector tasked to capture area up to the Jamuna River and secure two vital objectives; Rangpur and Bogra. Guarding the approach to this sector was the vital strongpoint of Hilli. Hilli was located bang on the International Border and had already seen some heavy fighting in the days preceding the war. It was well stocked and the defenses were well dug-in and coordinated. In some places railway coaches were dug into the ground to serve as pillboxes. Defensive positions had been prepared around houses and key localities by merely stacking sacks of cement around them and allowing the rains to solidify the cement into a solid impregnable mass. Hilli witnessed some of the bitterest battles of the Eastern Sector. It was invested on 6 December and captured after repeated attacks and heavy casualties only on 11 December. The resolute defense put up by its garrison is reflected by the fact that there were only forty survivors after the battle.

While the fighting at Hilli was still underway, the balance of the division moved on ahead with armor and infantry towards the depth objectives of Rangpur and Bogra. The area chosen for the advance was boggy and considered virtually impassable and the speed of the Indian advance surprised the Pakistanis. When a Pakistani post commander reported that he had seen Indian tanks, he was told that they could not have come through the *bils* and marshes and he must have seen buffaloes. His reply was a classic. "You may be right, Sir. But I swear the buffaloes have 100mm guns on them and are picking off our bunkers one by one".

The Division reached Bogra by 12 December and the town was outflanked and a road block established in the rear. A frontal attack was launched using armor and infantry which penetrated the centre of the town. Fighting was stiff and small groups continued holding out till 16 December, when the cease fire came in to effect and the Pakistanis began surrendering en masse. Around 16,000 officers, JCOs and other ranks were captured in this sector.

Operations in Northern and Eastern Sector

While 2 and 33 Corps applied pressure from the West, 4 Corps advanced from the East in conjunction with 101 Communication Area moving in from the North. 4 Corps was the strongest Corps of the offensive with three divisions (57, 23 and 8) tasked to advance up to the line of the Meghna River and from there pose a threat to Dacca. It is significant that in the initial planning, Lieutenant General Sagat Singh, the GOC had not tasked any of his divisions for the capture of Dacca. Plans for the crossing of the Meghna river and subsequent operations towards Dacca were to be made only as the operations unfolded.

A key element of his plan lay in ensuring that the enemy would not be able to fall back across the Meghna to reinforce the defenses of Dacca. He thus launched his three divisions simultaneously with 8 Infantry Division in the North tasked to capture Sylhet, 57 Division in the Central Sector heading for Akhaura and 23 Mountain Division moving in the South. Two Pakistanis divisions, 14 and 39, held the sector, their defenses based on the theatre fortress of Sylhet, Bhairab Bazar, Comila and Chittagong with other smaller fortresses along the approaches.

Moving from an unexpected direction, 8 Mountain Division contacted Sylhet from the South and Southwest. Yet even as these operations were underway, radio intercepts revealed that the Pakistanis were planning to withdraw through the town towards

Indian armour poised on the border prior to their rapid thrust

Indian Plan in the Eastern Theatre.

This was the only crossing on the river and while the destruction of the bridge delayed the Indian advance, it also prevented any Pakistani troops from this sector from withdrawing back into Dacca. Once again General Sagat used his small helicopter force to ferry two battalions across the Meghna and established a bridgehead on the other side. Guns and heavy equipment were ferried across the river on rafts and motor launches, and the engineers worked feverishly to repair the bridge. The Corps gradually built up across the river and on 14 December Medium guns fired into the heart of Dacca for the first time. A attack on Dacca was planned the next night and 4 Corps issued orders for its capture, – orders that were never implemented since on 16 December, Pakistani forces surrendered unconditionally to the Indian army.

The Fall of Dacca

As Indian troops advanced towards the three rivers surrounding the Dacca bowl, the threat to Dacca was also developing from its exposed Northern flank. Here, in the Central Sector, 101 Communication Zone advanced from Meghalaya with two brigades and rapidly captured the fortresses of Jamalpur and Mymensingh. To prevent the enemy withdrawal 2 PARA was para-dropped in the area of Tangail, to capture the bridge on the river Lohaganj and prevent the withdrawing enemy from falling back to Dacca.

The drop was eventful – a heavy wind dispersed the paratroopers and their equipment – one Dakota discharged its load 17 kilometers from the dropping zone. But the battalion soon regrouped. Many of the withdrawing enemy blundered in to the 2 PARA positions and were captured or killed. The drop caused far more confusion that was ever envisaged. The local commanders first cheered at the news, thinking that Chinese or Americans troops had arrived to rescue them. When they realized that they were in fact Indians troops, despondency set in. A BBC broadcast reported that 5000 troops had been dropped which further reinforced the panic.

INSTRUMENT OF SURRENDER SIGNED AT DACCA AT 1631 HOURS (IST)

ON 16 DEC 1971

The PAKISTAN Eastern Command agree to surrender all PAKISTAN Armed Forces in BANGLA DESH to Lieutenant-General JAGJIT SINGH AURORA, General Officer Commanding in Chief of the Indian and BANGLA DESH forces in the Eastern Theatre. This surrender includes all PAKISTAN land, air and naval forces as also all para-military forces and civil armed forces. The forces will lay down their arms and surrender at the places where they are currently located to the nearest regular troops under the command of Lieutenant-General JAGJIT SINGH AURORA.

The PAKISTAN Eastern Command shall come under the orders of Lieutenant-General JAGJIT SINGH AURORA as soon as this instrument has been signed. Disobedience of orders will be regarded as a breach of the surrender terms and will be dealt with in accordance with the accepted laws and usages of war. The decision of Lieutenant-General JAGJIT SINGH AURORA will be final, should any doubt arise as to the meaning or interpretation of the surrender terms.

Lieutenant-General JAGJIT SINGH AURORA gives a solemn assurance that personnel who surrender shall be treated with dignity and respect that soldiers are entitled to in accordance with the provisions of the GENEVA Convention and guarantees the safety and well-being of all PAKISTAN military and para-military forces who surrender. Protection will be provided to foreign nationals, ethnic minorities and personnel of WEST PAKISTAN origin by the forces under the command of Lieutenant-General JAGJIT SINGH AURORA.

Jagjit Singh

(JAGJIT SINGH AURORA)
Lieutenant-General
General Officer Commanding in Chief
Indian and BANGLA DESH Forces in the
Eastern Theatre

16 December 1971.

AAK Niazi Lt Gen

(AMIR ABDULLAH KHAN NIAZI)
Lieutenant-General
Martial Law Administrator Zone B and
Commander Eastern Command (PAKISTAN)

16 December 1971.

Indian Plan in the Eastern Theatre.

Over 93,000 Pakistani soldiers surrendered in East Pakistan

Niazi sent out a frantic message to Islamabad "Enemy landed one brigade in Tangail area. Request friends arrive Dacca by air, first flight, 12 December". By now an air of despondency had overcome most of Niazi's scattered command and their only hope lay in the arrival of the Chinese or the Americans. In fact till the closing days of the war, Niazi was constantly bolstered by promises that Chinese or US reinforcements were coming to their rescue, if only he held on long enough. None of this was forthcoming. The US Seventh Fleet did move threateningly towards the Bay of Bengal, but the promised troops and aid to Niazi never really materialized.

Within Dacca, the scattered, disoriented troops struggled without a cohesive leadership and morale was at its lowest ebb. On 14 December, a conference was held at Government house, by the Governor of East Pakistan, Dr Malik, with all senior military and civil representatives, including Niazi. By then Indian artillery was already shelling Dacca, its troops were at the doorstep and to reinforce its ability to strike at will, an Indian Air Force Hunter rocketed the Government House while the meeting was in progress. The roof collapsed, pandemonium ensued and the panic struck Governor fled to the sanctuary of the local Headquarters of the International Red Cross and wrote out his resignation. By now it was virtually all over.

That same day Niazi received a message from Yahya Khan to end hostilities. Niazi sent a message to the Indians through the United States Consul General in Dacca requesting a ceasefire. Manekshaw agreed and a gesture of goodwill all action over Dacca was halted from 1700 hours on 15 December.

Around midnight 15/16 December Niazi's issued a message to all lower formation asking them to ceasefire and surrender to their Indian counter-parts. On the morning of 16 December, the first Indian troops entered Dacca. By afternoon Major General Jacob, chief of Staff Eastern Command reached Dacca and conveyed the comprehensive terms of surrender – it was to be a complete surrender of all of Pakistan's Armed Forces in Bangladesh, not just a ceasefire. A reluctant Niazi agreed and at 4.30 P.M. on 16 December in front of a million strong crowd cheering "Joi Bangla" and "Indira Gandhi Ki Jai", General Niazi and General Aurora signed the instrument of surrender at Dacca Race Course. 93,000 Pakistani troops – the largest haul of prisoners since World War II – surrendered with their weapons and equipment. The war in the East was over. A new nation had been created.

The Western Theatre

Pakistan hoped to win the war in the East, by achieving decisive victories in the Western Theatre. In their scheme of things, an offensive here would automatically divert attention and force India to pull out its forces from the Eastern theatre. With ten infantry divisions, two armored divisions, two independent infantry brigades and two independent armored brigades in the Western Theater, she had the ability to hold territory and still launch at least two corps sized offensives in Punjab or Jammu and Kashmir. India's strategy in this theatre was one of offensive defense – to retain a balanced defensive posture and only go in for limited counter offensives.

Pakistan's offensive was preceded by air strikes against Indian airfields and vital installations, which though ambitious in scale did not achieve the desired results. On 3 December at 8pm, preceded by a heavy artillery bombardment, their ground offensives went in against Poonch and Chhamb. Poonch was a favored theatre which had been attacked in 1948 and 65, but this time the Indians were prepared and the vital element of surprise was lost to the enemy. Repeated enemy attacks were beaten back with heavy casualties to both sides. By around 10 December the attacks petered out and the Indian consolidated in the areas that were initially lost. The Indian counter offensive was launched which made limited headway and by the end of the war, there were very little gains on either side.

In Chhamb however, the Pakistani attacks made greater headway. Chhamb was always an obsession with Pakistan and had been attacked on 1947 and then re-captured. It was captured again in 1965, but returned after the ceasefire agreement (in exchange for the valuable Haji Pir Bulge). Chhamb and Akhnur controlled the artery to Kashmir and as before, Pakistani plans hinged on throttling that artery.

10 Infantry Division, which was holding the sector decided to thwart the enemy offensive designs by launching a pre-emptive operation directed at their launch pads. Yet the offensive plans were at the expense of the formation's basic defensive role and created gaps in its defenses. The Division was in a state of flux, and had pulled back some of its formations to concentrate for its impending offensive when the Pakistanis attacked on 3 December. Pakistan's 23 Infantry Division along with an armored brigade burst through the Indian defenses and reached the banks of the Munawar Tawi River by 10 December. After the initial disorientation, the Indians reorganized themselves and readjusted their defensive layout. Counter attacks on the enemy bridgeheads pushed the enemy back across the river. By 11 December, enemy attacks had petered out and the offensive was spent without achieving its terminal objectives. An Indian counter offensive captured the narrow Pakistani salient into Indian territory and helped reduce the threat to Akhnur. By the end of the war the initiative was back in Indian hands.

While the Pakistani offensives were underway in Chhamb and Poonch, the major Indian offensive was launched in the Shakargarh Bulge, the large, bulbous bulge projecting into Indian territory towards Pathankot, Jammu and Punjab. It was prime land and if captured, would pose a threat to the very heartland of Pakistan. Pakistan had prepared an elaborate series of obstacles across the Degh Nadi, Bein River and the Basantar River and had fortified the major towns and villages in the area. 1 Corps had been tasked to break into the salient and capture Zafarwal – Dhamtal – Narowal initially and then develop operations towards Pasrur. The offensive went in on 5 December with two divisions, 39 and 54 Infantry Divisions. The formations made initial headway and secured their objectives across the enemy's first line of defense, including a crossing on the Basantar River. 17 HORSE secured the crossing with their Commanding Officer, Lieutenant Colonel Hanut Singh leading the crossing across a dense minefield in his own tank. The rapid and unexpected crossing across the minefield provided a vital bridgehead which though counter-attacked, held on in the face of repeated enemy assaults. It was here that Major Hoshiar Singh of 3 Grenadiers and 2 Lt Arun Khetrapal of 17 Horse won the Param Vir Chakra for exceptional gallantry. Pakistani counter attacks were ferocious and launched with equal determination. The body of one of their Commanding Officers, killed while leading a counter attack, was handed back with a citation from the opposing unit, 3 Grenadiers, commending his bravery. He was subsequently awarded a posthumous Hilal-I-Jurrat – such acts of chivalry were rarely seen on the modern battlefield.

By 16 December, 1 Corps had broken through the covering positions, but had not yet contacted the main enemy positions. By the time the ceasefire was announced, 1 Corps had not captured its objectives of Zafarwal or Dhamtal, but its offensive had tied down much of Pakistan's strategic reserves and blunted its capabilities to launch an offensive in the sector.

Actions were also underway in Punjab. 15 Infantry Division captured the Dera Baba Nanak Enclave across the Ravi River.

However the Pakistanis blew up the bridge across the wide Ravi River before withdrawal and thus denied the launch pad for any offensive into their territory. Further south, the Pakistanis captured the crucial Hussianiwala enclave over the Sutlej River in a surprise attack on night 4 December, but the Indians evened the score by capturing the Sehjra bulge near Ferozepur.

Second Lieutenant Arun Khetrapal, PVC (Posthumous)

In Rajasthan, 11 Infantry Division launched its offensive and captured Khokrapar and Gadra City by 6 December. However the ultimate objective, Naya Chor proved elusive. 11 Division had advanced deep into the desert, and by then its build up was affected by lack of track laying material and duck-boards. When the much needed equipment did arrive and the Division finally built up for the attack on Naya Chor on 16 December it was too late. The cease fire put a halt to all actions in the theatre.

Further South, in the Jaisalmer sector, another action – though smaller in scale, but much romanticized due to its depiction in the movie 'Border' needs to be recounted. Here 12 Infantry Division was poised for an offensive towards Islamgarh, when the Pakistanis attacked on night 4 December in a limited offensive directed towards Jaisalmer. The spearhead of the offensive was halted at Longewala, which was held by nothing more than an isolated company of 23 Punjab. Enemy tanks halted at the sight of barbed wire fencing ahead of the post, anticipating a minefield (in fact, there was no minefield – the wire was laid to dissuade stray dogs and cattle from entering). In the clear moonlit night, the company beat back the enemy's infantry attacks with heavy casualties. Against all odds, the post held on throughout the night, aided by the reluctance of the Pakistanis to attack with armor. At daybreak, the Gods of War smiled- there was no fog and two Hunters from

The destroyed bridge at Dera Baba Nanak

Jaisalmer airfield took off and engaged the halted enemy with rockets and cannon fire. The results were devastating. The tanks maneuvered feverishly to escape, but in the open desert there was little cover and the sorties created havoc amongst the exposed enemy tanks. By midday 17 tanks and 23 other vehicles had been destroyed and this put paid to the enemy advance in this theatre. However their offensive, though unsuccessful had a spin-off. It halted the planned Indian offensive in this sector by 12 Division, which now went on the defensive. The campaign in Rajasthan ended with around 12,000 square kilometers of captured territory, but the green belt could not be reached and most of it was desert wasteland.

Barring their actions in Chhamb there was little to show for the much vaunted Pakistani offensives. In fact their armored division was not even fully engaged throughout the war. Later accounts revealed that they had been in fact, planning a counter offensive in the Punjab Sector, but could never really take off due to the rapid Indian actions across the entire border. On 16 December, after the surrender of the Eastern Army, Yahya Khan broadcast to his people that it was merely the loss of a battle and the war would go on. But it was bravado. He too realized the situation and when Mrs Gandhi announced in Parliament that Indian troops would cease operations from 2000 hours on 17 December, he accepted the cease fire offer with alacrity. The guns finally fell silent on both fronts on night 17 December.

By the end of the war, Pakistan had lost not only its entire Eastern wing, but vital territory in Rajasthan, Punjab and Jammu and Kashmir as well. It was the most decisive victory ever won by the Indian Army and with it the balance of power and the very geography of the sub-continent was permanently altered. This war forms a virtual case study in the successful execution of a campaign. None expected Dacca to fall in just 12 days – and achievement reminiscent of the German Blitzkrieg of 1940 – only executed over terrain twice as difficult. The political and military leadership were in unison and in Sam Maneckshaw and Mrs Indira Gandhi, there was a leadership of a caliber never seen before. The strategy was cautious and sound – the execution was bold and audacious. Yet, if one factor highlights the success of this campaign is just this – timing. Maneckshaw's moral courage in standing up to Mrs Gandhi's demands to launch the campaign in April and postponing it to December was perhaps the single most factor responsible for the complete and overwhelming victory; else it may have just been an inconclusive campaign.

And finally, what decided the issue was the Indian soldier. Given clear cut orders, adequate weaponry and ammunition, a tot of rum or two after the objective was captured and just the basic necessities

THE MOMENT

The decisive moment of the campaign came much before the war. General Maneckshaw's insisted on launching the war in winter instead of April. This provided much needed time for the army to build up its offensive capabilities. It also ensured that the Chinese passes were snowed-in and the Chinese threat negated thus enabling the Indian army to pull out much needed troops from that sector.

The decision was an example of perfect timing, which proved to be the most crucial factor in India's overwhelming victory.

THE TACTICS AND EQUIPMENT

The rapid action of the army was comparable with the German *Blitzkrieg* across France. In twelve days its forces overran an area the size of Greece.

The advancing troops simply by-passed the major strongholds and headed for the Dacca bowl. The Pakistanis on the other hand resorted to static holding of strong points in the mistaken belief that if they held on long enough, the Americans would come to their aid. The emphasis on fortress defence meant that adequate troops were not available for the defence of Dacca. No plans were made for troops to fall back.

The Indians revealed great flexibility as they approached Dacca. There were no plans to enter Dacca but the speed of the advance resulted in the bulk of the Pakistani troops being cut off behind them and Dacca was relatively undefended. Plans were now made to attack Dacca from the bridgehead across the Meghna River. This did not materialize because of the ceasefire.

of administration, he did all that was expected of him and more. In the words of Sydney Schanberg, war correspondent with the *New York Times*, "This army was something, they were great all the way, I lived with the officers and I walked with the jawans – and they were all great. Sure some of them were scared at first, they would not be human if they weren't, but I never saw a man flinch because he was scared. ... And they were the most perfect gentlemen, I have never seen them do a wrong thing, not even when they saw how bestial the enemy had been".

Yet the gains of the war were willingly given away in the bargaining table. 93,000 prisoners were released without extracting any concession in Kashmir or getting a permanent solution to the problem. A new nation was created and Pakistan cut to size, but the root cause of Indo-Pak hostility remained unaddressed. The victory of 71 brought two decades of peace in the sub-continent. Then the ghosts of Kashmir resurfaced in the 80s, first in the decade long insurgency, and then again in Kargil in 1999. The peace that the sub-continent sought remained as elusive as ever.

अमर
जवान

Index